The Long Pass

The Inside Story
of the NEW YORK JETS
from the Terrible Titans to
BROADWAY JOE NAMATH and
the Championship of 1968

THE LONG PASS

by LOU SAHADI

Introduction by DON MAYNARD

THE WORLD PUBLISHING COMPANY

New York and Cleveland

Published by The World Publishing Company
2231 West 110th Street, Cleveland, Ohio 44102

Published simultaneously in Canada by
Nelson, Foster & Scott Ltd.

Second Printing—September, 1969

Library of Congress Catalog Card Number: 71–87057
Printed in the United States of America

WORLD PUBLISHING
TIMES MIRROR

For

Maryann, Joseph, Helen, David, and Elizabeth

The five best reasons for this book.

Preface

The sports fan is a paradoxical person—he can be fickle, he can be loyal. In 1960, the Titans were born, the first new pro-football team in New York in eleven years. A new team, a new league, a new venture, yet not many people went to the Polo Grounds to see them play. The club lasted only three years. They were orphans compared to the New York Mets who played in the same stadium, with no better results, when they were born in 1962. While New Yorkers embraced the Mets, they ignored the Titans. Although no one of the present-day Jets likes to recall this chapter in their history, the fact remains that without the Titans there would be no Jets. Some of the current Jets, Don Maynard, Larry Grantham, Bill Mathis, and Curley Johnson, will tell you this. They fought an uphill battle as Titans and kept fighting simply because of the pride that drives professional athletes.

The old Titans, as well as the American Football League, were winners too when the Jets emerged victorious in the 1969 Super Bowl. They were the colorless, rejected part of the Jets' history. But some of the greatest moments in American sports history have been produced by underdogs—the Louis-Schmeling fight, the Pittsburgh Pirates' victory over the New York Yankees in the 1960 World Series. The Jets' Super Bowl victory over the Baltimore Colts stands among those moments. This is the story of the latest underdog to capture totally the imagination of every sports fan. Suddenly, derision changed to cheers and the New York Jets became the darlings of the sports world.

L. S.

Writing a book of this scope under a tight deadline couldn't have been accomplished without the cooperation of a number of key individuals. I would like to specially convey my thanks to Jane Wagner, the type of editor no author should be without; Murray Chass of the Associated Press; Frank Ramos of the New York Jets, and Jack Horrigan of the Buffalo Bills. And, of course, the 1968 New York Jets, who made it all possible.

Contents

Illustrations following pages *110* and *174*.

Introduction

It was late in the fourth quarter and getting dark. From the sidelines where I was sitting I glanced up at the scoreboard, and saw what all the world could see, Jets 16, Colts 0. Right then I knew we were going to beat Baltimore in the Super Bowl. The New York Jets were on the way to becoming the football champions of the world.

I yelled to the defensive team, "Hold 'em. Let's shut 'em out." I really wanted to shut out the NFL. During all my years in the AFL I was always being told how great the NFL was, that they had the best players, that they played superior football, that we weren't in the same league with them. That's why I wanted a shutout so much. I wanted to skunk them and put an end to all that hogwash.

I had been through it all during the past nine years. I don't think anyone, with perhaps the exception of Larry Grantham and Bill Mathis, had suffered as much frustration as I had all these years. We may be professionals in a violent and brutal sport, but even with us it can hurt to feel unwanted, to be looked down upon, to be ignored by the fans and ridiculed by the press, season after season. That one day, that single Super Bowl victory took care of all of the emptiness and frustration I had experienced.

It all began back in 1960 when I first reported to training camp with the New York Titans. It was a new team in a new professional league. There were over 100 of us who were trying for a place in the sun, unwanted by the other league. The players were faceless. They were nobodies who wanted to become professional football players in an unknown league. It was nothing like the year when I reported to the New York Giants training camp where I would recognize Kyle Rote, or Frank Gifford, or Charlie Conerly. It was simply a hundred guys with uncertain futures wanting to play football.

I never got the feeling of really belonging that summer until one of the veteran players, Bobby Dillon, came over to me after we had played an exhibition game in Bangor, Maine, and shook my hand and welcomed me to the team. It was like the President shaking my hand. Probably nobody remembers Bobby. But, I'll never forget him. In his way he accepted me and I became part of a team.

Finally Bobby was cut, but by then I had become close friends with Grantham and Mathis, and we could share the heartaches and disappointments. One of the biggest was that the New York fans never really accepted us. Even worse, the sportswriters often scoffed at us. I knew there was a great deal of front office politics with the owner of the Titans, Harry Wismer, but we were still professional football players trying to earn a living and, at the same time, respect. The Giants had New York all to themselves then and we were treated like intruders or worse, clowns.

But we never lost our desire as athletes. We were disappointed at the number of people who came out to see us play. We hadn't expected the fans to break down the doors, but, at most games you could almost count the fans in the stands. They were the smallest crowds I had ever played before. They just weren't comparable to my previous two years in professional football. Still, the team worked all that much harder and there was a close feeling with the players, a feeling that we would sink or swim together.

We thought we reached the end in 1962, just three years after the team was born. In mid-season, our paychecks bounced. We didn't know what to do. That was the first time a thing like that ever happened to any of us. It created a lot of doubt not only about the future of the Titans, but the AFL as well. However, the league office assured us that everything would be all right and that they would pay us for the remainder of the season.

Still, at season's end, we didn't know if any of us would be back again. As bad as the attendance was the first two years, it was even worse the third season. We all knew the club was in dire financial straits and we didn't know if there would be any New York Titans in 1963. We knew the club had to be sold but whoever bought it could move the franchise to another city. I remember shaking hands with my teammates and wondering if I would be playing with them again next season.

I was home in Texas the following March when I learned that the Titans had been sold to a group of businessmen headed by Sonny Werblin. I had never heard of him. The only thing I learned was that the club would remain in New York but that they would change the name Titans. I still was apprehensive and I pondered quitting football. The idea of returning to the Polo Grounds with new owners whom I knew nothing about didn't appeal to me.

However, when the club named Weeb Ewbank as head coach, most of my doubts were erased. I didn't know Ewbank personally, but I knew he was an experienced professional coach who had produced championships at Baltimore. I convinced myself that these new owners, by hiring a seasoned professional coach, were really serious about football. The two previous Titan coaches I had played for, Sammy Baugh and Bulldog Turner, had never had anything but playing experience. So, I was as excited as a rookie reporting to his first training camp.

I anxiously checked in at Peekskill the summer of 1963. The team was now called the Jets and a great many of the

Titans from the previous season were on hand. However, I got the feeling of not belonging all over again. Ewbank had made a statement that he would eventually get rid of all the old Titans. It gave me a scared feeling right away. I didn't know whether to pack up and leave, or give it a shot. I talked with Grantham and we decided that we were professional athletes and we would go out and show the new coaches that we knew something about playing football. I had the feeling of trying to prove myself all over again but I was determined to do it.

There was a lot of friction in that first Jet training camp. Every day, a couple of old Titans were cut from the squad and one or two ex-Colts came into camp. All the ex-Colts stuck together, as did the ex-Titans and the new players who came in as free agents. We felt we were the underdogs inasmuch as the front office wanted a distinct new image and took steps to completely remove all references to the Titans.

Many times during the practice sessions I felt I was an open target for the criticism of the coaches simply because I was a former Titan. A quarterback would throw a pass over my head or behind me and I would be the one they found fault with. If it wasn't for George Sauer, who was the only holdover coach from the Titan organization, I might have quit.

I can't say enough great things about George Sauer. He laid the cards on the table, and you always felt you would get a fair shake from him. Whenever I had a problem, I went to him. He was someone I felt I could go to to get something off my chest. He'd sit there and listen and look at the situation from the player's side and from management's and then explain it all in his own way. He made a lot of difference. He helped me personally a great deal. He'd make me see every possible angle to any problem I brought to him. As a result, after talking things out with him, I'd always feel surer of myself.

Everything turned out much better that first Jet season. More people came to see us play and I felt quite a bit more secure knowing that the new owners had a large amount of money behind them. I got to see Werblin quite a bit, but never any of the other owners except maybe at a club function like a Thanksgiving Day dinner.

In some ways Werblin reminded me of Wismer. The biggest difference was that Werblin radiated success. He looked and acted the part and tried to develop a more personal rapport with the players. The club's operation was much more organized. It was run on a major-league level, from the front office to the playing field. That was the biggest difference during the first year as Jets.

When we moved over to Shea Stadium in 1964, it was like another world. The plush locker room, the playing field, the stadium itself. The most heart-warming part was the fans. New York finally turned out to see us play. We had more fans that first year at Shea than all the years at the Polo Grounds put together. I didn't feel like an orphan any more.

Now I wanted a championship. I wanted to prove something to myself. I wanted the team to prove something to itself. The front office was getting good players in the draft and we were on the way. The first year at Shea, Matt Snell was the most exciting rookie in the league. He finished as the second-best runner in the AFL and he gave us a ground attack we had never had before. All we needed to make us go on offense was a quarterback and the Jets went out and got the best one around after the 1964 college season, Joe Namath.

Every football fan knew about Namath and his $400,000 price tag. It was a sum of money unheard of before in professional football. There were a lot of stories going around that the rest of the players resented Namath because of all the money he got. They were all blown up out of proportion. I, for one, never resented it. I felt that if a player could get that kind of money, I was all for it. The only unsettling thing I felt was that with that kind of money around, management could afford, and ought to give a little more to the veterans.

I had a great understanding with Joe right from the start. I told him privately, "If anything doesn't work out during a game, let's talk it over." I respect quarterbacks and I promised him, "You make me look good and I'll make you look good. We are both in this together." I understand quarterbacks' problems: "I know sometimes you throw off balance. I'll never knock you for a bad pass."

At the same time, I told him, "Let's you and I talk it over instead of you shaking your head and turning your back, and me talking to myself. Let's discuss it. We'll make it go the next time." Right off the bat Joe and I had a great thing going. We both laid it on the line to one another.

Joe went through some trying seasons, but he was learning. Nobody wants to win more than Joe. He's the greatest competitor I've ever seen. The rest of the team realized that he was the one player who could lead us to a championship. He has a great arm and all he needed was a little time to adjust to the pro-game. I don't think anybody was ever down on Joe, especially those first two seasons, 1965 and 1966, because he was learning.

We almost pulled off a championship in 1967. We had gotten off fast and by mid-season we were comfortably out in front. I told Grantham that this could be the year we had both waited for. However, Emerson Boozer, the other half of our running attack, got hurt and was finished for the rest of the season. We came in a disappointed second.

A significant change occurred before the 1968 season. Werblin sold out his share of the club and Ewbank came out of the shadows and took command all the way. Werblin, whose intimate relationship with Namath dominated the team, was gone, and the players all rallied behind Weeb. The first thing he did was to change our training camp from Peekskill to Hofstra University. He also got rid of some disturbing elements on the team and everything else began to change.

All season long we did the job. We won the Eastern Division title and then the AFL championship by defeating Oakland. But we all wanted one more win, the Super Bowl. A lot of people didn't give us much of a chance to beat Baltimore. We were confident we could do it. Namath had told the world that we would beat the Colts and we went out to do the job.

We were all a bit tense before we took the field for the kickoff. I went through the same routine I always do before a game. I'd rub the palms of my hands against the wall and then walk over to Grantham and Mathis and shake their hands. "Let's get this one. It's the one we all waited for."

Weeb called us all together and said he didn't know what team to introduce for the benefit of national television, the offense or the defense.

"Why not introduce the seniors," suggested Namath, referring to the high school football routine.

That broke everybody up. We all laughed and it broke the tension. We went out onto the field and did the job nobody ever thought we could do.

DON MAYNARD
April 28, 1969

The Long Pass

1

Champagne
and Roses

December 30, 1968. Champagne, roses, laughter, and speeches. And no one asked, "Would you have believed it?" Everyone in the Diamond Room of Shea Stadium was a believer.

The New York Jets had won the 1968 American Football League championship.

The man who once had seemed the biggest believer of all, Sonny Werblin, was not at the party. Six years earlier, in 1963, when he purchased the bankrupt New York Titans, Werblin had flatly stated, "In five years I will have champions."

It took the Jets six years: Sonny Werblin's faith lasted only five. In the spring of 1968 Werblin sold his share of the club he once had called "my team." For five years he had devoted most of his time and energy to grooming them, in his own fashion, for the championship.

Now, players, their wives, officials of the club, members of the local press, hastily assembled at Shea Stadium for the victory celebration. The jubilation, the exultant mood, were too strong for any nostalgia. Not until much later in the evening would anyone wonder why Werblin had been unable to see that his prodigious efforts to create winners had nearly killed the club.

Much later a young woman (a player's wife?) would ask, "But why didn't Weeb Ewbank stand up and demand his rights years ago?" And as you moved away from the group someone gently began to explain about the coach, Weeb Ewbank. After Werblin had left the club, Weeb seemed to have taken control and begun moving this team toward this celebration. (Though the question would rise, again and again: Who had really directed the Jets to victory, Ewbank or Joe Namath?)

When Joe Namath—Joe Willie, Broadway Joe—entered the Diamond Room, Phil Iselin, the Jets' president, was there to greet him. And you knew that everyone in that room, especially the players, had been waiting for Joe Namath to arrive.

The arrogance, the brashness, the flamboyance, whatever else he might have been tagged with over the past four years, were all there, but somehow they looked different in the light of victory. It was a handsome, confident, charming young man who came into the room with a lovely blond, Suzy Storm, on his arm. It was a gracious young man who turned to Wendy Hudson to ask her something. And it was a delighted young man who threw back his head with laughter at something Jim Hudson said in reply.

A little later, while we sat eating, Namath would get up from the table to seek out one or another in the room, moving from table to table. Something he wanted to ask or say, or just concern for each person he knew. When he'd return to the table, he'd bring back a small report, as if he'd been sent out for news.

While the strolling musicians hovered near us, I told Joe that Frank Litsky said his paper, *The New York Times,* had contacted Jimmy the Greek in Las Vegas to determine the odds on the Super Bowl. The Vegas crowd had established the Baltimore Colts an 18-point favorite on the opening line.

"Eighteen points," exclaimed Namath. "How do they figure that? Man, I wish I could bet. All those points. It doesn't seem possible." He shook his head in disbelief.

Throughout the room the conversation moved from the recent victory to the Super Bowl game. Bill Mazer, an NBC announcer, emceed a short program, which he began by praising Gerry Philbin. He had been a Philbin promoter longer than he had been an ardent Jet rooter. The players expected it, and it didn't bother them.

Several players spoke briefly, acknowledging that the team had pulled together to make the victory possible: the usual banquet remarks.

Then Mazer called on Ewbank. He had been through this sort of victory dinner with the Baltimore Colts in 1958 and 1959. He praised his players who worked hard all season long, and had a special word of thanks for his assistants, without whom he said no coach could attain any measure of success. In a final tribute, he thanked the players' wives, who had the patience to endure the efforts of the players throughout the season.

At last Mazer looked around for Namath. Joe approached the microphone, still limping a bit from the previous day's game. He kept his head down until he was ready to speak.

"The coach thanked all the players' wives. I would like to thank all the broads in New York." The audience howled its delight. Diffidence is not Joe's style.

"Seriously, though," he went on, "this championship was a great one for the players. However, I don't think anyone deserved it more than Coach Ewbank. Now, Weeb and I have had our little differences over the years, but we were both pulling for the same thing. Certainly no one worked harder than Weeb. He's a dedicated coach. I understand that he's at Shea every morning at eight o'clock."

Namath stood looking thoughtful, almost troubled. "Of course, I've never seen him at that hour because it's still a bit too early for me."

Ewbank grinned. The rest of the audience roared.

The Super Bowl war of nerves began as soon as the Jets stepped off the plane in Ft. Lauderdale later in the week. A number of local writers and television reporters greeted the Jets upon their arrival in Florida.

"Hey, Joe, what do you think of Earl Morrall?" asked one television reporter.

"I can think of four or five quarterbacks in the AFL better than Morrall," Namath snapped. "Myself, John Hadl of San Diego, Bob Griese of Miami, Daryle Lamonica of Oakland, and Len Dawson of Kansas City."

Morrall, the Colts' quarterback, had captured the imagination of pro-football fans with his dramatic performance during the 1968 season. He had been nothing more than a mediocre performer throughout his thirteen-year career, which had been spent with five different teams. Yet in his first season with the Colts, he took over for the ailing Johnny Unitas and guided Baltimore to its championship.

Of all the remarks Namath could have made, this was scarcely the most gracious or diplomatic. Namath's natural confidence and candor run counter to the tradition which demands that athletes, regardless of what they privately believe, always praise their opponents in public statements—a tradition which has produced an incredible amount of treacle and inanity. Honestly believing that there were five quarterbacks in his own league better than Morrall, Namath ignored diplomacy and named them. Overnight his remarks made headlines all over the nation. And most sportswriters—who would have privately derided Namath's sincerity had he gushed over Morrall's ability—chose to believe in print that Namath had put the rap on Morrall. Joe should have known, and perhaps he did, that his remark wouldn't be treated kindly. This kind of thing was to go on all week. The Ft. Lauderdale *News* correctly headlined it: "Namath Speaks, Controversy Results."

The next day the Jets began serious preparations for the game. Squad meetings with the coaches to review the Colts' game films were scheduled for noon. At two P.M. they would scrimmage on the practice field, Ft. Lauderdale Stadium, a baseball plant used by the New York Yankees' farm club.

But prior to the noon meeting, Larry Grantham, the team player representative, informed Ewbank that he wanted to hold a squad meeting without any coaches present. The players met behind closed doors.

The players had a number of grievances, mostly petty gripes, some exaggerated by locker-room rumors. But before any serious business on the field began, Grantham wanted a meeting to clear the air. The club had come too far to allow any kind of dissension to jeopardize the Super Bowl winner's share of $15,000 per man.

At the end of the meeting, Grantham asked Ewbank to join them. Ewbank listened to the grievances, one by one, and quickly succeeded in satisfying the players. First he assured: yes, they would be getting rings to symbolize their AFL championship. The players had voted for rings, but a source-less rumor had management substituting watches. Then the players insisted the club spend $3,000 for each ring; Ewbank informed them that no club in the past had ever paid more than $1,000, and this satisfied them.

Regarding the demand that the club pick up the expenses for their wives, Ewbank again referred to past experience. He emphasized that the wives had been welcome to take the charter that the club arranged, either flying down to Ft. Lauderdale or going back with the club to New York the day after the Super Bowl. Then he pointed out that the three previous Super Bowl clubs, Green Bay, Kansas City, and Oakland, had not made any special allowances for players' wives.

The other major concern of the players was the cost required to get the field ready for the AFL championship game in New York. The figure of $42,000 for field maintenance and another $12,000 for turning on the lights, which they had heard about, was, according to rumor, going to be deducted from the winner's share of the game receipts. Ewbank explained to them that he did not know what the costs were because the club had not yet received a bill, and besides, it would not come out of the players' pockets.

With these matters settled, the squad reorganized for the

noon meeting. Then Ewbank sent them out on the field for contact drills. This was their first heavy workout since the championship game. Ewbank liked the way they hit.

Johnny Sample, defensive captain of the team, came on the field with high-topped shoes and leg weights attached to both ankles. He sprinted up and down the field, stopped to catch his breath, then assumed a defensive stance and began to run backward. Sample, according to some sportswriters, is getting old and starting to slow down. This backbreaking training technique, Sample claims, improves both his speed and stamina.

Just after the workout started, Ewbank noticed people watching from a tower on the roof of the stadium.

"Who are they?" he asked. "From the Federal Aviation Administration," he was told. The steel structure was used in the operation of an adjoining municipal airport.

A similar incident had occurred the previous year when the Green Bay Packers trained on the same field. However, coach Vinnie Lombardi didn't ask who was in the tower. He had stalked over and found out himself.

Pro-football clubs, when they hold secret workouts, always worry about spies. During a workout in Denver a few seasons earlier, Jet officials had spotted someone watching from a tree. John Free, the club's traveling secretary, chased the observer, who succeeded in getting away.

Frank Ramos, the Jets' publicity director, also had an experience with a self-appointed secret agent. "One year a guy tried to sell me information on the Kansas City 'I' formation, claiming it was something new," said Ramos. "Kansas City had been using the 'I' for two years. There are always people trying to sell you things like this for a price."

The Colts did not arrive in Ft. Lauderdale until after dinner the next day. There were some 250 people, most of them kids seeking autographs, awaiting their arrival. They cheered the players as they filed out of the plane one by one, and the biggest cheer of all was for Morrall. Forgotten by the crowd was yesterday's hero, Johnny Unitas, who walked alone, in shirt sleeves, to the buses at the end of the runway.

"Yeah Earl . . . Attaboy Earl . . . Way to go, Morrall," yelled the kids. It was all new to Morrall, who had mostly heard boos in his pro career.

The reporters failed to get Morrall to react to Namath's statement that there were five quarterbacks in the AFL better than he was. Cautiously, Morrall refused to engage in a controversy.

"Joe Namath is entitled to his opinion," was all he said. Earl has always had the reputation of being a nice guy. He is reserved and does not encourage feuds or hold grudges, even though he has been treated unfairly on numerous occasions throughout his NFL career.

Baltimore coach Don Shula, however, did speak in defense of his quarterback. "How Namath can rap Earl is a thing I don't understand. How the hell can you rap a guy that's the National Football League's Player of the Year? Particularly when Earl's had the percentage of completions he's had, the touchdown passes he's had, and the big yardage he's accumulated for us. Earl's not a guy who dumps things out in the flat to flare men to get a completion percentage built up. This guy is only interested in winning and doing the job. Namath can say whatever he wants to say, but I don't see how he can rap a guy who's accomplished the things Earl has for us all year. Anybody who doesn't realize what he's done for us is very wrong. He adapted quickly to an unfamiliar numbering system, and he recognizes how to improvise if necessary after the ball is snapped. That's the name of our game. He's a guy you have to chase off the practice field. He's well liked by everybody, and I have nothing but admiration for him."

Whether he intended to or not, Shula appeared defensive, as if he were trying to bolster his quarterback's confidence. While praising Morrall, he declined to compare him with Namath.

"I don't see how anybody can compare them," Shula said. "They haven't been throwing against the same kind of defenses. Namath has a quick release and sets up with good depth and vision downfield. He back-pedals more than the quarterbacks in our league, and he doesn't get caught with the football. If his deep receivers are covered, he manages to dump the ball off. It's a problem getting to the guy because he gets back deep and gets back in a hurry. He has what we call fast feet. No overall speed, but quick feet."

If psychological warfare means anything at all in professional football, then Namath emerged triumphant by trapping Shula into a defense of Morrall that studiously avoided any comparison of the two quarterbacks.

Sunday's heavy rains made it impossible for the Jets to practice outdoors. Instead, they spent nearly two hours in squad meetings and still more in review of Baltimore's game films. The coaches would run a single play over and over again to detect, and commit to memory, certain mannerisms a particular player employed. It could be any number of little things that go unseen by the average fan, a certain stance a lineman takes, a move a receiver makes before running his favorite pattern, a pattern the quarterback establishes. These things provide the edge that coaches search for in designing their game plan. By Wednesday the Jets would have already formulated their offensive and defensive strategy.

Walt Michaels, the defensive backfield coach, had detected a weakness in the Colts' pass coverage. Frequently they combined a zone defense with a linebacker blitz. Michaels felt that Namath would be able to read the blitz easily and that his deep dropback and quick release could beat it, particularly if he went to the short man or to receivers coming out of the backfield whom the zone could not cover.

After the session, several of the players walked around the lobby, while others sought the quiet of their rooms either to read or take a nap. Randy Beverly and Johnny Sample, the Jets' cornerbacks, stared out at the rain. They were supposed to be the two weak links in the team's secondary, Beverly because of his inexperience and Sample because he was slowing down. One too young, and one too old.

Beverly was only in his second season on the squad. He

was signed as a free agent in 1966 and spent that year on the taxi squad. In 1967 he was brought up to the parent team and barely got past the final cut. When Cornell Gordon suffered an injury in the opening game of that season, Beverly got his chance and made the most of it.

"Sure we've heard a lot about the Colts and their great receivers," said Beverly to a few sportswriters, "but we haven't seen that much of the Colts yet. We've only watched half of the film of their game against Cleveland. On Tuesday we'll study the films some more. Right now, all I know is what I hear and what I read in the newspapers. We know they have great receivers. We don't worry about them picking on one individual. We play a team defense. Everything is a team effort. That's the way we play defense."

Johnny Sample was a cagey veteran, having played professional football for eleven years, eight of them in the National Football League. He had played on Ewbank's 1958 and 1959 championship clubs. He began his career with Baltimore before being traded—first to Pittsburgh and then to Washington—not because he lacked ability but because he was an intense and outspoken individual who had great difficulty in keeping his observations to himself.

"When you hear about the Jets you hear about Namath and the offense," said Sample. "But our defense happens to be the best in the league. We gave up the least first downs, least total yards and the least yards rushing in the AFL. Our defense has been the difference this year. Al Atkinson is the best middle linebacker in all football. Guys like Dick Butkus and Tommy Nobis of the Falcons may be great against the run, but nobody compares with Atkinson on pass defense. Our front four is as good as anybody's."

Sample was referring to Gerry Philbin, defensive end Verlon Biggs, and defensive tackles John Elliott and Paul Rochester, along with Carl McAdams, who alternated with Rochester during the course of a game. "We played two NFL teams in the preseason and didn't give up a touchdown. I'm not saying that preseason games compare to the Super Bowl. They don't.

But we have a terrific defense to go along with Namath and our offense. This is my fourth championship game, counting Oakland last week, and I've never been on a loser. I intend to keep my winning streak going." Sample's grin had more determination in it than humor.

Monday the tension began to ease up a bit. It was an off-day, following the same routine that the Jets had followed all season long. A nice, quiet day after a Sunday of violence. The players' only obligation was a picture session that had been ordered by the commissioner's office. The Jets were to put on their game uniforms and pose for photographers for about an hour, beginning at noon.

Three of the more celebrated Jets, however, failed to appear. Snell and Boozer, who roomed together, were absent. So was Namath. League officials were upset, and the Jet coaches did not know what had happened to the three. In a disciplinary move, Ewbank fined them all. Snell and Boozer claimed that they did not receive a wake-up call, awoke by themselves, saw the day was dark, and went back to sleep. Jim Hudson, Namath's roommate, claimed he tried to awaken Joe but that he was sleeping too soundly and did not respond. The fines stuck.

What no one noticed, neither the press nor the AFL officials —not even Ewbank, at first—was that a fourth player had been missing at the photo session. Carl McAdams had not shown up, but no one asked for him and no one missed him. Anonymity has certain advantages. In spite of all the complaining, or possibly because of all the complaining, when the missing players finally arrived, no one bothered to take their picture.

The same day, word spread that on Sunday night Namath and Lou Michaels, Baltimore's field-goal kicker and defensive end, had been embroiled in a heated exchange of words that nearly resulted in a fight. Lou, the younger brother of Walt Michaels, the Jets' defensive backfield coach, is as well known for his temper as Namath is for his personality. So it was a credible tale.

The incident occurred in Fazio's, one of the popular Italian restaurants in Ft. Lauderdale. As the story goes, Michaels greeted Namath, and Joe cheerfully replied, saying that the Jets were going to kick the hell out of Baltimore. Michaels sat with his teammate, Dan Sullivan; Namath was with Jim Hudson.

"Haven't you heard of the word 'modesty,' Joseph?" asked Michaels.

"We're going to beat you, and I'm going to pick you apart," said Namath.

"Joseph, I do believe you are the man who could do it," admitted Michaels. "But it's kind of hard throwing out of a well."

Michaels seemed to be trying to scare Namath. He was implying that the Colts' defensive unit intended to ignore the Jets' running game in order to bury Joe under their line charge and blitzing backs.

"Don't worry about that," said Namath, "because my blockers will give me time."

"I never heard Johnny Unitas or Bobby Layne talk that way."

"I believe that."

"If we get into trouble, we'll send in the master, Unitas."

"I hope you do that. It will mean the game is too far gone," was Namath's final observation.

It is not an unlikely conversation. Ball players often exchange this kind of banter. But then the tone of the story changed: Michaels asked Namath to step outside. Before the situation could get out of control, Sullivan calmed Michaels down, and conversation ended abruptly. Quietly and separately they finished their dinners, and when the checks came, Namath not only paid his but Michaels' as well.

Much of the story seems confirmed by a statement Michaels made later. "When everything was said and done, I was ready to take back the things I said when we first met. I learned you might as well hear Namath out. He strikes you as being cocky, but I came away thinking that he's a real gentleman. There's a lot of good in this guy." That was an unusual remark for Michaels. He is not known for going out of his way to like people—or to have them like him.

"The only reason I showed any resentment toward Namath to begin with was because he said the Jets were going to whip us and kick the hell out of us as well." Then switching the subject, Michaels recalled with some awe: "He must have had a wad of dough, close to two thousand dollars, and he peeled off a one-hundred-dollar bill to pay the entire check. I don't know how he tips; I didn't see that."

Later Namath laughed off the incident. "It was all good clean fun, and we parted the best of friends," he said.

Joe ended the evening by graciously driving Michaels back to his hotel. If there is an advantage to be gained, Namath had scored again in the psychological war.

Although it didn't rain, the weather was cloudy on Tuesday. The players gathered for their noon session indoors and watched the remainder of the NFL championship game between Baltimore and Cleveland. They observed the compelling Colt defense shut out the Browns with a strong rush from their front four. One defender in particular, Bubba Smith, was of special concern to Dave Herman. Like Herman, Smith played his college football at Michigan State. After a mediocre rookie season at tackle, Smith had come alive this year. He was big and rough and, having been shifted to end—where he had played at college—he was making his reputation as an effective pass rusher.

Dave Herman's mission was to keep Bubba Smith out of range of Joe Namath. And Herman, at 6 feet, 1 inch, and 250 pounds, seemed no match for the 6-foot-7-inch, 300-pound Smith.

Most of his professional life, Herman had operated as a guard, and he had become one of the best in the AFL. But in the championship game against Oakland, he was shifted to tackle to handle Isaac Lassiter, a giant who, even at 6 feet, 5 inches, and 270 pounds, is not as big as Bubba. Herman became a tackle when Sam Walton, a big rookie, had failed to do the job in some key games. Herman's experience as a tackle amounted to only four and a half quarters in the entire 1968 campaign.

Although he is not tall, Herman's shoulders and torso are so large that during most games his jersey will not stay tucked in his pants. Off the field, his quiet manner, conservative clothes and hornrimmed glasses give him an almost scholarly appearance that his teammates tease him about. After the practice session, he sat in the dressing room and talked about the forthcoming game.

"There's been talk about Bubba's swollen ankle, but I guarantee you that by Sunday he'll be ready to go—he's a pro. He is just bigger and quicker than anybody I've had to face, but we've got to protect Joe if we are going to do anything at all. We must hold our blocks longer than most linemen do. Not because of Joe's legs, but because of his deep, drop-back style. Hell, I'm glad he's a drop-back passer. At least we know he's right behind us instead of roaming around back there."

In the back of another part of the dressing room, some forty reporters were waiting to interview Namath. They waited in vain. Joe did not want to give interviews to any writer he did not know. The club officials respected his wishes. The forty left with empty notebooks.

"Joe says there's been enough written about him already," announced Ramos, the Jets' publicity director, to the press corps.

"You've got to try to understand his side of it," offered Ewbank. "All year long, just in New York, there are twenty or more writers trying to talk to Joe all the time. The kid can't get undressed. He can't take a shower. He can't live his life. Magazine writers, newspaper reporters, television people, they're all over Joe."

A friend tried to change Namath's mind about one writer

whom Joe didn't know. "You'll like this guy's stuff, Joe," said the friend.

"Really?" Namath raised his eyebrows in mock surprise. "I haven't seen anything yet that I've liked down here." Another endearing remark.

After dinner that night Namath and Jim Hudson began to study films of the Baltimore–Los Angeles game. They were viewing a part of the game in which the Rams were on offense. One particular Ram pass pattern caught Joe's eye. He kept running the sequence through over and over.

"Did you see the safety on that pass pattern, Jim? Watch. Look how he moves to the inside. Did you see that? Now watch again. Did you see how he played that?"

Namath, who can read films as well as anyone in the business, detected a flaw in the Colts' pass coverage on a particular type of pass pattern. It would provide at least one approach for him to pick the Colts' pass defense apart, as he had told Lou Michaels he would.

On Wednesday the sun shone brightly and the squad was again scheduled for contact. After their film session, they trotted out of the dressing room for another closed workout. The session was brisk. The offense was sharp and displayed good timing. The defense reacted well and made sharp contact. Ewbank was pleased.

Later, lounging in the sun at the pool, Jim Hudson and Billy Baird talked about Sunday's game, and specifically about John Mackey of the Colts. Hudson, the strong-side safety and Baird, the weak-side one, would be chiefly responsible for neutralizing Mackey, a big tight end who runs like a halfback in the open field. Some experts felt that Mackey was one of the keys in Baltimore's offensive scheme.

"I don't know if he's the key or not," said Hudson. "We won't know that until the game is over. If he ends up catching ten passes, then I'd say he was the key."

"I think we know how to neutralize Mackey," added Baird. "I was a rookie with the Colts the same time Mackey was."

"They keep talking about Mackey's size," said Hudson, "but we've gone up against tight ends in our own league who have that kind of size: Fred Arbanas of Kansas City, Jacque MacKinnon and Willie Frazier of San Diego. We've handled ourselves pretty well with them and also with guys with good speed and good moves. But this is the first time we'll be up against anyone that has the size plus speed and good moves. Mackey likes to line up in the backfield while the flanker slides up into the line. The idea is to anchor the safety in the middle of the field to see which way Mackey is going before he commits himself."

Hudson relaxed. "Hell, I've seen that before. Kansas City uses it, and we've handled it pretty well. We'll just wait and see. We're ready for Mackey."

Hudson's plan was not to wait for Mackey to commit himself —inside or out—but to pick him up as soon as he crossed the line of scrimmage. This would probably keep Morrall from passing to him, but in the event Morrall did hit Mackey with a quick one, he would not have running room.

After Thursday's indoor meeting, the players gathered around Ewbank on the practice field. The squat coach, wearing a short-sleeved Jet T-shirt and a white baseball cap with a green J in front, stood dwarfed in the middle of the circle and lectured the men.

"You hit too hard and moved too fast yesterday. I don't want to see anything as rough as Wednesday's contact. We don't want to lose a ball player."

Later he admitted frankly, "The way they were going at it, they scared me for a while. We certainly don't want to come up with an injury at this point. And besides, we don't want to leave the game out on the practice field. We were at our peak earlier in the week, and I've told them that there won't be any more contact the rest of the way. That's the problem, you have to try and calm them down."

Like Namath, Ewbank could not understand the smart money's insistence that the Jets did not have a chance. "If you listen to people talk, it would be foolish for us to dress Sunday, but we're going to. My boys are ready."

Later that night Namath went to Miami to receive the city's Touchdown Club's FAME Award as the pro-football player of the year. The dinner was held at the Miami Springs Villa, and it was sold out, with most of the audience lured by Namath's presence. Astronaut Gordon Cooper and Indianapolis 500-mile race winner Jim Rathman were also present, but the evening belonged to Namath.

AFL president Milt Woodard presented Namath with the award and stepped back to let Joe express his gratitude.

"The Jets will win Sunday, I guarantee it," Namath announced matter-of-factly.

The statement brought a loud jeer from a heckler, obviously a Baltimore fan.

"Who's that? Lou Michaels?" asked Namath, smiling at the crowd.

"I didn't intend to cast any slur on Earl Morrall when I said there were five quarterbacks in the AFL who could throw as well or better than he can. I wasn't rapping Morrall. He doesn't rate such treatment. He stepped in and took the Colts to the NFL championship. That speaks for itself. But I am entitled to my opinions and have the right to express them, just as any of you do."

Joe grinned like a mischievous little boy. "They say the Colts are going to take my statement and put it up on their bulletin board. Psychologically it's going to lift them up for the game. If the Colts need anything like that to lift them up for the game, then they're in trouble from the beginning."

Having finished the Colts off publicly for the third time in a week, Namath then turned toward Woodard and launched into a dissertation on hair styles.

"How can the league say it's wrong to have long hair? What's hair got to do with being a football player?"

Joe acknowledged the league's tonsorial problem. "They have to go along with public opinion, and people say it creates the wrong image for kids. If that's so, it's the parents' fault, because they shouldn't tell the kids it's wrong."

Namath stood there modeling his long hair which curled around his ears and lay over his collar at the back of his neck. He looked mod, and the audience loved it and applauded his remarks.

Before stepping down from the podium, Namath gave his detractors one glimmer of hope. "In closing, I hate to say it, but I'm afraid it's true: The name of the game is kill the quarterback, and you have a chance to win."

Namath's free-wheeling candor made the next day's headlines, creating more excitement. It was only forty-eight hours until kickoff, and ticket scalpers were asking and getting $50 to $75 for a $12 seat. Namath had created more interest in this Super Bowl than the holy Green Bay Packers did in the two previous ones, and the guys who hustle tickets for a living thought Namath was just beautiful.

The clamor for tickets reached a point where even we sportswriters refused to answer our telephones. We would collect our messages three times a day, sorting out the ticket seekers from the other calls, comparing notes on oddly or uniquely phrased requests. No matter where we turned, we were asked for tickets.

The bartender at the poolside bar of the Hilton Plaza—press headquarters for the game—was looking to nail a couple for a friend who said he could make a buck on them.

A lawyer from Ft. Lauderdale was desperate for tickets for a couple of his clients. He said he would pay $50 apiece for them. His desperation reached a point where finally a friend of his from Brooklyn offered his own two tickets.

Namath's name dominated not only Ewbank's press conference, but Shula's as well.

"What would they have talked about if there were no Joe Namath?" one writer asked.

"I'm sure Namath has provided extra interest in the game," admitted Shula. "You very seldom run across a colorful guy like Namath, particularly a guy with his kind of ability. Joe's comments definitely have helped the overall interest in the game. Our football team is conscious of everything that is written, everything that goes on. Joe makes it more interesting. We had a pretty good laugh out of the thing that happened between Lou Michaels and Namath. I think it happened in a restaurant. Lou assured me it was not in a bar. Actually, Joe is the 837th guy that Michaels has threatened to deck. If Lou had punched Joe, it would have been just the 37th guy that he actually hit."

Ewbank found himself trapped by Namath's words. He was asked if he was as confident as his quarterback. He gulped, then repeated the question while searching for a cautious answer.

"I don't think any ball player should start in a game or even show up if he doesn't think he has an opportunity to win. So Joe guaranteed it, huh? Well, I'm for Joe."

As Ewbank promised, the Jets began to taper off in their workouts later that afternoon. The heavy morning rain subsided by the afternoon, and the Jets were able to suit up and work on their time drills for about an hour. Actually, with the heavy work concluded, they concentrated on keeping their timing sharp.

Saturday morning, the players moved leisurely about their hotel. The sun was warm, and a great many of them preferred to sit outside. Some chose to stay in their rooms, welcoming the solitude while waiting for their final pregame drill of the long season. It all had begun in the heat of the previous July, when they assembled for the preseason training camp. Few, if anyone, felt it would come down to this. The sportswriters had not given them much of a chance to win their own division title, let alone to play for the world championship. Six months of incredible work, of injuries, early fall heat when some of them were so fatigued that they wanted to drop, and winter cold when the wind would cut across their faces and the ground would come up hard. Now it came down to one game and a $15,000 booty.

The final Super Bowl drill lasted less than an hour. The coaching staff just wanted the players to get the feel of the three-P.M. sun—the hour the game would start—and to keep the hone on their timing. There was nothing left anybody could do but wait.

The Jets knew what waiting was all about. They had waited nine years. One more day would not make any difference.

2

Texas Origins

The National Football League was formed in the 1920's with ten teams. It remained as the only professional-football league in existence until 1946, when the All-America Conference was founded with eight teams. However, with poor attendance throughout most of the league cities, the new league was disbanded after three years. Its better franchises, such as Baltimore, the Cleveland Browns, and the San Francisco 49ers, were absorbed into the NFL. When the seeds for the American Football League were planted in 1959, the NFL had 12 teams in operation. The AFL launched its campaign in 1960 with eight teams, and once again professional football had two leagues. Most experts at the time predicted that the AFL would fold in two years. But it survived.

There have always been men—and some exceptional women—who want to own a piece of a prizefighter or a good percentage of a professional athletic team, even if it is not the best financial investment.

Lamar Hunt was a man who wanted to own a football team.

In 1959 Lamar Hunt was wealthy enough not only to want a professional football team but wealthy enough to look around on the open market for a franchise to purchase. There were twelve such properties then, and two of them happened to be in the city of Chicago. Chicago football, however, belonged to George Halas. He was one of the pioneers of professional football, and his Bears were a household word in Chicago. The other team in town, the Cardinals, were the orphans nobody wanted.

Hunt reasoned, and correctly so, that the Cardinals would make an ideal purchase. He would buy the club and transfer it to his hometown of Dallas. He chose to ignore the fact that Dallas had an ill-fated experience with professional football some years back in the All-America Conference. True, that was years back, before the advent of television and its profound effect on the economics of professional football.

The owners of the Cardinals, however, were interested in selling only twenty percent of the team. The figure was not enough for Hunt to be considered the owner. A part owner, yes, but nothing more. Still, he tried. He had enough money to buy any existing franchise, and he wanted to spend it. He was confronted with another obstacle, Halas.

Halas was the patriarch among the owners. He was also the head of the National Football League's expansion committee, whose duty is to accept or reject proposals for new franchises. Actually, whatever Halas decided was law, committee or no committee. He informed young Mr. Hunt that the league was most definitely against any franchise shift to Dallas. He reminded Hunt that in 1952 a professional football team had failed dismally there.

But Lamar Hunt was not easily deterred. He was shy, wore glasses, and had the outward appearance of a choir boy. He was only twenty-six years old, but he had guts, and he had money.

Hunt was a frustrated football player at Southern Methodist University, where he had graduated three years before and where he had sat on the bench as a member of the varsity for the same number of years. He sat so far down on the bench that no one knew him.

"I had received two letters at SMU," recalled Hunt somewhat sheepishly. "The first letter came from Coach Matty Bell at the end of my senior year. It read: 'Dear Lamar: Please stay off our football field. You have cluttered it up long enough.'

"The second letter I got was also from Matty Bell: 'Dear Lamar: Please return to the athletic department the twelve T-shirts you've taken the past three years.'"

If he could not play for a team, he could buy one, and if he could not buy one, then he would have to start his own league.

"I had been trying to buy the Cardinals from the Wolfner family," admitted Hunt. "They had mentioned that a number of other people also wanted to buy the team, and it was becoming obvious to me that they wouldn't sell. Then I began thinking that if there were these other people trying to get into football, maybe we could start our own league.

"I remembered some of the people the Cardinals mentioned. Bud Adams of Houston stood out in my mind. Then there were people in Minnesota and Seattle, and it went on from there. It was up to me to go out and recruit the owners."

The first person that Hunt contacted was K. S. "Bud" Adams, another wealthy Texan. They had never met. In January of 1959 Hunt went to Houston to meet Bud Adams.

Hunt and Adams are complete opposites. Lamar is quiet, unassuming, dresses conservatively, wears glasses, and appears soft. He could easily pass for a librarian. Adams, on the other hand, is what a typical Texan is supposed to be: Flamboyant in his ten-gallon hat and cowboy boots, he likes to wear a startlingly white leather coat.

Their meeting was amicable. They talked for three hours but never mentioned football. Finally, as Adams was driving Hunt to the airport, the subject came up. Apparently Hunt was impressed enough with Adams.

"If I could get four other people in four other cities to

sponsor teams in another professional-football league, would you come in?" Hunt asked.

Adams did not hesitate. He simply answered, "Yes."

Adams had also made overtures to the Chicago Cardinals and reportedly could have purchased forty-nine percent of the club. However, Adams, who certainly had money enough to buy an entire team, was not interested in being a part owner, and a minority one at that.

Adams and Hunt had somewhat similar backgrounds. Adams had played football at Kansas University. And, although Adams did not inherit his wealth like Hunt, his fortune is enormous. He owns the Ada Oil Company, and is also a rancher, investor, cattle breeder, and real-estate developer. Stories abound about wealthy Texans. Some are about Adams.

In a group of persons sitting around a Texas barbecue, one Texan bragged, "I own three thousand acres."

"I own five thousand," another said, and turning to Adams asked, "And how many do you own, son?"

"Just one hundred."

"Poor boy, and where is your spread?"

"Downtown Houston," answered Adams.

In 1968, another story goes, Adams attended an oil convention in Chicago. A friend accompanied him in the limousine which was moving through downtown.

"See that building being constructed over there?" asked the companion. "That's going to be one-hundred stories high when it's completed."

"How much is that in acres?" inquired Adams.

His friend continued, "Jerry Wolman [the former financially torn owner of the Philadelphia Eagles] started that building. He had to sell out because he was pressed for money."

"Lamar Hunt and I warned him about that," replied Adams. "We told him he should always keep a hundred million or two in the cashbox. Might need it sometime."

The chauffeur interrupted for a second. "Excuse me, sir," he addressed Adams, "you got yourself a hotel here, Mr. Adams?"

"Not this time," said Adams, looking straight ahead. "I'm only staying a couple of days, so I just took a floor."

"By the way," the friend remarked, "I understand Lamar has offered to put fifty million dollars behind a new stadium in Kansas City."

"That's his allowance the kid's spending, not mine," snapped Adams.

These were the two pivotal men who launched the American Football League. As Hunt promised, as soon as he returned to Dallas he began contacting people who were interested in owning professional-football franchises.

The first person Hunt reached was Bob Howsam in Denver. Howsam had a background in professional sports, being an executive of the Denver Bears baseball team of the American Association, a high-ranking minor league. Howsam acknowledged that he would be interested in another league.

Hunt then turned to Minnesota and received the pledges of three prominent Minneapolis businessmen, E. William Boyer, chairman of the Minneapolis Chamber of Commerce; Max Winter, owner of the Minneapolis Lakers professional-basketball team; and H. P. Skoglund, vice-president of Raven Industries.

With four cities verbally committed, Hunt reasoned it was time to tap the New York market. He was well aware that no new national sports venture could be successful without the nation's largest city. Hunt arrived in New York for a meeting with William Shea, a prominent attorney who was spearheading a drive to launch the Continental League, a new major baseball league.

Shea's involvement with the baseball movement prevented him from even thinking of a new football league. However, he suggested Harry Wismer, who was a well-known sportscaster and a stockholder in the Detroit Lions and Washington Redskins. Wismer had an effervescent personality and a ready smile. He came on strong and liked to be the center of attention. When he had been drinking, he came on loud. Always sharply dressed, Wismer loved the good times and, better still, publicity. He agreed readily to Hunt's proposal because he was feuding at the time with Washington's principal owner, George Preston Marshall, and realized he would never own the Redskins.

The sixth city on Hunt's list was Los Angeles. He telephoned a friend, former tennis star Gene Mako, and Mako arranged a meeting with Barron Hilton, the handsome younger son of hotel tycoon Conrad Hilton. Hunt went to Los Angeles and met Hilton, who expressed interest in the new venture but asked for a little time to consider.

It was now July, and Hunt almost had six teams in the fold. The rival NFL was operating solidly with twelve teams, but Hunt envisioned only eight for the first season. Still, the young Texan was wary. He decided to meet with Bert Bell, the commissioner of the National Football League. Somehow, Hunt still envisioned owning an NFL franchise in Dallas. Bell convinced him that there would be no expansion by the NFL for years and that a club in Dallas was definitely out of the picture. The meeting convinced Hunt that he had to go ahead with his new league if he ever hoped to own a professional-football team.

After several phone conversations with Hunt, Hilton decided to join the league. Again, Hunt sought a meeting with Bell. He asked Davey O'Brien to set it up. O'Brien was in the oil-drilling-equipment business and worked for Lamar's father and was a natural go-between. He had been the star quarterback when Bell coached the Philadelphia Eagles in the late 1930's. Hunt wanted Bell's reaction to the possibility of a second football league and also wanted to know if he would consider being its commissioner.

Bell seemed receptive. He felt certain the new league would succeed and added that the NFL would not do anything to harm its chances.

However, Bell was playing it shrewdly. A congressional committee, spearheaded by New York Congressman Emanuel Celler, had begun an investigation into the monopolistic tendencies of professional sports. He knew that as commissioner of the NFL he would be appearing as a witness. If he had to play cards with congressmen, he wanted a stacked deck.

At the end of July Bell phoned O'Brien and asked that he and Hunt meet him in Washington. He informed them of the congressional hearings and that he would like to discuss the new league. Hunt consented and supplied the names of the individuals involved. Bell had the marked aces he needed to allay the congressmen's fears.

Hunt and Wismer were in the back of the hearing room when Bell testified. He spoke mostly in generalities but apparently convinced the congressmen, as well as Hunt and Wismer, of the open, fair play of professional football.

"I'm all for the new league and would help nurture it," announced Bell. "The more teams and the more competition, the better."

Despite Bell's statements, the owners in the NFL privately were against any new league. Actually Bell did want pro football to expand, with him the commissioner of both leagues. The owners nevertheless felt that a new league could not survive. The disbanding of the All-America Conference just ten years before was still fresh in their minds.

Bell's remarks dispelled Hunt's apprehensions about the older league. He felt it was now time to herald the new league in the press and on television and informed Adams to announce the inclusion of Houston in a new professional league, which still had not been named.

A large turnout from the news media attended the press conference in Houston the first week in August. Adams made the announcement and then Hunt told the members of the press that they would soon reveal the rest of the cities who had franchises in the new league.

Hunt and Adams, on a suggestion of Wismer, agreed to hold the first meeting of the league on August 14 in Chicago at the Hilton Hotel. Wismer, ever publicity-conscious, suggested the date because that was the weekend of the All-Star game, and writers from all over the nation would be there to cover the game between the collegians and the champions of pro football.

At the meeting, six cities were represented by eight individuals: Lamar Hunt (Dallas); Bud Adams (Houston); Harry Wismer (New York); Bob Howsam (Denver); Barron Hilton (Los Angeles); and Max Winter, E. W. Boyer, and H. P. Skoglund (Minneapolis). They announced that the league would begin play in 1960 and that they would hold another organizational meeting in Dallas on August 22.

On that day, articles of the new league were approved by the members. They also agreed that each owner would provide a $100,000 performance bond and would place $25,000 in cash into the league's account. There was no turning back now.

August had been a busy month for Hunt and Adams. Before he announced his entry into the league, Adams had received a telephone call from Craig Cullinan of the Houston Sports Association, who asked him not to commit himself. Then Ed Pauley, one of the owners of the Los Angeles Rams, made a peace bid to Hunt. He said that if Hunt and Adams would disband their plans for a new league, the NFL would give them franchises in Dallas and Houston. All of this was being done to keep the AFL out of Texas. Hunt would not yield. The battle lines were drawn.

The new league began to move much more quickly. They met for the third time on September 12 in Beverly Hills, and the prospects of adding a seventh city, Boston, appeared bright. William H. Sullivan represented a group of businessmen and felt that he could convince his associates to join the league. On October 28 the principals met for the fourth time in Wismer's apartment in New York, and Ralph C. Wilson, who owned an insurance company and a trucking firm in Detroit, joined as a franchise holder for Buffalo.

Two weeks prior to the New York meeting, Bert Bell had died on October 11 in Philadelphia. Austin Gunsel, the NFL's treasurer, was named acting commissioner, and a month later, the war between the rival leagues burst into the open.

The setting for the battleground was the November meeting of the fledgling league in Minneapolis. At first everything appeared normal, and optimism permeated the meetings. Sullivan attended the session to be formally accepted as the league's eighth team, and the owners were going to conduct their first draft of college players.

"I will never forget that first meeting, because that was the first time I actually met Lamar Hunt," recalled Sullivan.

"I'd heard about Hunt, this fabulously wealthy young guy, and I was prepared to meet a flamboyant big Texan wearing high-heeled boots, a big hat, and a cigar to match.

"I walked into the room, and there was this young fellow with his foot up on the edge of the table. There was a hole in the bottom of his shoe. Then he took his foot down and put the other one up. So help me, there was a hole in that one too.

"He noticed that I was looking at him. He grinned kind of shyly and said, 'It just proves that I'm twice as good as Adlai Stevenson. Hello, you're Bill Sullivan, aren't you? I'm Lamar Hunt.'"

That was the lightest part of the meeting. The bomb exploded at a dinner given by the Minneapolis owners. Some two hundred local citizens turned out, as Wismer put it, "to look us over."

A few minutes after the dinner began, Wismer received a telephone call. Sitting between Hunt and Winter, he excused himself and left the room. It was a long-distance call from a friend of Wismer's, Mims Thomason, president of United Press International in New York.

Thomason didn't waste any words. "Harry, you've been taken. We just received a tip that the NFL has offered a franchise to Minneapolis, and the parties have accepted it. Your people are out."

Wismer was stunned. He listened to Thomason for another few minutes and then hung up. He jauntily returned to the dining room, approached the microphone in the center of the dais, and asked for quiet.

"Ladies and gentlemen. I think so far as the AFL is concerned in Minneapolis, this is our Last Supper."

The room burst into noise. Hunt was excited. He wanted an explanation, and Wismer asked him and Winter to come outside and he would tell them what he had learned. Wismer demanded that Winter admit that he had received approval for an NFL franchise. Winter denied it. Wismer was furious, and Hunt asked him to calm down. He said they would resolve everything at the meeting later. The dinner broke up, and everyone headed back to the hotel for the meeting.

Wismer rode in Boyer's car and tried to get an admission from him. Boyer just replied that he did not feel well and was going home. He dropped Wismer off at the hotel. Hunt tried to maintain order at the meeting, but Wismer was in a rage. He repeated his accusations to Winter and Skoglund, but both remained silent. Wismer screamed at both to leave the meeting, and Sullivan, who had come to Minneapolis to formally join the AFL, sat stunned by all that was taking place.

Finally Wismer, Wilson, Adams, and Hilton agreed to convene the next day, to accept Boston as the eighth and final franchise, to conduct the college draft, and to select a commissioner.

The next day, November 22, the league announced that Boston had been accepted as the eighth city. They then proceeded to conduct their first formal draft of college players, drafting 264 players, 33 for each team. Each team was allowed a wild-card pick, in that their first choice could be any player they wanted. After that, they each had to pick according to position in order to complete an eleven-man offensive team. Then, continuing to alternate who picked first on the subsequent rounds, the teams completed the full selection of 264 players.

Drafting alphabetically, the first-round choices were: Boston—Gerhard Schwedes, halfback from Syracuse; Buffalo—Richie Lucas, halfback, Penn State; Dallas—Don Meredith, quarterback, SMU; Denver—Roger LeClerc, center, Trinity (Conn.); Houston—Billy Cannon, halfback, LSU; Los Angeles—Monty Stickles, end, Notre Dame; Minneapolis—Dale Hackbart, quarterback, Wisconsin; New York—George Izo, quarterback, Notre Dame.

After the draft was finished, the league adopted a television policy fostered by Wismer. It was Wismer's most important contribution. The plan called for the league office to negotiate a television contract with one of the major networks, the proceeds from which were to be divided equally among the member clubs. It was a plan later adopted by Pete Rozelle when he became commissioner of the NFL.

The owners then approached the task of selecting a commissioner. Twenty-five persons were considered, but only eight were interviewed. One of the prime candidates was Fritz Crisler, the athletic director of the University of Michigan. He supposedly asked for $100,000 for five years, and a big insurance policy. There were, however, certain misgivings about Crisler. He was a champion of college athletics and never looked with much favor on professional football. He was turned down.

Wismer suggested Frank Leahy, the former Notre Dame coach, and was voted down. He then nominated Ed "Moose" Krause, the athletic director of Notre Dame. Krause, however, did not want to leave Notre Dame.

Still Wismer tried. He came out for Rip Miller, the athletic director at the Naval Academy. And, for the third time, Wismer came up empty-handed.

The owners finally agreed on Joe Foss. He was not a Wismer man, but he was everything else. A former World War II flying ace, who was awarded the Congressional Medal of Honor, Foss had served two terms as governor of South Dakota. A ruggedly handsome forty-four-year-old, it was said that he could not be more honest if he tried.

There are many stories about Foss, but one simply and purely displays his style. During a war-bond tour in the spring of 1943, a rally was held at New York City Hall, and Mayor Fiorello La Guardia introduced Foss to the crowd.

"Now, ladies and gentlemen," began the mayor, "I want

to introduce the only man to ever survive a head-on collision with a Japanese Zero."

Acknowledging the applause and cheers, Foss addressed the crowd: "I don't know who the hell the mayor is talking about folks, but I'm Joe Foss."

The new commissioner was as folksy as Mark Twain. He treated everyone alike—owner, player, writer, or fan. He liked nothing better than to appear as an after-dinner speaker, especially with youth groups.

Surrounded with glory, he had also suffered tragedies in his personal life. His father had died when he was twelve years old, and he had helped run the farm while still attending school. Working his way through Augustana College and the University of South Dakota, he took six years to complete his education. His first son was born dead; his second died shortly after birth; another son survived polio, and his daughter had cerebral palsy. Yet, in the face of tragedy and hardship, Joe Foss prevailed. Whether they realized it or not, the owners had selected a stalwart man.

Foss reportedly received a three-year contract at $30,000 a year plus expenses. The league office would be in Dallas, and Foss scheduled the first annual meeting there for January 26. Then he extended an olive branch to the NFL.

"I hope to arrange a meeting with NFL officials to work out some type of salary agreement so the leagues won't get into a money war. We have no intention of trying to outbuy the NFL. For our part, we'll be more than happy to keep salaries as they are now in professional football. Naturally, though, there'll be some bidding for the top stars. We understand that and are equipped for it.

"Let me emphasize that there is no fight with the NFL. I'll recognize a fight if there is one, and I'll know what to do about it. We want the NFL to be successful, and we want to be successful too. There is room for both. And, thanks to the NFL and television, more people are interested in football than ever before."

On December 7 the new league completed its college draft

for the approaching 1960 season. They drafted 161 more players for a total of 425, a total of fifty-three for each team.

By then, despite the owners' original denials, Wismer's report proved correct and the Minnesota group made a formal application to withdraw.

When the owners convened under Foss for the first time, three cities were in contention for the franchise: Oakland, San Francisco, and Atlanta. The Eastern Division of the league was complete with New York, Buffalo, Boston, and Houston. The Western Division needed another entry to go along with Los Angeles, Denver, and Dallas. Hilton argued strongly for the Oakland group, represented by Y. C. (Chet) Soda. He repeated that it would be foolish for him to operate alone on the coast, and the other owners agreed.

The owners then elected Hunt as the league's first president, an obvious selection in that the young Texan was primarily responsible for the birth of the new league.

The meeting, which began on Tuesday and was scheduled to run only two days, lasted until Saturday. The owners had accomplished a great many things. They approved a fourteen-game schedule and adopted the two-point conversion rule which had been employed by the colleges the year before.

Wismer was the center of attention throughout the extended meetings. He would often leave the room and leak information to Ed Fite, the Dallas bureau manager for the United Press. Wismer was probably returning a favor to Mims Thomason for the information about Minneapolis. Typically, Wismer's information was frequently in conflict with many of the announcements Foss made at the press conferences.

No one suffered more than Howard Tuckner, of *The New York Times,* which was the only New York newspaper covering the meetings. Tuckner was on his first out-of-town assignment, and he was a little nervous. He kept getting phone calls from his New York office complaining that the United Press was saying one thing and he was reporting another.

Finally, as Wismer was leaving the room to have a private

meeting with Fite, Tuckner yelled: "Harry, could I have a word with you?"

The entire press group burst into laughter. The writers all knew that Tuckner was getting short-changed by Wismer.

Wismer gladly accommodated Tuckner. They went outside for a private discussion, and Wismer denied he was responsible for the information the United Press was reporting.

"Harry, could I have a word with you?" became a standing gag line for the rest of the meeting.

The press recognized the wayward, even irresponsible streak in Wismer.

3

The Wismer Way

Harry Wismer first met Lamar Hunt in July of 1959 at the Belmont Plaza Hotel in New York. Although he had never met Lamar, he had met his father, Harold L. Hunt, a number of years ago.

Wismer was impressed with the elder Hunt, who told him he had acquired his wealth by borrowing fifty dollars and wagering he could discover oil on land where geologists said there was none to be found. Hunt claimed a man would succeed if he kept plugging along and was willing to gamble.

That was Wismer's philosophy too. He had scratched for everything he had gained. He was born in Port Huron, Michigan, where his father managed a clothing store. Although he had already left high school, in order to acquire a college education, he applied for football scholarships at all the Big Ten schools. No offers came, but Harry, enterprising even as a teen-ager, got a letter of recommendation from his old high-school coach and headed south. He tried Vanderbilt and then the University of Georgia. He was rejected at both. Undismayed, Harry kept plugging and finally was successful with coach Charlie Bachman at the University of Florida. Bachman was not ecstatic but was sufficiently convinced that young Wismer had enough football background to give him a scholarship, room, board, tuition, books, and a number of odd jobs for spending money.

While not exactly a con man, Wismer certainly was an opportunist. He knew how and when to take advantage of situations, and by doing a favor here, and getting one in return, he progressed much more rapidly in the game of life than in that of football. He managed to help Bachman get the job of head coach at Michigan State and then returned there as a member of the team to finish his education.

Harry did not play much football. An injury sidelined him for the season, and as a result he did not finish his education. Bachman told him to forget football, probably so that he could forget about Wismer as a player, and got him a job broadcasting State's football games on the university's station.

Watching Bill Stern and Graham McNamee broadcast one of State's games in the radio booth opened Wismer's eyes. He saw the glory and color in sports broadcasting and decided this was his new game. With a microphone in his hands, Wismer felt power. He met George "Dick" Richards, the owner of the Detroit Lions, who also had vast business interests, including radio stations. Within a year Wismer quit college to take a full-time job as sportscaster over WJR in Detroit at $20,000 a year. By the time he was twenty-five, Wismer's voice echoed throughout the Midwest as the play-by-play announcer for the Lions on Sunday and Big Ten games on Saturday. Young Harry was grossing $100,000 a year.

He had scratched for a buck, the way H. L. Hunt said you could, and he had made it. He joined NBC in New York in 1941, broadcasting a number of Notre Dame games on Saturdays and NFL games on Sundays. Wismer was now a national name.

The following year he went to Washington to cover the Redskin games on Sunday, and he became a public-relations expert for Harry Bennett, one of the top executives at the Ford

Motor Company at Willow Run, and still found time to broadcast a big college game on Saturday.

In 1959 Harry Wismer looked at young Lamar Hunt in the Belmont Plaza and knew that Hunt had never scratched and hustled for a dollar. The meeting lasted for about two hours. Hunt explained that he wanted Wismer, who at the time owned part of the Redskins and the Lions, to own the league's franchise in New York.

"I listened to Lamar and he appeared sincere enough. He told me I was the best person to have as a partner in organizing and publicizing the new league. I told him I would be willing to look into it but that I had to determine the extent of my financial involvement." When Wismer later decided to join, Hunt seemed relieved.

But Wismer's love of publicity soon caused trouble. As head of the television committee, Wismer made a premature announcement that upset the colleges: "We will play all seven games in the Polo Grounds on Saturday afternoons," said Wismer. "This returns Saturday football to a city that has virtually been without it in the last ten years."

He immediately heard from enough college presidents and athletic directors to change his plans. In November he made another announcement: "No games will be played on Saturday afternoons. They will be played Friday nights, Saturday mornings and nights, Sundays, and holidays. If the American League were to play on Saturday afternoons, it would undoubtedly injure attendance in the immediate area, and the broadcasting and telecasting would hurt the college games all over the country.

"We had an offer of one and a half million dollars from television if we agreed to play on Saturday afternoons. That would have meant a lot in getting us off the ground, but we didn't want to hurt the colleges."

So, without wanting to hurt anybody, at least for the time being, Wismer went about organizing his football team. The new missile launching gave him the idea for the name of his club: He called them the Titans.

"Besides," Wismer explained, "Titans are bigger and stronger than Giants."

Then Wismer was called in by the district attorney's office for questioning. It was the result of one of the meetings in Wismer's apartment. In some of the previous meetings of the new owners, a lot of talking was done and very little progress made. It reached a point where few of the owners could agree on what had been said.

"For that reason alone I decided to have minutes kept of the third meeting, which was scheduled to be held in my office."

Wanting to make an impression with the other owners, Wismer told his secretary to locate a specialist in tape recordings. The electronics expert arrived early the day of the meeting to set up his equipment. He placed a number of microphones around the living room of Wismer's apartment and connected them to the recording instrument. A specially erected sound box was added to identify each owner as he spoke.

The meeting got under way, and the electronics man was there to make sure everything worked perfectly. The first day's session was lengthy, and the owners adjourned until the next day. When they convened again, one of the owners noticed, for the first time, the technician's presence and demanded that he leave. Wismer defended the need for taping the session, but after a long and heated argument Wismer agreed to dismiss him. The recording expert then became angry about the way he was being treated and refused to turn over the previous day's tape unless he received an exorbitant fee, which the owners refused to pay.

The whole experience appeared forgotten until a few days later, when some of the details appeared in a local sports column. The account was exaggerated to the degree that Wismer's apartment was secretly bugged and certain testimony was being recorded. The next day Wismer received a call from the district attorney's office asking him to come in and explain what was going on in his apartment with confidential recording equipment. This Wismer did. If there is one thing Harry could do, it was to talk his way out of difficult situations.

The episode over, Wismer began thinking of a coach for his newly minted Titans of New York. He wanted a name coach. He favored Duffy Daugherty of Michigan State, where Wismer himself began it all. Wismer offered him something in the neighborhood of $25,000 for five years. Daugherty was interested. He presented Wismer's offer to the university officials and came away with a bigger contract from them. Then Wismer turned to Dick Gallagher, the former coach of Santa Clara, but Ralph Wilson got him first.

Watching the New York Giants–Washington Redskins game on television, Wismer found his man. Sammy Baugh, already a legendary figure in pro football, was being interviewed as a halftime guest. Sammy Baugh? Why not? Baugh was an extremely popular player during his time. He held just about every passing record in the NFL, was one of the game's foremost punters, and also had played defense. He had a Texas twang, a warm smile, and was loved by everyone. He had been immediately elected to pro football's Hall of Fame when he retired.

Wismer put in a call to the press box and asked to speak to Baugh. Since Baugh had to fly to New York the next day to get a plane back to Texas, where he was head coach at Hardin-Simmons University in Abilene, they agreed to meet at the airport.

"I met Baugh at nine A.M. Monday at Idlewild," said Wismer. "We sat on a bench outside of the Brass Rail restaurant. I had to talk fast, because Sammy had to catch a nine-fifty-five flight. I presented the whole picture to him, pointed out the importance of Texans in the league. He knew the ones involved, and he also felt that with television, the league had a chance. We shook hands before he departed, and Baugh agreed to coach the Titans. He said he wanted a few days to talk things over with the people at his college and to hold any announcements until then."

So, Wismer had his big-name coach, and he could barely wait to break the news. He set up a press conference in his apartment on December 18 to make the announcement.

"We had quite a large turnout," said Wismer. "Baugh and I agreed to a twenty-eight-thousand-dollar contract for three years. However, before he met the press to be introduced, he wanted to get paid. I quickly turned to Joe Arcuni, who was a ten-percent owner of the Titans. All three of us went to my bedroom to talk things over. Fortunately, Joe always carried a lot of cash around with him. I never thought he'd have that much. But, he counted out twenty-eight thousand and Sam signed the contract. Then we went before the press to announce that Sammy Baugh was the first coach of the New York Titans."

Baugh had played for sixteen years in the NFL for the Washington Redskins. He retired after the 1952 season when he was thirty-seven years old.

"Would he play with the Titans?" asked a writer.

"I reckon not," remarked Baugh. "I'd rather rassle a steer than meet up with those linemen playing pro ball today."

Baugh quickly lined up his staff. He named as assistants George Sauer, Bones Taylor, Dick Todd, and John Steber. The latter was his line coach at Hardin-Simmons. Taylor, a former Redskin star, was named end coach, and Todd, also another Redskin standout, was made backfield coach. Sauer had been released as head coach at Baylor University.

Wismer then needed a general manager. As he put it, he luckily got Steve Sebo, a classmate of his at Michigan State. Sebo had just been released as coach of the University of Pennsylvania after having led the Quakers to the Ivy League championship. Despite Sebo's 9-0 record, the alumni considered his type of football dull and succeeded in having him removed as coach.

Wismer still had one more vacancy, and an important one at that, defensive line coach. He looked across the river to Yankee Stadium, where the Giants' popular defensive end Andy Robustelli was nearing the end of his career. Like

Daugherty, the Michigan State coach Wismer first approached, Robustelli benefited from Harry's approach with a raise in pay for one more season as a player along with a promise of a Giant coaching job.

A short time later, Wismer thought he had landed one of Washington's assistant coaches as his defensive coach. That would gall George Marshall, his old rival. Wismer believed the deal was set. The Redskin aide even sent his biography so that Wismer could prepare copies to distribute at a press conference scheduled in his apartment.

Everyone appeared except Turk Edwards, the coach who was going to be introduced. Unknown to Wismer, Edwards had decided to remain with Washington. Wismer called Sebo into his bedroom for a quick consultation.

"How many reporters know that we were going to announce the name of a coach?" asked Wismer.

"Just one," replied Sebo.

In a desperate move to avoid embarrassment, they decided to announce the signing of a player, Don Maynard, the biggest name of the fifteen players they had offered contracts to at that time. Happily, it worked: Inasmuch as Maynard was a former Giant, his signing received good space in the newspapers.

Wismer was still resolved to secure an NFL coach for the opening that remained. Again he stared out at Yankee Stadium, and this time succeeded in hiring John Dell Isola, line coach of the Giants, as his defensive line coach. The coaching staff completed, Wismer turned to other matters.

He still had to secure a field to play on, and all he could negotiate for was the ancient Polo Grounds. The old horseshoe-shaped structure at the tip of Manhattan, directly opposite Yankee Stadium and the financially prosperous Giants, was practically a deserted arena except for some midget auto racing. It was barren, desolate, and badly in need of repair and painting. Still, Wismer had no choice.

Wismer had to pay $7,500 rental per game, for all seven games, and in advance. But he had no alternative but to sign and deliver the money, which would be forfeited if the club disbanded.

All that was left now was to sign players. That was Sebo's job. He began an all-out search to find playing talent, while Wismer began to study the economics of running a professional football team. Adding all his projected costs and expenses, Wismer figured it would take more than $800,000 to operate the first season. Television revenue would take care of some, but no one knew exactly how much, as a contract still had to be negotiated with one of the networks. Inasmuch as Wismer needed a winning team to compete with the Giants, he conceivably would have to pay high prices in the player market.

Don Maynard actually was the first player to be signed by the Titan organization. His career with the Giants had lasted two years, most of it spent as a kickoff and punt-return specialist. He was lean and had excellent speed, but he never enjoyed much success with the Giants. They released him in 1958, and he played the next year in the Canadian League. When he learned that Baugh had been named coach of the Titans, he wrote him asking for a chance to play. Baugh consented.

"I couldn't wait to sign and play pro football in the States again," sighed Maynard. "I didn't haggle over any money. I signed the first contract they sent me." Another good player the Titans signed was Larry Grantham. He wasn't big, weighing less than 200 pounds, but he had displayed quickness and savvy as a lineman at the University of Mississippi. He had also been drafted by the Baltimore Colts, but Grantham felt he had a better opportunity with the new league, and the Titans showed more interest in him than the Colts had.

Sebo traveled extensively that spring looking for players, and before the season began he had traveled some 35,000 miles.

Meanwhile, Wismer was busy with league affairs. Besides being the chairman of the television committee, he was also head of the expansion committee. In the spring he released a story saying that Atlanta and Chicago were added to the league and that they would begin play in 1961. Like other Wismer releases, it was premature and inaccurate.

Wismer said that two groups were seeking an AFL franchise in Chicago. One was headed by Bill Veeck, the president of the Chicago White Sox, and the other was being led by Tom King, Jr., who was vice-president of Chicago's Merchandise Mart, and John Rigney, a former vice-president of the White Sox. King denied it.

Wismer identified the Atlanta owner as Eaton Chalkley, a lawyer and businessman. "The only thing that keeps Atlanta from being able to play this year is a segregation issue," explained Wismer. "The team wants to use Grant Field, but a Georgia law prohibits Negroes from playing with whites in a state-owned arena. If this law is repealed before the 1961 season, Atlanta will use that park. If not, the Atlanta team will use the park to be built for the Atlanta entry in the Continental Baseball League."

If this episode marked a particular low for Wismer with Foss and the owners, it was forgotten in June. The dynamic Harry finally completed the television deal the new owners direly needed. The league signed a five-year contract with the American Broadcasting Company. The first year's revenue was $1,785,000, with graduated increases for each of the remaining four years.

It was the first positive financially rewarding deal the league made. That was on June 9. Some ten days later they hoped for another when Foss announced that the AFL filed a $10,000,000 antitrust suit against the NFL, charging it with consipiring to monopolize professional football. The suit, however, did not receive a hearing until 1963. Judge Roszel Thompson ruled that although the AFL was excluded from some markets, a conspiracy was not involved.

By July 9 close to 100 players had been invited by Sebo to report to the Titans' first training camp on the campus of the University of New Hampshire in Durham. One group of players assembled in New York to take the eight-hour journey to New Hampshire. They gathered in the lobby of the Manhattan Hotel, twenty-six of them, most of them waiting for another—and perhaps their last—chance to play professional football. They waited, hardly talking, but wondering about the future. Some were casually dressed. Maynard was conspicuous with his long sideburns, which were unheard of then, and his cowboy boots; Grantham was close by, wearing a sport shirt and sweater, while Hubert Bobo, a fullback from Ohio State, had his shirt open at the collar.

Shortly after ten A.M. Baugh entered and shook hands with each player. He had never met most of them. But they all knew who he was. Baugh was unpretentious and introduced himself, saying, "I'm Sambo."

"You know," he remarked a bit later, "some of these boys will be eating dirt from the first day, but they won't quit. Then you have to tell them that they didn't make the team, and some will turn away and cry."

Sid Youngelman, a 260-pound tackle with five years' experience in the NFL, stood to one side looking at the group. He was now twenty-seven years old, and getting another chance in pro ball after having been released by the Cleveland Browns.

"You know, they're all suspicious and nervous and maybe even scared of the next guy until that first scrimmage," he observed. "That's how it is at the beginning. But then, everything is okay after they knock the daylights out of each other."

Another prospect, Bill Worhman, stood alone from the group talking to his wife and two little children. He, too, was twenty-seven and had had a brief trial with the Cleveland Browns as a halfback. He had been head football coach at Dickinson High School in Jersey City the previous season but had quit because he felt sure he could make the team.

"I can always get a coaching job," he argued with himself, "but I can't always get a shot at something like this. I can't get football out of my system. I have to find out. . . ."

The players boarded the bus that was waiting on Eighth

Avenue. The weather was hot, and the players carried their jackets over their arms. They silently found their seats and sat down.

Bill Worhman's wife watched them. She was like a wife bidding farewell to a husband going off to war. She stood there with her two youngsters.

"Scott," she said, "hold Valerie's hand. Daddy's going away now. Wave to him."

Bill Worhman never saw them. He was sitting on the opposite side of the bus. Despite his wife and two children, he left a secure coaching job to embark on his great adventure. He lasted only a few days.

On July 10, in New Hampshire, under a hot sun, the Titans had their first workout. Baugh, lean and hard in a T-shirt, shorts, and a baseball cap, blew his whistle, and 100 athletes ran up to him. He broke the players up into squads and told them to go to work.

"I'd like to bring my men around slowly, but there isn't enough time."

He was right. Of the 100 players on the field, only forty-five would remain when the team broke camp on August 1. Twelve more would then be cut during the next five weeks. He had a lot of trimming to do.

"This is like waking up Christmas morning and looking at the pretties," Baugh said. "I reckon it's time to find out which toys will hold up."

Baugh concentrated on the quarterbacks. There were eleven of them seeking a fling at glory, but only three would get the chance. When a passer hit his target, Baugh would smile. When one would throw the ball wildly, Baugh would look down at the grass and carefully spit tobacco juice at a target only he could see.

"I don't give a damn for pretty form or pretty passes if the passer can't get the ball to the receiver. You can't throw spirals when you're running for your life."

"Sam, which quarterback do you like best out there?" an observer asked.

"It wouldn't be fair to say now," drawled Baugh. "But I'll tell you this. I can see five quarterbacks out there who won't make it."

Players have a way of complaining when it comes to training camps. It's as guaranteed as death and taxes. After three days the players began to bitch about the food. Strangely enough, this time they were right, and the coaches agreed too.

The manager of the dining hall was Sarah Thames, a sweet and understanding woman who had been feeding students and athletes for thirty-one years. The meals invariably consisted of ham, cottage cheese, and hot tea. The lack of variety upset the players. Many of them were constantly hungry, and second helpings were out of the question.

"The food sure better improve around here," said Jack Patterson, a halfback candidate from Houston. "If it doesn't improve soon, then we won't be here. Maybe we'll trim Houston when we play them, but from what my friends write me, they're beating the hell out of us on food."

Even Baugh was dissatisfied. "If I had to vote whether we had a good meal here, I'd vote no every damn time. I'm not saying cottage cheese is no good for you, but I'm sick of looking at it and at ham, too. I want to see a lot of iced tea and cold tomatoes 'cause that tastes good to the boys going down." He then yelled to Jack Copeland, the team trainer, "Hey, Jackie, go see what the heck is going on here with the meals."

Copeland made his way to Miss Thames's office. She smiled as he greeted her. "Miss Thames, we've got to come up with a good meal tonight," he pleaded. "It's a critical situation so far as morale is concerned. Let's have lots of tomatoes and iced tea and cut down on the cottage cheese and ham."

"Oh, I see," she said. "But I thought that each player was to have only forty-four hundred calories a day."

"Look, ma'am," answered Copeland. "The coaches' philosophy on the subject is this: We don't really care about the calories, we just want them satisfied."

Actually, the officials at the university had good intentions regarding the food. In fact, they went out of their way for the Titans. Pete Janetos, the director of the school's extension and summer session, who handled the arrangements for housing and feeding the Titans, had driven 200 miles to St. Michael's College in Winooski Park, Vermont, where the New York Giants had trained for several years. He brought back the menus that they had used and gave them to Miss Thames. The ham and cottage cheese apparently had not bothered the Giants. But they knew who and what they were: winners.

After only three days, the Titans began their first scrimmage. Baugh had an accelerated program, and he had to find answers quickly. He scheduled two scrimmages a day, one in the morning and the other in the afternoon. Players in the early session escaped the heat of the day. But it was hard work nevertheless, and a period of reckoning for many.

There was nothing complex about Baugh's method of coaching. He was a simple man who had been a great football player, and he relayed his expertise to his men in the most direct way he could. He told the players the correct way to do things without any detailed explanation of the whys and wherefores. If a quarterback's pass was wide of a receiver, Baugh would simply and starkly point out how important a receiver is to a passer.

Baugh ordered sixty-three players to scrimmage. The remaining thirty-seven athletes were spared because they had already been screened by the staff as the best prospects. They toiled in sweat suits and shorts while the others bumped heads for a chance to remain alive.

Just before the scrimmage started, Baugh walked over to the offensive huddle.

"Boys, we're scrimmaging you people because everyone's going to get a fair shake here. If you've got something to show me, now's the time to start showing."

The players got the message. They disregarded the heat and hit and smacked each other like dying men trying to escape execution. When the sweat and bruises of the day were over, a couple of quarterbacks, some running backs, and about a dozen linemen joined the select thirty-seven.

When the Titans broke camp two weeks later, Baugh had trimmed his squad to the necessary forty-five. They left Durham on July 31 to embark on a two-game trip to the West Coast against the Los Angeles Chargers and the Oakland Raiders. During the five scheduled exhibition games, Baugh would have to cut twelve players before the club's regular season opener against the Buffalo Bills on September 11.

In the opening game of the exhibition season the Titans were handily beaten by Los Angeles, 27–7 before a crowd of 27,778 in the 100,000-seat Los Angeles Coliseum. A Charger official had expected at least 40,000, since a high-school all-star game the previous night had attracted 46,000 people.

The following week the Titans did not fare any better, although their margin of defeat against Oakland was smaller, 23–17. The Titans were then walloped by the Dallas Texans, 35–14, in Abilene. It was the same story the next weekend against Houston.

Not until their final preseason game did the Titans register a victory. New York beat Buffalo, 52–31, a week before they opened their regular season against the same club at the Polo Grounds. Coming off a big victory, Wismer figured that ticket sales would boom.

Ralph Hawkins, a defensive back, was one of the last players to be cut. He thought he had made the squad. No other team picked him up, and two weeks later the Titans offered him $6,200 to return after he had originally signed for $8,500. Hawkins refused and remained in Maryland as a high-school coach.

The week before the opener, the Titans moved into the Polo Grounds. The field was in horrible shape, and Wismer said it cost him $15,000 to get it in playing condition. The grass was high, almost knee-high in some spots. After it was cut, a number of barren spots left gaping holes. Wismer had it sprayed green so that the field wouldn't look bad on television.

No matter what Wismer did, he could not change the decrepit condition of the Polo Grounds. It was a dismal half-concrete, half-wooden structure. There were no escalators or elevators. The fans had to walk up long, narrow ramps.

At least every other row in the stands had a broken or missing seat. The seats that remained were rickety and unpainted. The lavatories and concession stands were inadequate, and there was little space for parking. The members of the press worked in small, cramped quarters that were often dusty and dirty and always drafty, with little heat.

One night, after a game with Oakland, the players left the small, crowded clubhouse carrying their shoes and socks and with the bottoms of their trousers rolled up high. There was about six inches of water on the floor.

Still, the shoddy ball park brought back a lot of memories to Baugh.

"When I think that this is going to be my home now, I get a good laugh," he remarked. "I used to have to run for my life here, playing against the Giants."

On the Saturday before the game, Chuck Burr, the sportscaster for the Bills' games, and Jack Horrigan, a sportswriter with the Buffalo *Evening News* who was assigned to cover the Bills, went to Wismer's apartment to get their press credentials.

Wismer's apartment address was 277 Park Avenue, but the entrance to the building was on 49th Street. Pity the poor ticket buyer who was looking for the Titans' office on Park Avenue. Wismer used the living room for his office, while the coaches used the dining room. A small foyer served as the ticket department. The publicity man's office was the butler's pantry, while the bathroom served as the mimeograph room, where releases were turned out. It was the only office like it—then or now—in the American Football League.

Horrigan and Burr entered the apartment and were greeted

by Bob Kelly, one of the club's publicists, who told them they would have to wait for their credentials because Wismer was asleep. They waited. They talked and were shown around the apartment, and they still waited.

Finally Horrigan told Kelly they had to leave and they wanted their credentials. Kelly slowly opened the door of Wismer's bedroom, got down on his hands and knees and crawled into the room. He reached the bed, gently lifted up the covers, and carefully pulled out a box which contained the press tickets. He tiptoed out of the room. Wismer never woke up, and Horrigan and Burr had their tickets.

That night the weather in New York was balmy. The temperature was around seventy degrees, and Wismer and the rest of the Titan staff were optimistic that good weather the next day would bring out a crowd of at least 20,000. Wismer had hired Angelo Bertelli, the former great Notre Dame All-American quarterback, to be the public-address announcer, and Baugh had served notice to the public that the Titans would be an exciting club by saying, "We'll throw the ball until we make 'em dizzy." Everything was ready.

Sunday morning broke dark and windy, with the first signs of Hurricane Diana. By game time, at 2:05 P.M., the rain had started to come down steadily. Wismer was bursting with pride before the kickoff. He walked up and down the sidelines in a camel-hair coat looking like a boy on Christmas morning with too many presents. He had designed dark-blue jerseys with gold lettering and gold pants with a blue stripe. The helmets were gold, and the stockings were blue with gold stripes. This was Wismer's team. His very own, wearing the colors of the school he revered above all others, Notre Dame.

You needed a scorecard to identify the players. The Titans' opening lineup was: Thurlow Cooper, right end; Gene Cockrell, right tackle; John McMullan, right guard; Mike Hudock, center; Bob Mischak, left guard; Joe Katcik, left tackle; Art Powell, split end; Bill Shockley, halfback; Dick Jamieson, quarterback; Pete Hart, fullback; and Don Maynard, flanker.

Although the game was an artistic success, 27–3, it was a financial flop. It was the first of a succession of never-ending losses at the gate. There were 9,607 people in the stands, but only 5,727 paid. It was hardly enough to pay for the rental of the field. Still, Wismer was satisfied with the efforts of the club and overjoyed that the players had presented him with the game ball.

Al Dorow, a journeyman quarterback who had played for Washington and Philadelphia, came off the bench in the second quarter and captured the fancy of what crowd there was. He sparked the Titans to their victory, by running for two touchdowns. Despite the muddy field, Bill Shockley kicked two field goals and three extra points. The final Titan touchdown was a thirteen-yard pass from Jamieson to Powell.

Until halfway through the season, the Titans challenged the Houston Oilers for the lead. But Dorow and then Jamieson were injured, and the club turned to a taxi-squad quarterback, Bob Scrabis, for help, which he was ill-equipped to provide. By the time Dorow and Jamieson fully recovered from their injuries, the club had dropped out of contention.

Friday's game with Boston had to be postponed until the following night. The New York Yankees were playing an important game against the Baltimore Orioles on Friday, and Wismer wanted to avoid a conflict. Saturday's game had a wild ending, the Patriots winning on the final play, 28–24, with Wismer lodging a protest after viewing the game films the following day. He said a Boston player, Chuck Shonta, had kicked a loose football and the play should have been dead. He invited Foss to fly to New York to see the infraction for himself. Foss sent his representative, Bob Austin, supervisor of officials, who viewed the films and detected a double infraction, spotting Rick Sapienza of the Titans also kicking the ball.

That set the pace for the remainder of the Titans' year. They reached an all-time low when one of their guards, Howie Glenn, died as a result of a broken neck suffered in the game against the Houston Oilers on October 9. In the history of pro football, there were only two recorded deaths at the time.

The Titans finished the season at 7–7, breaking even on the field if not on the gate. Officially the club had attracted only 114,628 in seven games, an average of 16,375 for each date. The biggest crowd they drew was 21,000 for the Houston game. Even these relatively low attendance figures, released by Wismer, were scoffed at by the press. One New York writer, George Vecsey, wrote, "The fans came disguised as empty seats."

"There were so few fans at the games that we used to wave to our wives in the stands," quipped Grantham. "During the game we'd hear the announcement that there were nineteen thousand or twenty thousand people. We knew there were only two thousand or three thousand in the park. I used to tell a story at some dinners that the Titans didn't line up on the field for the pregame introductions. We went into the stands and shook hands with everybody."

The Giants, directly across the river, attracted sellouts to their games. Wismer broke his last ties with the NFL when he sold his 200 Redskin shares to William B. McDonald of Miami for $350,000. The first year of Harry Wismer, his Titans, and the AFL had ended.

Houston had emerged as the Eastern Conference champion, and Los Angeles took the Western Conference. On January 1, 1961, the Oilers defeated the Los Angeles Chargers, 24–16, to become the first champions of the AFL.

In 1961 Wismer and the AFL first heard the name Sonny Werblin. Barron Hilton brought him in to serve as the league's television agent, and Wismer and Werblin never hit it off. Wismer always suspected that Werblin was waiting around to acquire the Titans, his Titans!

The 1961 season showed much the same paltry box-office receipts as the year before. Except, now, Wismer became irritated and began to lash out. He brought the Titans closer to

New York for training camp, to the Bear Mountain Inn, in an attempt to get more publicity. This move failed—at least the fans were not breaking down the door at his Park Avenue apartment to purchase season tickets.

Angrily, Wismer struck out at the press, Harold Weissman of the *Daily Mirror* in particular. Wismer accused Weissman of favoring the Giants in his columns because the writer's son was a ball boy for them. Weissman answered that this was news to both him and Mrs. Weissman, since they had no children.

Then Wismer began a season-long tirade against Foss. He insisted that the league office belonged in New York. Foss simply ignored him.

Wismer's most celebrated feud occurred with Buffalo coach Buster Ramsey. The Titans were playing the Bills in Buffalo, and quarterback Al Dorow ran out of the pocket and was chased to the Buffalo sideline. Richie McCabe, who played cornerback on that side for the Bills, charged after Dorow and hit him after he was out of bounds. Dorow managed to stay on his feet, spun around, and threw the ball at Mc-Cabe.

Immediately Coach Ramsey charged Dorow, and the Buffalo players followed him. While no witnesses will say that they saw any punches thrown, Dorow did go down from two right-hands to the jaw. Calm was eventually restored, and the game continued without further incident.

After the game Wismer was incensed. He wanted Ramsey banned for life from football. Baugh looked the other way. He said that any player dumb enough to get into a fight on the other team's side of the field deserved whatever he got. It is an unwritten rule among players that you never start a fight in front of the other guy's bench. Baugh's traditional attitude, however, did not endear him to Wismer.

Later in the season, when the Bills came to New York to play the Titans on Thanksgiving Day, the ever-enterprising, publicity-conscious Wismer telegraphed the police commissioner of New York for added protection. The newspapers gave the story good play, but still the fans did not come out in large numbers.

Instead, Wismer came out against Foss after the game. He called a press conference in which he declared that he was going to ask for Foss's ouster as a commissioner at the end of the season. He pointed out that he felt Foss was an outstanding person and cited his war record and such. But Wismer insisted that the league office had to be in New York and if Foss would not agree to the move, Wismer would see that he was removed at the January league meeting in San Diego.

The Titans finished the 1961 campaign with another 7–7 record. Wismer, however, had become disenchanted with Baugh, saying that he was too soft and that he could have gotten more out of the players. Baugh felt that the players required little supervision. It was obvious why the players liked him.

At times Wismer, always on the sidelines, would send in plays during a game. One time, when an opposing runner burst through the middle for a long touchdown, Wismer grabbed one of his players and asked what kind of play it was.

"It was a draw play."

"Good," Wismer noted, and added, "let's run it the next time we get the ball."

Wismer criticized Baugh for not having a play book. Larry Grantham said of Baugh, "He knew the game inside and out, but kept it in his head."

Baugh was a calm person and seemed unaffected by anything going on around him. He approached his job with a nonchalance that drove Wismer to distraction.

One time, as the team was lining up for the television introductions on the field, one of the players began to throw up as the camera began to swing down the line.

"Hey, coach, get this guy out of here; he is getting us all sick," yelled one of the players on the field to Baugh on the bench.

"Better he stays out there than being over here and getting twenty-two of us sick," answered Baugh.

At the end of the second season, Houston again won the Eastern Conference, and San Diego, which had operated as Los Angeles the previous year, took the Western title. In the championship game at San Diego, the Oilers won their second straight title, 10–3. But after two years of operation, none of the eight teams in the league showed a profit, and the Titans appeared to be the biggest losers.

At the annual league meeting in San Diego in January of 1962, Foss and some of the owners—Ralph Wilson, Lamar Hunt, and Billy Sullivan—were sitting around a table at the El Cortez Hotel. Wismer came up, and without even acknowledging anyone else, stared straight at Foss. Everyone's nervousness was apparent.

"Hello, Joe," Wismer bellowed. "Have a cigar; in fact, have two cigars, pal."

Everybody laughed. But that only temporarily ended Wismer's attempts to have Foss removed as commissioner.

Despite the heavy financial losses the first two seasons, Wismer was feeling a bit better about things for the 1962 campaign. A few days before the San Diego meeting, Wismer sold thirty percent of his club to Royal Raidle of Palm Beach, Florida, for $500,000.

"In view of the fact that I have lost one million, two hundred thousand dollars in the past two years with the Titans, this is about the best thing that has happened to me," Wismer remarked.

Later in the month, however, he suffered a setback when Sebo resigned to become the athletic director at the University of Virginia. He still had a year remaining on his three-year contract with the Titans.

"There is no friction between me and Wismer," Sebo emphasized. "I'm just tired of traveling and want to settle down on the campus. I have my family to consider. I spend Christmas and New Year's Eve on planes."

That spring Wismer made another move in his publicity department, which had been like a revolving door the first two years. Attending the turf writers' dinner-dance in Saratoga, he approached Murray Goodman, the publicity director of Yonkers Raceway, on the dance floor, of all places.

"Murray," he yelled, "I'm going to get you to work for me. Just wait and see."

A month later Wismer called Goodman at his office at Yonkers. He again made Goodman an offer.

"It so happens that I decided to leave Yonkers at the time," recalled Goodman. "I told him that I would meet him the next day in his office."

Goodman was accompanied by his son, Robert, who that morning had received his discharge from the Coast Guard. They both went up to Wismer's office.

"Hey, that's a fine-looking boy you got there," said Wismer.

"He just got out of service," replied Goodman.

"That's fine, son," said Wismer. "Do you have a job yet?"

"No, sir, I don't."

"Well, you got one now," remarked Wismer. "You can start working for me at one hundred dollars a week." Goodman signed a two-year contract with Wismer.

Goodman, a veteran publicity man, was well liked by the members of the New York sports fraternity. Short, with wavy hair, big blue eyes, and an ever-present cigar, he looked and acted tough, but was always generous and fair. That was his strength, and the writers loved him for it.

"As soon as I announced the fact that I was working for the Titans, my friends told me I was crazy," said Goodman. "But I had a two-year contract, so I began to apply myself."

Actually Goodman walked right into a hornet's nest. Wismer's disenchantment with Baugh had reached a point of no return. Before the team was scheduled to report to East Stroudsburg, Pennsylvania, for training camp, Wismer replaced Sammy with Clyde "Bulldog" Turner, a former center with the Chicago Bears. Baugh had one year remaining on his contract, and Wismer said that he could spend it as an adviser and kicking coach.

It was obvious that Baugh's presence at training camp

could create an embarrassing situation for Turner. Goodman told Turner that he was now head coach and that it would be better for all concerned if he told Baugh not to remain on the field.

"I can't do that, Murray. Sammy is my idol."

Goodman approached Baugh and got him to sit down with Wismer and the lawyers and to work things out. They did, and Wismer and Baugh parted as friends, with Sammy getting paid the remainder of his one-year contract.

"I think the world of Sammy," remarked Wismer, "so this is the way to do it. We're both good friends. He'll be paid off for the remaining year of his contract."

"I think the world of Harry," said Baugh. "I'll take the money. Harry gave me my chance to coach pro football. If there is any way I can help the Titans, I'll be happy to do it. I'll be glad to scout for the club, talk to a prospect, anything."

"I may even make him a director of the club," snapped Wismer. "If he gets a job, God bless him. In fact, I'll do everything I can to help him land one."

But after Baugh left, Wismer sat in a big overstuffed chair and there were tears in his eyes. Baugh was his idol too.

Goodman tried to build a new image for the Titans. He would precede the club on their preseason exhibition road games and feed the old boxing publicity angle he had practiced in past years of building up the underdog. He told the out-of-town sportswriters that the Titans under Turner had a new killer instinct and they would run up four or five touchdowns before they would ease off. Goodman got headlines, and Turner got the jitters.

"What are you doing, Murray?" he screamed. "I never said any of those things. You're going to get the other teams angry, and they'll kill us. I'm going to tell Harry."

"What are you worrying about," exclaimed Goodman; "you wanna sell tickets and make money, don't you? This is the way to do it."

Turner did tell Wismer, and the two agreed that Goodman's tactics were not right. Wismer informed Goodman that he could not release anything without written permission from either himself or Turner.

"Can you imagine getting written permission when I am working on the coast and they're both in New York?" asked Goodman.

Relations between Goodman and Wismer became strained. Shortly after, Wismer suspended but did not fire him, so he would not have to pay off on his contract.

"I tried to get him to fire me in the worst possible way, but he wouldn't," said Goodman. "I've never seen anybody like Wismer. He had a multiple personality which could run its course in an hour's time. He could be a charmer, kind, vicious, or mean. But the guy really loved football. He was proud of his team.

"I don't know how he did it, but he used to be drunk by ten in the morning. I knew he didn't stay up all night drinking. Then I found out how he did it. He'd take beef broth and vodka for breakfast, and it would knock him for a loop. I tried it one day, just to see. It worked."

It was apparent that Wismer knew the end was in sight. The first crisis came at the beginning of the season, when the players' paychecks bounced. The players refused to practice all week. Finally, on their own, they worked out Friday, went to Buffalo on Saturday, and defeated the Bills that night. In the dressing room before the game someone said, "Let's go out and win one for the gypper."

From then on, Wismer's troubles began to mount quickly. Foss continued his open warfare with Wismer by calling for his ouster.

"It would be better for New York if the Titans got a new owner," stated Foss. "Wismer gets only the worst kind of publicity. He feels any publicity is good publicity. He's unreasonable. He'll say anything, and he'll stick anyone in the mud."

Wismer fought to keep his team. "There's no way in the world anyone can make me sell my stock," he fumed. "I'll go to every court in the land. That goes for Foss or anyone else. I have no intention of getting out. I've spent one million, two hundred thousand dollars to bring football to New York, and no politician from Sioux Falls, South Dakota, is going to get me out."

Finally, the first week in November, Wismer gave up. He called Milt Woodard, the assistant commissioner and treasurer of the AFL, to say that unless he received substantial help immediately, he was finished. The league assumed the cost of running the club from November 8 until the end of the season.

Harry Wismer, still wearing his camel-hair coat, although a bit worn from the years, still walked the sidelines in the remaining Titan home games.

4

Werblin
to the Rescue

"Joe, I'm broke, I don't know what I am going to do."

Harry Wismer said it plainly enough. He forgot his feud with Commissioner Joe Foss that first week in November. When you are completely out of money, you quickly forget who your enemies are. Wismer was desperate and had no choice but to talk to Foss.

"Now, just hold on, Harry," said Foss, "and sit still long enough for me to work something out."

For once Wismer kept his mouth shut. The AFL was faced with a serious crisis, and Foss realized its significance the moment he spoke to Wismer. They could have lost their television deal, the one reliable source of funds. Quickly Foss telephoned the remaining seven owners. He bluntly informed them of the situation, emphasizing the necessity of a team in New York. They all agreed that whatever he decided would be all right with them.

Foss made certain the Titans would finish the season on the playing field. Four days after Wismer's call, he received an accounting of the Titans' operations from Milt Woodard, the league's treasurer, and learned it would take $362,000 for the club to play the remainder of their games. He assessed each of the seven other clubs an equal share, even though it strained Denver and Oakland.

Foss then asked the owners to attend an emergency meeting in Houston on December 19. Until then, Wismer would remain as president of the Titans, and the players would be paid by the league.

The owners assembled in the Shamrock Hotel in Houston to solve the New York dilemma. Wismer attended the meeting with his attorney, Bill Richter. Foss and the owners felt the best thing for Wismer to do would be to sell the club. Wismer and his attorney agreed. The rest was up to Foss.

"People had approached me when the Titan situation unfolded," said Foss. "I compiled a list of the interested parties and made it known to the other owners. I told them that I would check out each prospect individually and see how serious their intentions were.

"I began calling the prospects the day after the meeting ended. The list of potential buyers, however, quickly dwindled. Most of them offered ridiculous prices, ranging from six hundred to eight hundred thousand dollars. The top figure would not come close to covering the owners' expenses, plus the other liabilities.

"Then, I thought I had one individual who sounded enthusiastic. I spoke to him on the phone and arranged to meet him the following day in New York at the Waldorf-Astoria. It was a futile trip. All the guy wanted was to pay the existing bills of the Titans and then assume ownership. I told that bird he was on dream street and returned to Dallas.

"I continued the search for prospects, but time was getting short. I had gone to my home in South Dakota for the weekend and talked with Sullivan Barnes, one of the league's attornies, on the phone and he mentioned the name of Sonny Werblin, recalling a remark Sonny had made a year before at the 21 Club in New York.

"I remembered the incident well. We were having dinner,

Sonny, Barnes, Wismer, and I. Sonny was the league's television agent at the time, and he had made a remark to Wismer during the course of our conversation: 'I'd like to own your ball club and show you how to run it.'

"The statement infuriated Wismer. He quickly became suspicious of Werblin and accused him of having designs to take over his club. Werblin assured him that it was no such thing. Still, Wismer wasn't convinced and was quite upset until I calmed things down.

"So, I placed a call to Werblin in New York in December. His secretary told me that he was vacationing at his home in New Jersey and that he couldn't be reached. I told her that it was an emergency and that I had to talk to him. She gave me the telephone number and I called him.

" 'Sonny, would you be interested in buying the Titans?' He said that he might be and that he'd talk to me about it sometime in the next month or so. I told him there wasn't time and we had to talk now. We set up a lunch date the next day at the 21, and I flew all night from South Dakota to make the appointment. We had a friendly meeting and Sonny agreed to a one-million-dollar price.

"Now I figured that the problem was over. I told Wismer that I had a buyer for the club. He asked me who, but I wouldn't tell him. He got mad and told me that he had changed his mind about selling. He said he was going to throw the club into bankruptcy and continue to run the Titans with refinancing.

"I thought we'd hit a snag. Wismer was like a drowning man going down for the third time. He put on a three-ring circus in court. There was a newspaper strike on at the time, and the only interested people in court were the creditors and a bunch of winos who came in to get out of the cold.

"Almost every other day Wismer came into court with a new lawyer. Each lawyer used a different approach, which resulted in the hearing moving very slowly.

"Wismer was quite vociferous. He'd stand and yell at witnesses, often challenging the veracity of their statements. The judge warned Wismer that he would hold him in contempt if he didn't remain quiet.

"Just before the case went to court, Tom Granatell, president of New Jersey Chemical Company, tried to buy the club. Granatell met with Wismer, who told him, 'Kid, all you have to do is attend the hearings in court, and when the judge asks for bids on the club, you offer one and a half million dollars. That's all you have to do, and leave the rest to me.'

"But Granatell couldn't get any satisfaction from Wismer on what the one and a half million would get him, and he never bothered to show up in court.

"By now Werblin was beginning to lose interest," said Foss. "I couldn't let that happen, because it was March already, and the 1963 season was right around the corner. We had a schedule to make up and television commitments to resolve. Finally the federal bankruptcy referee ruled against Wismer and the way was open for Werblin's group to buy the Titans. On March 15 the referee approved the sale for one million dollars of the Titans to the Gotham Football Club, Inc."

After three years of stormy controversy, haphazard operations, and financial chaos, Harry Wismer was completely removed from the American Football League. He left something of a legacy. He was one of the founders, and without him there possibly might not have been a television contract and subsequently no league.

At the time of the purchase, Werblin, in his early fifties, was president of Music Corporation of America-TV. There were four others connected with him in the purchasing group: Donald Lillis, a partner of Bear, Stearns & Co., Wall Street brokers; Townsend Martin and Leon Hess, directors of Monmouth Race Track in New Jersey; and Philip Iselin, vice-president and treasurer of Monmouth. Lillis was also connected with horse racing, as president of Bowie Race Track in Maryland, while Werblin was a director at Monmouth.

Like Wismer, Werblin was a hustler. He had been raised in Brooklyn in a middle-class neighborhood. His father was a partner in a paper-bag company and he planned to send

Sonny to Dartmouth. Just before Werblin was to leave for college, his father died suddenly and Sonny decided to enroll at Rutgers in New Brunswick, New Jersey, to be closer to home.

Sonny wanted to play football, but he broke his shoulder playing on the freshman team and gave up the sport. He then turned his efforts to making money, at which he proved quite adept. By the time he was a junior, Werblin was a correspondent for a total of seven New York and New Jersey newspapers. The dean called him into his office one day and told him that no one student would be allowed to monopolize all the newspapers.

"I was making so much money that they broke me up as a monopoly," claimed Werblin.

After graduation he was offered a job by *The New York Times*. The salary, however, was disappointingly low, so Sonny took a job with a paper-bag company. Upset at the fact that his late father's partners had purchased the family interest, he decided to prove that he could make it on his own.

"I went to work in a mill and served as a salesman. I was making seventeen dollars a week during the depression, but at least I was doing something."

A couple of years later he was doing something else. In 1934 he went to work as an office boy in the New York branch of the Music Corporation of America. The outfit had been founded ten years before in Chicago by Dr. Jules Stein, an eye doctor, and Billy Goodheart, a piano player, who represented bands for a flat ten-percent commission.

Goodheart had the most profound influence on Werblin. He would purposely arrive in the office ahead of Sonny and then yell at him for being late. He would mess up his desk and break pencils and then scream at Werblin for having everything so untidy. Goodheart would also send Sonny on any number of worthless errands all designed to test the youngster. Finally, after months of harassing him, Goodheart sent Werblin on the road as a band boy for Guy Lombardo.

"I remember one time on the road we were being taken by

a local dance-hall promoter," recalled Sonny. "I knew we were
getting swindled. The promoter had relatives all over the place
taking up the money. He was a big man in shirt sleeves and he
wore suspenders. I asked him if he could change a couple of
thousand-dollar bills. He said he could, and he began empty-
ing his pockets, which were filled with money. I caught him off
guard. I grabbed whatever money I could and then ran as fast
as I could for the bus."

Werblin was learning quickly. Following his education on
the road, he was called back to the New York office and began
booking bands all over town, in hotels, nightclubs, and
theaters. When MCA moved into radio, Werblin got his first
exposure to Madison Avenue. And, when Goodheart retired
in 1941, Werblin took over, having recovered from a heart
attack the previous year.

As Werblin assumed command, television created a new era
in the entertainment business, and Werblin moved quickly and
ably to take advantage of it. He became a shrewd salesman
and a pioneer at the same time. For a while, during the early
days of television, big-name stars refused to appear on the
video tube. It was not yet financially attractive enough, as the
big advertising money had not yet begun to pour into the
industry. Werblin devised a solution: give the big stars part
ownership in their own shows.

It worked, and Werblin became one of the most important
men in the industry. Strangely, for a man who was a genius
with the most public of all the media, Werblin always remained in the background. He refrained from interviews but
worked quietly and effectively. It was not unusual that on a
given day he would appear in the top executive offices of all
three networks. He was well respected in the sense that he had
not only the client at heart but the customer as well. In 1962,
when he learned that the Titans were having financial difficul-
ties, Werblin recommended that MCA purchase the team.
However, the company's lawyers, fearful of antitrust action,
advised against it.

Then, a year later, Werblin became the dominant figure of

a syndicate that owned the Titans. And Werblin immediately applied show-business techniques.

"Pro football is the ultimate in entertainment," he said. "It's got everything—action, violence, color. Look at the kids on the vacant lots these days. They aren't throwing a baseball around anymore, they're playing catch with a football. Timing is everything, in show business and everything else, and this is the time for pro football."

The Titans had been a bad show on television the past three years. So, like a show that the networks would reject another time, Werblin discarded the name of the Titans forever. He decided not to rebuild a sick product, but to build a new one.

He began with a new name. Less than a month after they purchased the Titans, Werblin announced that the new name of the team would be the Jets. At the same time, he introduced Weeb Ewbank, who two months before had been released as head coach of the Baltimore Colts, as the new coach and general manager.

Ewbank was well known in professional football. He had won two championships for the Colts after having taken over in a situation similar to the Jets', namely, a vast rebuilding job.

Bulldog Turner, who had a year remaining on his contract, was paid off and released. So, too, were Turner's assistant coaches. Werblin wanted a new beginning. The only organizational man retained from the Titan regime was George Sauer. He impressed Werblin with his honesty, dedication, and knowledge of football players. He was made director of player personnel and turned loose to scout the nation for players.

Sauer also had a good rapport with the players. Maynard, for one, always sought his advice when he was troubled.

"You really felt you'd get a fair shake from Sauer," explained Maynard. "When the new owners came in, I was happy to learn that they would retain him. I felt I had one vote for me already.

"He was a guy I felt I could go to. I had some problems at times, and he made a lot of difference. He helped me a lot. He would see the problem from my side and at the same time relate it to me from the other side. He'd make me see every possible angle."

Werblin even changed the colors of the Jets' uniforms. Werblin was born on St. Patrick's Day, and green was his favorite color.

The next person Werblin hired for the organization was Joe Cahill, the sports-public-relations director at West Point. He had deep ties at the Point and left with mixed emotions. Cahill was so well liked and respected by the metropolitan sportswriters that they gave him a dinner when he resigned his Army post. Joe Cahill was an immensely likable Irishman, with a warm, infectious smile.

Werblin worked incessantly to rebuild the organization, and relished the work. "The final signing (for the purchase of the club) took place at the attorney's office, Ed Neaher, at Twenty-five Broadway. It was snowing pretty hard, as I remember, and I had tried to hail a cab, but with the weather being what it was, I couldn't get one. It was already after four o'clock, and I had gone without eating throughout the day-long discussions.

"I started walking a few blocks looking for a cab, and then I walked into the first coffee shop I found. I was hungry and wanted a sandwich. The prices were unbelievable. Here, I had just signed a check for one million dollars, and I was eating a tuna-fish sandwich for nineteen cents and drinking a cup of coffee that cost five cents."

Werblin secured offices for the Jets not far from his apartment. The entire office decor radiated with green, from the carpet to the stationery to the ribbons in the typewriter. As he had said, everything would change, and there would not be any reminders of the Titans.

The only things he could not change were the Polo Grounds and the players. Although he hoped Shea Stadium would be completed in time for the football season, he expected to play the Jets' home games on the scene of the Titans' demise. And, since no one in the demoralized Titan organization had signed any of the players that had been drafted, it would be the same

Titan personnel running up and down the field, unrecogniz-
able in their new uniforms.

Construction on Shea Stadium had begun in 1962. It was
named after William Shea, a New York attorney who had led
a civic drive to bring National League baseball back to New
York. Shea and Branch Rickey, the former owner of the
Brooklyn Dodgers, were the main architects of the Continental
League, a new baseball league that was spawned in 1959. The
league never did get off the ground, but Shea's and Rickey's
efforts resulted in the birth of the New York Mets, an expansion team in the National League in 1962.

The AFL tried to help. They gave the Jets the first opportunity to pick up any players cut by the other clubs. It was
hardly a way to build a franchise, but if some talent could be
found to supplement the hold-over Titans, then so much the
better.

Baseball's newborn New York Mets had spent close to
$50,000 in refurbishing the old Polo Grounds, but it still was
not very appealing, and parking remained a major problem.
If any club needed the flair of a showman, it was the Jets.

Werblin began to promote in the best show-business tradition. As it turned out, the Jets were possibly the first sports
enterprise to depend so heavily on radio and newspaper advertising. When some of his associates questioned his strategy,
Sonny convinced them by asking: "When was the last time
you watched a commercial?"

Werblin built a female symbol, "Jet-Set Janie," for the radio
audience. It was a takeoff on Adelaide, from Damon Runyon's
Guys and Dolls, a dumb broad with a Brooklyn accent. Janie
would tell her listeners that she became interested in football
because she had recently begun keeping company "with a
soitan party wot plays football for the New York Jets." Now,
she said, she knew the difference "between a pass and a
huddle."

Then Janie would talk a little about coach Weeb Ewbank.
"Weeb Ewbank" she would ask, "now wot kinda name is dat?
Anyway, anyone wot don' go to see the Jets is got some noive."

Werblin was out to sell a new product in the best way he knew how. He wanted no affiliations with the past. He even resented any misconceptions concerning his purchase of the AFL's New York franchise.

"I acquired the club on my own terms. I did not buy the franchise from Wismer, but from the receivership court, and thereby purchased only the assets. I wasn't responsible for any of the team's debts. I set up the club as a subchapter S corporation, which meant that I could deduct from my personal income any losses that I incurred from the club. I figured any sports franchise in New York was worth one million dollars."

Werblin was dedicated to making the Jets a successful operation. He turned all his energy toward that goal. However, he didn't delude himself into thinking that he could do it in one short season. But the first step would be an important one. His emphasis on detail, coupled with ample energy, had been largely responsible for his success in the business world.

"I'll work twenty hours a day or more if necessary."

Those close to him didn't have to be assured. Some swear that it is not unusual for Werblin to go to sleep at four A.M., wake up two hours later, go to his office, and then catch an early-morning flight to Miami to watch one of his horses run at Hialeah. He'll return to his office in New York in the evening, work until midnight, and then go out for supper before returning home.

Werblin is gregarious by nature, has a puckish smile, and likes to tell stories and to entertain. Being short and slightly built, he seemingly could get lost in a crowd. But somehow, when Sonny Werblin walks into a room, everyone knows he is there. He has a certain charm that quickly travels across a room. He was well liked by the writers because he not only freely mingled with them, but often gave lavish press parties when making announcements.

A gentle-looking individual with a soft voice, Werblin wears glasses with clear-plastic rims and dresses conservatively. He answers questions thoughtfully, and if any question in particular disturbs him, he answers it with a question himself.

He admitted that a lot of his approach to football originated in the entertainment world. It motivated his thinking and his actions.

"Too many people make the mistake of trying to salvage something out of a bad investment, and they end up losing more money," he pointed out. "In the *George White Scandals* many years ago, Willie Howard worked a wonderful comedy routine. He was in a subway and he spit out the tip of a cigar. A policeman came up to him and said that would be a two-dollar fine. Suddenly another man ran up and shouted 'I'm a lawyer, and we'll fight this injustice.'

"So, the lawyer began fighting Willie's case, and the more he fought, the more Willie got pushed around. Finally, after weeks and weeks, Willie was thrown in jail for thirty days. Through it all, the weeks in court, the pushing around, Willie kept repeating one plea to the lawyer, 'Please, please. Pay the two dollars.'

"In show business we have an expression: 'Pay the two dollars.' Take your loss. I believe in that."

Although he is not a dramatic individual, Werblin resorted to theatrics the very first day the Jets reported to preseason training camp. He did it to make a point.

"I walked into the locker room, and the equipment manager was repairing a flap on a pair of shoulder pads. He was repairing them with adhesive tape.

"I went over to him and looked at him for a moment. Then I yelled, 'What are you doing? What in the world are you doing?' "

This was the first time that most of the squad had seen Werblin. They were sitting around relaxing and then looked up startled when Werblin began shouting.

" 'I'm repairing the shoulder pads,' answered the equipment man.

" 'Not on the Jets,' I snapped. 'We use new equipment on

the Jets.' I then yanked the shoulder pads away from him and flung them with all my strength into a garbage can.

"I'm not normally a dramatic man, but I was there for a purpose that day. I wanted to get a sense of pride into the players. I wanted them to know that things were different now.

"You know what that was? That was the Ziegfeld Method. Florenz Ziegfeld used to dress his showgirls in hundred-dollar hats, five-hundred-dollar gowns, and sixty-dollar petticoats. People used to ask him: 'Why the petticoats, Flo? No one can see them.' Ziegfeld's reply was that the girls knew the difference and it gave them more pride. That's the way we have to operate."

Certainly no one else in professional football ever operated that way.

5

Ewbank's Plan

"I was shocked. It all happened so suddenly, I haven't thought where I go from here. I'm waiting."

Weeb Ewbank said it all in three sentences the morning after he was released as head coach and general manager of the Baltimore Colts. He had been asked to rebuild a tottering ball club in 1954. He was asked to build a winner in five years. He did. He won a championship in 1958 and another in 1959, and suddenly, after a 7–7 season in 1962, Ewbank was released. There were no complicated reasons given, just the fact that "it was felt a change was needed."

He sat in the living room of his four-bedroom colonial house just outside of Baltimore, his wife Lucy handing him a cream soda, his favorite soft drink. He was in his stocking feet, trying to relax as best he could, with an uncertain future an intruder in the quiet of his home. All the Colt mementos—a small foot rug, a team photo, several ashtrays, an age-worn football—suddenly were strangers to him. Weeb Ewbank was no longer a Baltimore Colt. He was trying to hold back the tears.

"No reason was given, nothing was said except that they felt a change was in order," Ewbank kept repeating. "Coaching is like riding a motorcycle: you ride it long enough, and you're going to get killed."

Only a few years before, in the glory days of Baltimore championships, Colt owner Carroll Rosenbloom had referred to Ewbank as "my crew-cut IBM machine." He was that and more, a plain-looking man who could eat corn on the cob every day and talk football every minute of the time. He was as dedicated to his profession as any coach could be. After each day's workout he would write a report and file it in the basement of his modestly furnished home.

Ewbank is a mild-mannered individual who rarely displays his emotions. He is short, five-foot-seven, and heavy, 190 pounds, and one of his rare, but widely observed, displays of emotion occurred during the sudden-death championship game between the Colts and the New York Giants in 1958.

The little field general took off after Sam Huff, the celebrated Giant linebacker, and began flailing away with both fists at the New York hero. Huff fended him off until players from both sides raced over and pulled Ewbank away.

"I'm not proud of what I did," Ewbank remarked after the titanic but extraordinarily mismatched struggle. "I thought I saw Huff jab his knees into Ray Berry's ribs."

Weeb, who got the nickname from a younger brother who couldn't pronounce his given name of Wilbur, was born in Richmond, Indiana, in 1907. At the age of seven he helped make deliveries on a horse and wagon for his father's two grocery stores. He liked sports, football and baseball, and played both when he entered Miami University in Oxford, Ohio, in 1924.

In the fifteen years following his graduation, Ewbank coached high-school sports—football, baseball, and basketball —and earned a Master of Science degree from Columbia University during the summer months. He later coached at the Great Lakes Naval Training Station during World War II, then moved into the college ranks at Brown and at Washington

(Missouri) University. From 1949 he was the tackle coach of the Cleveland Browns until, in 1954, he went to Baltimore as head coach.

Now he was out. He accepted his firing gracefully. He did not strike back at anyone, and even wished his successor, former aide Don Shula, and the Colts nothing but the best of luck. Financially he was secure. He had two years remaining on his Baltimore contract and had invested in an oil business which was starting to expand. Still, it could not satisfy him. He had too much football left in him. His wife, Lucy, knew it, and she also knew that he would be back coaching before the 1963 season came around.

"When he sits at his desk, peering through his glasses at plays he has doodled on the back of envelopes or any other scrap of paper, I can see a little football in each eye," she said affectionately. "He always kids us and says that football comes first and the family is a necessary evil."

While waiting like an Army wife for orders to arrive, the inevitable happened. The telephone rang and Lucy answered it. It was from Joe Foss. The commissioner of the AFL was on the line and wanted to talk to Weeb. Foss was acting as a feeler to see if Ewbank would be interested in coaching the New York entry in his league. It was like a call from heaven.

"Why don't you just retire?" asked Lucy.

"Well, I don't know," answered Weeb. "I just like the game so much. We'll wait and see."

A couple of days later Sonny Werblin called from Miami. He said he had talked to Joe Foss, who told him that Ewbank might be interested in coaching in New York. Weeb repeated that he was, and then Werblin asked him to come down to Miami to discuss it.

"I went to Miami with an open mind," said Ewbank. "I knew that I wanted to coach again. But I wanted to wait and see what the situation was before committing myself. I met Werblin and we talked, rather casually at first, for two days. I told Werblin that I would like very much to coach the ball club but that I wanted to talk the situation over with my wife.

We had lived in Baltimore for quite a number of years and we had a lot of friends and our roots were there.

"Lucy knew where my first love was, and she didn't object. She said we'll just sell the house and buy another. I called Werblin back and said I'd be his coach. But then I also told him that for me to be head coach I must also be the general manager too. He said he didn't know about that part. But I was firm and told him that was the only way I'd take the job as coach. A few weeks later he agreed.

"Being the general manager, as well as the coach, was important, to my way of thinking. If you go down through the years in pro football, the success coaches are the ones who are both. I'm talking about George Halas, Paul Brown, and more recently Vince Lombardi. They had control. They had a better opportunity to succeed. I have to have complete control of my football team."

The deal almost fell through over the general-manager stipulation, but Ewbank remained firm, and finally the new owners relented. The agreement was signed April 12, and that night Werblin, Foss, and Ewbank celebrated privately at Le Pavillon, a fashionable restaurant on New York's East Side.

Werblin's office called a major press conference on Monday afternoon. Over the weekend the newspaper writers speculated that Ewbank would be named coach, after word had gotten out that he had been negotiating with the new owners of the New York franchise for the past several weeks. On April 15 Ewbank was introduced to the press as the club's head coach and general manager for the next three years. Werblin also announced that the club's new name would be the Jets.

"I've seen sicker cows than this get well," Ewbank told the large turnout of press representatives. "I don't know a lot about the players. But I don't think they are any worse than the Colts when I took over after a 3-9 season in 1953. I'll feel right at home. I'm used to challenges. We won't panic. It will take time to sit down and analyze our problems.

"In Baltimore I said it would take five years to make a contender. We took five years and eight minutes, the extra time it took to beat the Giants in overtime for the championship. Our aim is to beat the record of the Colts."

Despite the many problems facing him—and it was already the middle of April—Ewbank looked at the situation optimistically. He was aware that the old owners had not signed a single draft choice the previous fall and that the club finished last in the Eastern Division with a 5-9 record.

"As far as I know, the club drafted only one player, Bill King of Dartmouth, who hasn't signed with somebody else. We'll have to go into the free-agent field. Don't forget, Johnny Unitas was a free agent when I got him at Baltimore. Two or three college coaches have already called me about players who were missed in the draft.

"We are going to comb every area we can. And there is another league. Some coaches over there have already contacted me. I'm not too familiar with the existing personnel, and I'll be spending a lot of time the next few months looking at films. Some players I know about. I've seen Lee Grosscup, and I think he has potential. National League coaches tell me that Johnny Green, another quarterback, has a lot of potential. I know about Larry Grantham, the linebacker. He was high on our list at Baltimore. Dick Guessman, a tackle, used to be with us at Baltimore.

"Let me say this. I hope this will be my last move. I hope to start a new era for the American Football League here."

Ewbank had to start organizing the Jets first. The first thing he had to do was to acquire an office. He wanted to have his operations at the Polo Grounds. Werblin preferred midtown. Ewbank's position was that all the successful clubs, the Browns, Colts, all operated out of their stadium. Werblin wanted to inaugurate a new image for the Jets and felt it would be much better if the office was in the center of town. Sonny won out, and the new club secured offices, even though they were small, at 660 Madison Avenue.

The biggest problem, even before they could sign any players, was a training-camp site. Because the old regime had not paid its bill at East Stroudsburg, the Jets could not return there. Training sites were difficult to come by. The Titans' reputation had preceded the Jets, and they were turned down at a number of places. It was already May, and still no training-camp location.

"Finally a friend of mine, Andy Marciano, suggested the Peekskill Military Academy," explained Ewbank. "He had gone to school there and figured that it would serve the purpose. So we went up there and explored the possibility. It wasn't an ideal situation, but I was getting perilously short of time. I decided that it would have to do. So, Peekskill was it."

Before Ewbank could set up quarters in Peekskill, he had to assemble a coaching staff. Knowing the task ahead, Ewbank selected young, energetic assistants. Only one, Walt Michaels, 34, had any previous pro experience. He had been the defensive line coach for the Oakland Raiders for one year. The rest were all new to professional football: Clive Rush, 32, backfield coach; Chuck Knox, 31, offensive line coach; and J. D. Donaldson, 36, defensive backfield coach.

Ewbank quickly put his house in order. He had Sauer out trying to sign whatever players were available, anyone from college players to free agents. The league made a gesture by allowing the Jets to select one seasoned player from each of six teams, allowing Oakland, which was also weak, the same deal. The clubs would freeze twenty-five veterans and half of their rookies and free agents. The Jets and Raiders would then be allowed to pick up from the remainder of the list. Ewbank and Sauer did not expect much help from that quarter.

The first contact the new management made with the veteran Titan players was through a mimeographed newsletter. There was nothing personal about it. The player's name was typed on top and the contents of the letter merely invited the player to attend training camp at Peekskill at a certain date.

Don Maynard, a three-year Titan veteran, received the letter at his home in El Paso, Texas. The flanker back had never heard of Werblin, but he knew of Ewbank. Being a frugal youngster, he decided that he would drive with his wife and two children to New York for the training months. He reasoned, however, that he better place a call to Ewbank to see if Shea Stadium, which was under construction, would be ready for the Jets to play that season.

"Weeb assured me that Shea would be completed by the time the football season came and that we'd be playing our games there," recalled Maynard. "So, when it was time to report to training camp, I decided that it would be best to find an apartment in Queens to be near the ball park.

"I got to New York and drove past Shea and couldn't believe my eyes. I stopped the car and looked around, and there wasn't anything going up. It was just one big wasteland. I had participated in the original ground-breaking ceremonies with Mr. Wismer near the end of the 1962 season, and it was no different now than it was then, just an empty lot.

"I know something about contracting, and I knew there was no way that a stadium would be built in time for football. I called Weeb and told him how upset I was. I felt he wasn't honest with me, inasmuch as I had my family to worry about and now I had the added worries of driving the car twenty-three hundred miles back home."

Maynard finally decided to get an apartment in Queens anyway. He had come that far, and there was no time to turn back. So he settled his family in a two-bedroom apartment and headed for his new club at Peekskill.

Although he was a veteran, he was not greeted with open arms. A lot of changes were taking place, particularly in personnel. Ewbank had made a statement that he would eventually get rid of all the old Titans, which did not give Maynard a feeling of security, even though he was one of the team's leading pass receivers.

"Like a bunch of baby chicks, some of us old Titans huddled together," recalled Maynard. "It was me, Larry Grantham, Billy Mathis, and Curley Johnson who stayed pretty close to each other. It was a heckuva way to start a training camp, what with a scared feeling and all.

"Weeb kept his word, like he said he would. He began to cut players that first week, and players were coming in and out of Peekskill like an Army depot. There were free agents coming in, along with a number of ex-Colts that Ewbank brought over from Baltimore. Right away there were three factions in camp, the old Titans that remained, the ex-Colts, and the new players. It caused a bit of friction in that, rather than pulling together in the beginning, everyone was out for themselves.

"The changes that were taking place were quite a shock to us. We had a countless number of meetings. We had so many of them that the guys used to kid around and ask when the next meeting was. You can have too many meetings, which could be a problem too.

"We were given play books, which we never had under Sammy Baugh. Everyone was responsible for his book, and we had to take them to all the meetings and study them at night. I must admit, everything was well organized. The meetings were serious and strict. It was like going back to school.

"Weeb was a great one for films. It got so that we watched so many NFL films that we were getting a bit disappointed. We weren't interested in the other league. Weeb was showing us the films to reveal to us how the Colts had done things over the years.

"I know one thing, every player, I don't care who they were, griped about the conditions at Peekskill. Everything was wrong—the poor facilities, the poor eating arrangements, even worse than the meals we had with the Titans. Peekskill was undoubtedly the worst place I have ever been.

"It wasn't just a football player's lament. The league had sponsored a training-camp tour of sportswriters from all the different cities, and they had all agreed, which is something when writers all agree on one thing, that the Jets' camp was the sorriest one they had visited.

"There could be eight of us sitting down at a table for lunch, and they would serve us six slices of bread," said Maynard. "Now, that was silly, because everybody eats two slices of bread. We would tell Weeb, and he would brush it off and say that he would see about it. But that's as far as it went.

"I like mayonnaise, love it, in fact. But when you leave it on the table overnight instead of refrigerating it after it's been opened, as the instructions on the jar tell you, it's the most ghastly thing I ever saw. It's enough to turn your blood.

"You wouldn't believe the facilities. I think there were four good showers for about eighty players. Now, that's unreal. There wasn't any room in the dressing room. The dormitories were pitiful. Why, the termites would even turn their noses away from the furniture. It was all very pathetic."

Maynard made a statement one time that anybody who would send their son to Peekskill Military Academy does not deserve a son. He meant it, but he did not know at the time, but he learned a year later, that Werblin's son was attending the school.

"Still, with it all, I personally felt optimistic about the approaching season," claimed Maynard. "We were starting to melt together into a single unit, despite the fact that there were three groups prevalent. We got to respect one another's ability, and in the final weeks each guy was trying to do his best.

"Weeb did a good gesture, for the most part, by bringing into camp the players that were released by the Colts. He knew them, and he'd tell them to come on over here. He did see good possibilities in a majority of the cases, and with the exception of a few, he made some good decisions.

"One player in particular I thought shouldn't have been released was Thurlow Cooper. He was a good tight end. We played together for three years. But they cut him and kept Dee Mackey, who was dropped by Baltimore. Personally, I liked Mackey, but I felt that Cooper was the better player.

"Mackey didn't do much in camp, and almost everyone on the squad noticed it. If he caught one ball a week it was something. Weeb would look up and yell, 'Come on, Dee, catch it like you used to.' Cooper was considered to be a better receiver and a great blocker.

"I'm a receiver too, and I used to take the brunt of criticism, not at the meetings, but on the field," revealed Maynard. "A quarterback would throw a pass ten feet over my head, and I would get hell for not catching the ball. Nobody would yell at the quarterback to throw a better pass. They figured the receiver should be able to come up with an outstanding catch. Right away you're on the defense. You know you're right, but what can you do? It happened to me so much that maybe I was more aware of it than the next guy."

The ex-Colts were not insecure. They felt they deserved to be there. Each old Titan tried a little harder because he wanted to prove he belonged. Besides, they never knew if they would be there the next week.

"Grantham and I got to be real close," said Maynard. "He's real smart. He's an officer in one of the banks in Mississippi. And he's one heckuva football player. He isn't big like most linebackers go, but he's got a lot of savvy. He knows the game, studies it. He has to, to make up for his size. He's like a coach out on the field. He's the sharpest defensive player I have ever known."

Grantham and Maynard figured out a way to get to showers first. At the end of a workout, Weeb would call everyone around him for a little talk. The two of them would work their way around the circle toward the north side of the field, which was the closest to the dressing room.

When they broke, Grantham and Maynard would lead the run to the dressing room. One of them would be sure to get to the showers first. A lot of the players would run harder to the showers than they did on the field.

While Ewbank was left with the problems of the training camp, Werblin was busy trying to promote season-ticket sales. He hired Vinnie Ayles away from the Mets to be his full-time ticket manager. Ayles had previously worked full time for the Mets, and when their season was drawing to a close, he would work for Wismer.

Werblin made one of his ingenious moves by renting a billboard near Yankee Stadium with a simple message: "Want Jet Tickets? Call TE 2-9200 Anytime and Ask for Vinnie."

People would go by the stadium, futilely wish they could get tickets to a Giant game, and then see Werblin's sign. Anytime meant twenty-four hours a day. Ayles would work all day and often into the night setting up a ticket system. When he would get through working, in many cases at two or three in the morning, he would go to sleep on the couch in the office. It worked. Their first year in the Polo Grounds, the Jets sold 4,000 season tickets compared to the 500 that the Titans sold.

"Werblin was one of the greatest promoters I ever met," said Ayles. "He would create the action, and I would handle it. Very often he would be out at night with a lot of friends and associates, and they'd get to drinking pretty good. Then he would give them the season-ticket sales pitch, and they, feeling no pain, would say okay, put me down for two or four, whatever the case might be.

"Sonny would be right there with a notebook and pencil. He'd write their names and addresses down, and the very next morning he would come into the office and give me the information. I'd send the individual the tickets, and most of the time they couldn't remember ordering them. He said not to worry about it but to keep after them to send in the money.

"He was quite different from Wismer, although I liked Harry. I think Wismer suffered from a personality complex. He got to drinking pretty good, and it reached a point where his wife used to hide the liquor from him. The poor guy turned out to be an alcoholic.

"I remember one time before the final Titan season began he was in the hospital on the East Side. He called me and told me to come up because he wanted to go over the ticket situation with me. Well, I got up to his room and happened to walk into the bathroom a bit later. I couldn't believe my eyes. The tub was filled with ice, and he must have had a case of beer there getting cold.

"He was really something. Every figure we used to give out with the Titans was a phony. We had nowhere near the people we announced. He never missed a game. He would stand on the sidelines and scream to his players, 'You're throwing the game.' "

Werblin was never deluded into believing the Jets would make money their first year, despite the increase in the season-ticket sales. He figured to lose about $300,000 but was quite optimistic about the future. He was certain New York was a two-team town and was not concerned about competing with the Giants.

"What was it George M. Cohan said about America?" posed Werblin, as he again turned toward show business to make a point. "He said, 'If it's not New York, it's Bridgeport.' Between Asbury Park and Poughkeepsie and Bridgeport there are 16,000,000 people. The Giants can only get 60,000 into their park. So we can make fans from the 15,940,000 who are left out.

"We have to make our own stars. We know the players we have are better than the ones we let go. We're building a solid organization, the best coaching, the best front-office management. We're going first class, and we're spending a lot of money. We want the players to feel like they're the Yankees, so that they'll play like the Yankees.

"Take Billy Mathis, for instance. We think he's going to be a great running back, except we have to tell him that every day. We paid a dentist bill of his left over from the old management. We told him to call his sick father long distance on us.

"Those things are matters of pennies, but they impress the players. We're building a fine attitude on this squad. We know we have a tough row to hoe, but we are making progress. In New York nobody knows much about American League football. But you travel around the country and you will find the league has a real acceptance. Television did it. We've got a good chance with the Jets, but we are just beginning."

On the playing field the Jets made an inauspicious beginning. After stumbling through the exhibition season, in which they dropped three of four games, the Jets opened their season in Boston and were soundly beaten, 38–14.

Still, the Jets had an advance of 7,000 tickets for their home opener the following week against Houston. It was a warm sunny day, and some 10,725 fans turned out. In one day Harry Wismer was beaten. Werblin had a band dressed in green jackets to provide music before and during the game.

When the Jets trotted out to the field, they lined up on both sides of the field and tossed autographed footballs into the stands. There was one with Ewbank's signature on it, and whoever caught that one was rewarded with an all-expense-paid trip for two to Buffalo later in the season. It was quite a prize—that is, if you like Buffalo. Werblin was promoting.

The Jets shocked the league by defeating the highly touted Oilers, 24–17. The excitement was provided by defensive back Marshall Starks, who ran back a field-goal attempt 97 yards for a picture-book touchdown just before the first half ended. The play seemed to stun last year's Eastern Division champions, and the Jets produced their first big win when just two weeks old.

For the next few weeks the Jets continued to shock the rest of the league, which caused people to wonder what Sonny Werblin's magic was.

They succeeded in beating Oakland and Boston, and after one month the Jets were leading their division! It was something out of *Damn Yankees*, and maybe it would never end.

But Broadway is one form of entertainment, and pro football another. You cannot write happy endings, players have to build them with controlled violence dominating equally well-drilled and fiercely motivated opponents. The Jets finished last, with a 5-8-1 record.

Still, the season was not without its memorable moments. One occurred just four days before the opening game against Boston. Ewbank activated his defensive line coach, Walt Michaels, who had joined him in June, leaving a similar job with Oakland. Michaels had played eleven years with the Cleveland Browns but had not been active for the past two seasons, operating solely as a coach.

"It was rough getting back," sighed Michaels. "I could give

it a pretty good go for about three quarters, but I'd be winded by the time the game ended."

Starks, who was the hero of the opening-game victory against Houston at the Polo Grounds, was lucky to be playing football. He was a draft choice of the St. Louis Cardinals the previous season and was cut very early.

"I talked it over with my father later, and we figured I deserved it," revealed Starks. "I didn't give it my all. I had been sought after and had money thrown at me and had a fake feeling of security."

How did he land with the Jets? He was working in a YMCA in Buffalo the previous year and learned about the Jets' mass tryout at Van Cortlandt Park. He was the lone survivor of 150 hopefuls.

The Jets' 10–7 victory over Oakland was a tribute to the defensive efforts of safetyman Dainard Paulson and linebacker Larry Grantham. Paulson intercepted three of quarterback Cotton Davidson's passes, while Grantham intercepted the other in leading the Jets to an upset win. The victory gave the Jets a 2-1 record and lifted them into first place, a half-game ahead of Boston.

The stage was set for the Jets' return meeting with the Patriots. It was the first crucial game in the club's history. Despite the fact that the Jets were ahead of the Patriots, the experts established Boston as a three-point favorite, even though they were starting Tom Yewcic at quarterback in place of the injured Babe Parilli.

Quarterback Dick Wood was voted the outstanding offensive player of the game. He completed 14 of 21 passes for 201 yards, getting the Jets started with two touchdowns in the first period.

Wood first hit Maynard with a 30-yard scoring pass and then sent in Mark Smolinski from two yards out for the second touchdown that sent the Jets into a 14–0 lead.

Even when Boston came back with a touchdown, in the second quarter, Wood never rattled. He dropped back and tossed a 53-yard bomb to Bake Turner, providing the Jets with a 21–10 halftime lead and ultimate victory.

After a month's play, the surprising Jets were leading the Eastern Division by one and a half games over Houston. They were starting to generate some enthusiasm.

"We're happy with the results, and I think things will get better when we move to Shea Stadium next year," said Werblin.

The Jets' fortunes for the entire season might have revolved around their game against the powerful San Diego Chargers. A victory would undoubtedly send them soaring to unprecedented heights. It can happen that way with a new club.

They almost did it. It took a touchdown by the favored Chargers in the final period to break the Jets' three-game winning streak, 24–20. On the first play of the game, Wood stunned the crowd of 27,189, the largest to see the Jets play that season. He looked around for Turner and fired a 51-yard scoring pass. The Jets jumped with joy on the sidelines. They lifted Turner off the ground and patted Wood on the back. The inspired defense held the Chargers' vaunted offense in check for most of the half as the Jets trotted off the field with a 10–3 edge. However, quarterback John Hadl came in the second half to spark the Chargers to their victory.

It appeared that the Jets' bubble had burst in the following month. They lost three games and tied one and fell all the way to last place with a 3-5-1 record.

However, they somehow managed to bounce back. With Wood connecting on touchdown passes to Turner and Maynard, the Jets defeated Denver 13–9.

No eyebrows were raised until the following week, when the Jets blanked the defending champions, Kansas City Chiefs, 17–0. It was the first time the Chiefs were blanked in fifty-three games, fifty-two in regular season and one championship contest. Wood and Maynard got the Jets in front with a 20-yard pass, and Mathis added the other touchdown with a two-yard run, and the defense did the rest. The victory raised the

Jets' record to 5-5-1, which was only a half-game below first-place Buffalo.

But it was too much to ask for the first-year Jets. As the luck of the schedule would have it, the Jets faced the Buffalo Bills the next week, and they were routed, 45–14, as Buffalo fullback Cookie Gilchrist personally tore them apart. He scored five touchdowns and gained 243 yards, which is still an AFL record.

Considering the fact that they were barely put together by the time the season opened, the Jets were relatively successful on the field. Ewbank was pleased with the results. The Jets played exciting football, and the overall caliber of play improved throughout the league.

Although Werblin was not particularly pleased with Wood, the lanky quarterback did a lot for the offense. His experience helped to knit the unit together, giving it direction. At times he was erratic. Wood liked to throw the long pass, and when he connected, he looked like an All Pro. When he lost his accuracy, he looked like something out of the sandlots.

He was excellent against Kansas City, yet bad against Buffalo the following week. The Jets had played the Bills almost even during the first half, before Gilchrist exploded in the second half. When the Jets fell behind, Wood tried to play catch-up football and forced many of his passes. Buffalo's defense managed to pick them off all too frequently, and the Bills' offense took it from there.

Werblin expected to lose money in his first year, and he did. Still, he was undismayed. The Jets had drawn considerably more people than the Titans had the previous season. The future looked bright indeed, with Shea Stadium yawning like a newborn baby in 1964.

6

Bonus Babies and Baby Sitters

It is possible that Joe Namath did not receive $400,000 when he signed with the New York Jets in 1965. No one has ever admitted the figure—not Namath, not Werblin, and not the Jets. The figure is pure speculation. The only certainty is that the St. Louis Cardinals of the NFL and the Jets were caught in a bidding war over the Alabama quarterback. The reported figure kept rising, and nobody bothered to deny the reports. It generated good publicity, and in the talent war between two leagues, publicity was the name of the game.

Namath's inflationary contract opened a money war unprecedented in the history of professional sports. Ultimately it resulted in the merger of the two factions a year later. The undercover war was the dirtiest and most vicious campaign imaginable, with an army of secret agents stopping at nothing —broads, booze, blackmail, and just short of kidnaping—to sign athletes for the league they represented.

The success of the Jets in their first season at Shea Stadium in 1964 made it obvious that the AFL was permanently established in New York. This franchise, which Foss had maintained was so vital to the success of the young league, was on solid ground after four years of unsure footing. Real progress was being made: A lucrative television contract was offered by NBC, and the league's owners prepared to spend big money to corral highly publicized college stars.

Werblin began modestly enough in 1964. The Jets had made Matt Snell of Ohio State their number-one draft choice following the 1963 college season. The New York Giants also thought highly of Snell and made him their number-three choice. It was the first direct confrontation between the two New York clubs. The American League held its draft a few weeks earlier than the National League that year. While the Nationals were conducting their draft, Werblin was in Miami. As soon as the Giants announced that they had selected Snell on the third round, Ewbank put in a call to Werblin.

"The Giants just drafted Snell," said Ewbank.

"On what round?" asked Werblin.

"On the third round."

"I'll meet you in Columbus tomorrow morning and bring some contracts along. We've got to sign him."

The Jets' scouting reports on Snell rated him highly. George Sauer had personally scouted the fullback, and his confidential report on Snell read: "On a team that features a power offense, he is the strong man. Outstanding quickness to veer and change direction without losing power. Coach very high on the boy. Calls him a natural."

The next morning Werblin arrived in Columbus accompanied by a tax expert. Ewbank was there with the contracts, and all three of them sat down with Snell and Ohio State coach Woody Hayes. It was a pleasant session. It went smoothly and quickly, and within an hour, Snell, with a $50,000 bonus, was a New York Jet. The tax expert's deferred-income plan had impressed Snell and Hayes, and Werblin's charm did the rest.

"I just felt Mr. Werblin was the kind of man I would like to be working for," said Snell. "Coach Hayes felt the same way and advised me to sign with the Jets. They are young and the league is young and I feel there's a good future for a young fellow like myself just starting out as a professional."

Matt Snell's signing signaled two important events. It indicated that the American League was now willing to pay whatever price was necessary to obtain top college stars. Even more important, the acquisition of Snell was a severe blow to the prestige of the Giants. They could no longer ignore the *other* team. The four years at the Polo Grounds had ended, and the Jets were moving into position to compete for old fans and to cultivate a new breed of fans in a multi-million-dollar structure in Queens.

In Snell, the Jets had an enormously talented player. He was, moreover, a hometown boy, from Long Island, which added to his boxoffice appeal. He got off to a fine start and led the league in rushing for a good part of the season, which in itself is unusual for a rookie.

Snell is an unusual type of man to be a star professional athlete. At 6-1 and 215 pounds, he is not big compared to most pro-football fullbacks. He has a disarming calmness. He reacts the same way if he runs for two yards or breaks away for fifty-two. He quietly walks back to the huddle with his hands on his hips and waits for the next play. His appeal, in an incredibly violent sport, is gentle. He never really exudes any confidence, yet he consistently gets the job done. Even when he was drafted by both leagues and offered large bonuses, he was apprehensive about playing pro ball.

"If Bob Ferguson, whom I considered the greatest fullback I have ever seen, couldn't make it in the pros, how can I?" asked Snell.

However, it was immediately obvious that Snell was going to make it, and make it big. In his very first exhibition game against the Boston Patriots, only a few days after reporting to the club following his appearance in the College All-Star game, he gained 117 yards in twenty attempts.

He was a natural athlete who responded to excellent coaching. An outstanding star at Carle Place High School on Long Island, Snell had received offers from sixty colleges. Even after he decided to attend Ohio State, he wondered if he was not too small to play college football. But coach Woody Hayes rapidly developed Snell's natural ability.

The turning point for Snell came on the practice field. Hayes had used him primarily at defensive end and linebacker, but one day tried an experiment. He inserted Snell at fullback during a scrimmage and instructed him to run an off-tackle play. Snell ran the play seven straight times, knocking down a few teammates and gaining a few yards. Hayes stopped the drill for a moment.

"Matthew," he called, "the object of this game is not to go out looking for people to run over. It is to get the ball into the end zone. Now, let's try it again."

Snell did. He was so careful in trying not to knock people down that he found himself running all alone. He ran so carefully, avoiding tacklers, that he broke away for a 65-yard touchdown. Snell became a fullback.

Before the Jets launched their 1964 season at Shea, Werblin began to spread the Jet gospel like a barker at a circus. It was all show business. Every youngster who had attended the Jets' training camp at Peekskill was given a white T-shirt inscribed: "I'm a Jet Fan." Close to 3,500 of them were handed out. Werblin was making new friends with the kids. The Jets even awarded trophies for a slow-pitch softball league at Jones Beach. There was a Jet Day at the World's Fair, Jet uniforms on display in some fifty business establishments around town, including banks, and there were some twenty reels of the Jet highlight film available for showing to groups anywhere.

The Jet campaign continued all summer long. Jet ball-point pens and Jet matches were available for the asking, and most times you did not even have to ask. Werblin and any member of the publicity department would hand them out in the course of a conversation. Enormous Jet schedules were attached to the sides of buses throughout Long Island, and Jet newspaper ads were as common as the daily television listings. It was a crash campaign, and it was effective. Over 17,000 season tickets were sold, making attendance prospects bright. With 17,000 guaranteed, the Jets could look for 30,000 or better for every home game.

Werblin was not finished. He wanted to project the Jet image at Shea which had been a popular rallying point for hysterical Met fans during the baseball season. The ticket takers, ushers, and even members of the ground crew were given green-and-white uniforms. They numbered 400, and each was given two sets of uniforms, summer and winter. Jet matches replaced Met matches, and Jet souvenirs, not Met ones, were to be sold throughout the park. In the restaurants, Jet waiters and waitresses would serve the fans on Jet doilies and dishes.

On the field, a motorized Jet plane would travel around the field and a 110-piece band would entertain the customers. The only thing that Werblin did not change was the grass. It was already green. Werblin had his theater open for business. It was one of the costliest pretheater openings in sports.

"Before I got into football, I had one particular show that did a capacity business one week, something like ninety-three thousand dollars," recalled Werblin. "The next week, I booked another into the same theater that did only eleven thousand. I stood in the back of the theater one night with an associate, lamenting the situation.

" 'Well,' my associate said, 'it's the same theater. The carpets, the seats, the lights . . . they're the same as last week. I guess the difference is on the stage.'

"That's about the size of it. People demand quality. And they'll come out for it."

And Werblin had begun to provide quality. A week before the season was over, Snell was named the AFL's Rookie of the Year. He was a runaway choice, earning sixteen of the twenty-four votes cast.

Of course, not all of Werblin's deals involved players of Snell's caliber. Some were more in line with Sonny's promotional ideas. Before the season, the Jets completed a nine-player trade with the Denver Broncos. No one to this day can name the eight other players involved. The only one anyone quickly remembers is Wahoo McDaniel, a 240-pound Choctaw-Chickasaw Indian, who was a middle linebacker.

If Werblin ever wanted a carnival attraction, it was McDaniel. Actually, he was nothing more than a journeyman player who had tried to make a go with four other teams—Dallas, San Diego, Houston, and Denver—and attained little success. He was a wrestler in the off-season and was quite popular with wrestling fans as Chief Wahoo, the good-guy Indian.

Being a wrestler, Wahoo also had some show business in him. He knew the value of publicity and knew how to get it. In this sense he was a natural, and in him Werblin saw all the color and appeal of a sideshow Indian in a traveling circus.

"This place ain't big enough for me and Sam Huff," claimed Wahoo with a serious look, in reference to the former Giant linebacking star. "It's a lucky thing for him that he moved out of town."

McDaniel was something special. Instead of his last name stitched on the back of his jersey, "Wahoo" was flashed across the shoulderblades. He was the only player in the league to be identified by his first name.

"Why not?" asked Wahoo. "The 'McDaniel' never earned me twenty-five cents in sports. It's the 'Wahoo' that brings in the money."

The crowds responded to the "Wahoo" from the opening game of the season. He was a fierce tackler when he wrapped his arms around an enemy runner. However, he was a bit slow reacting to pass plays, something the opposing teams discovered and exploited later in the season.

But Wahoo was the crowd's hero on the defensive unit. It reached a point where the public-address announcer, instead of identifying the tackler, would blurt out: "Tackle by you know who." And the crowd would immediately respond, "Wahoo! Wahoo! Wahoo!"

"I've played hard every year, but I've only had so-so recognition," admitted McDaniel after the opening game against Denver. "This year I am playing harder than ever. But the way the crowd reacted the first night surprised me. I am anxious for the second game to see if they will keep it up."

A Denver writer covering the game could not believe his ears. "All the applause Wahoo got in three years at Denver wouldn't amount to half of what he gets in one yell in New York," he remarked.

"I don't think the other players resent the attention I'm getting," said Wahoo in a moment of seriousness. "They know how I am. I'll play just as hard whether those people holler or not. But it sure does sound sweet."

It was sweet to Werblin too. This was show business in a new dimension. It had made its way into pro football, and it was selling. Even though the Jets finished the 1964 season with a 5-8-1 record, they attracted a new army of fans. It was Snell on offense and Wahoo on defense, the squad's first two heroes. When the club signed better players, Wahoo was made available to the expansion team to stock the new Miami Dolphins a few years later. The Wahoo legend lasted a couple of more seasons there before he was released and returned to wrestling all year round.

When the heroes arrived, so, too, did the Jets. On November 9 they drew 60,300 fans for their game with the Buffalo Bills, establishing a new league attendance record. They did it on a Sunday afternoon when the New York Giants, playing a few miles away in Yankee Stadium, attracted over 63,000 against the Dallas Cowboys. New York was a two-team football town, and for the American League that meant prosperity. In the seven home games, the Jets drew 298,000 fans, a substantial increase over the 91,000 of the previous year.

"This is the greatest town in the world," beamed Werblin. "It's a tough town to crack, but we did it. You can be the best opera singer in all of Denver, but you're nothing until you've sung at the Met. If you make it here, the rewards are tremendous. We lost money, but not as much as the first year. Promotion's fine, but what we need most of all is a winning football team."

The Jets had opened their first season at Shea impressively. They won three of their first five games, losing one and being tied in the other for a 3-1-1 record. The first game they ever played at Shea was a smash. They walloped the Denver Broncos, 30–6.

Wood had a flawless game. He connected on nine of 18 passes for 144 yards and two touchdowns, and none of his passes were intercepted. With Snell at fullback, Wood could mix his passes with a running game and the Broncos' defense was kept off balance most of the night.

Snell carried 22 times, for 82 yards, proving that a passer's best friend is a powerful runner who keeps the other team honest. When he was not running, Snell provided excellent blocking for Wood's pass plays.

As good as they were the opening game, they were as bad the following game. The Patriots analyzed the Jets' success over Denver precisely. They keyed on Snell and stopped the Jets' running attack, allowing them a good rush on Wood. He hurried his passes, and Boston intercepted five passes to fashion a 26–10 victory.

After playing a 17–17 tie against San Diego, the Jets came up with a big win over the Oakland Raiders, 35–13. Snell and an alert defense provided the victory, as Wood completed only three of fourteen passes.

Running inside and outside the Raiders' line, Snell had the biggest game of his young career. He carried 26 times for 168 yards, both club records, and scored two touchdowns. The defense, led by Grantham and McDaniel, contained the running of Clem Daniels and Billy Cannon while the secondary intercepted four Raider passes.

When the Jets defeated the Houston Oilers, 24–21, the following week, hopes for an Eastern Conference championship rose. It was Snell again who made it possible, shattering the two records he had established the previous week. He carried 31 times and gained 180 yards. On one series of downs he ran the ball six consecutive times, once bursting through the middle for 38 yards.

In their last seven games, however, the Jets managed only a single victory, a 27–14 triumph over the Kansas City Chiefs. Just prior to going into a downward spin, the Jets put it all together in a 35–14 rout of Boston. Wood enjoyed the finest day of his three-year career by connecting on 22 of 36 passes for 325 yards and three touchdowns. Wood befuddled the Boston defenses by throwing long and short, reading the enemy moves without any difficulty.

The defense was impressive. Again sparked by Grantham, McDaniel, and Billy Baird in the secondary, the Jets limited Boston's ground offensive to 34 yards and Baird intercepted his seventh pass of the season. McDaniel even scored the first touchdown of his five-year career when he ran 38 yards with an interception.

However, the Jets' weaknesses were evident the rest of the season. Although Ewbank had built a good defense, the offense was badly limited. With Snell as the only running threat, it was too easy to key on him, then put pressure on Wood, who became inconsistent when an effective rush developed. He became so erratic that Ewbank reverted to his two other quarterbacks, Mike Taliaferro and Pete Liske, during the final month of the season. Despite the fact that the club produced the same record as the year before, Ewbank nevertheless felt his squad was improving.

At the end of the 1964 season, Werblin quickly took a giant step toward building a winner. What the club needed above all else was an outstanding quarterback. The one they had in mind was Namath. The Houston Oilers, who finished last in the Eastern Division, and therefore who would have the first draft choice, was the only stumbling block in the Jets' path. Even before the college season ended, the Jets and the Oilers got together. Since it was known that Namath would prefer to play in New York, the Jets secured Houston's draft rights to deal with Namath, so that he would not be lost to an NFL team.

In Namath's three years on his college team, Alabama turned in an impressive 29-4 record, including three Bowl appearances. Namath left a number of Alabama passing records before he was finished: most passes attempted, 428; most passes completed, 237; most yards passing, 3,054; and most touchdown passes, 28.

By the time Namath graduated, Alabama coach Bear Bryant referred to him as "the greatest athlete I have ever coached."

Sauer's confidential scouting report on Namath was glowing. He was given a number-one rating in quickness, agility, reaction time, coordination, size potential (for a quarterback), intelligence, aggressiveness, and pride. He received a number-two rating in strength, durability, speed for position, and character. On the pro rating guide he received the highest evaluation: one plus. Sauer wrote: "An outstanding passer with big, good hands and exceptionally fast delivery. Has good agility and sets up very well. Throws the short pass very well and can also throw the bomb with great accuracy. Is smart and follows the game plan perfectly. Is a fine leader, and the team has great confidence in him. Will be everyone's number-one draft choice."

The last sentence was underlined. The stage was set for the first big bidding of the player war. The Jets' rivals were the St. Louis Cardinals, but neither could sign him until Alabama played its final game of the season against the University of Texas in the Orange Bowl on New Year's night.

However, weeks before the game, negotiations had been begun by both the Jets and the Cardinals with Mike Bite, a Birmingham attorney who represented Namath. All Bite had to do was wait for the telephone to ring, either from the Cardinals or the Jets. The bidding went back and forth, first one raising the price and then the other.

"Coach Bear Bryant had asked us not to talk to Namath during Alabama's season, and we respected his wishes," disclosed Werblin. "On the Tuesday after the regular season, we went to Birmingham and talked with Namath and Bite. Terms were discussed, but no commitments were made.

"Then Namath and Bite came out to our game in Oakland, and we talked again. It's a funny thing. Bear had told Joe, 'Don't you accept so much as a Coke,' and damned if he would. I ordered Cokes, and the kid wouldn't take his. In Oakland Joe said that he would like to play for the Jets.

"When they got back to Birmingham, Mike Bite called me. He told me that Joe would like to get his professional future settled before the Orange Bowl, but he thought he should listen to the Cardinals. I said of course he should. Then Bite asked, 'What if they offer more money?'

"I told Bite to tell Joe that if they offer more we'll see that he doesn't lose anything because of his promise to us. We'll match it.

"Bite and Namath met with Billy Bidwell, the vice-president of the Cards, in St. Louis. His brother, Stormy Bidwell, who was president, wasn't there. Every time an important point came up, Billy would excuse himself to go out and call his brother. While he was gone, Mike would call me and ask, 'What do we do now?' "

Werblin was suspicious. He couldn't understand why Billy always had to report every offer to his brother, Stormy. Weeks later it was discovered that Stormy had been acting as a go-between for the New York Giants, who had acquired the negotiation rights to Namath when the bidding got too high for the Cardinals.

"After that happened a few times, I told Mike that I wasn't sure they were dealing for the Cardinals. 'Next time he wants to call his brother, tell him that you would like to talk to him also,' I advised. 'And if Stormy agrees to your terms, tell him Joe will play for St. Louis. We can get out of that later.'

"Sure enough, it happened again, and this time Bite got on the phone with Stormy. Mike said, 'Mr. Bidwell, these are our terms. If you agree, Joe will play for you.'

"Stormy replied, 'Just a minute, I have to call somebody else.' Mike said to forget it, that Joe was signing with the Jets."

Nothing more happened. The Cardinals didn't call back with any more offers. Werblin, feeling confident that he had Namath all but signed, went to the Bahamas for a few days.

"I received a call from Namath, who was in Miami for the Orange Bowl," said Werblin. "He wanted to fly over and see me. All I could think of was that he wanted to back out of our agreement. He came over with a friend, and this time he let me buy him dinner.

"After dinner he asked to talk to me privately. I figured that this was it. He wanted to tell me that he was going to sign with St. Louis. That's all I could think of all throughout dinner.

"We were alone and Joe said, 'Mr. Werblin, I knew three weeks ago that the Giants were dealing for me. I just wanted to tell you not to worry about anything you hear. I'm going to play for the Jets.' "

Werblin flew to Miami to watch Namath. Ewbank joined him there. Because of his injured right knee, Namath did not start the game. In fact, it was doubtful whether he would play at all.

Then, in the second period, with Alabama trailing by two touchdowns, Namath limped onto the field, a protective brace protruding from his right knee. On one leg, he rallied the Crimson Tide to within a foot of the winning touchdown minutes from the end. His leadership and inspiration were apparent. The Jets had a prize.

"You should have seen the way everybody came forward on the edge of their seats when Namath came into the game," exclaimed Ewbank. "I never saw anything more exciting than that boy. That's the greatest trade we ever made. I see in him the same things I saw in Unitas."

Werblin saw other things, beyond the playing field. He saw a handsome, dark-haired youngster who generated sex appeal. He was instant box office, an athletic hero and Hollywood star all rolled into one. There was no question in Werblin's mind that Namath was the one player who had the ingredients of a superstar.

The very next morning Werblin began with the Hollywood buildup. Under high-powered lights and before grinding cameras Namath was introduced for the first time to the press as a member of the New York Jets. He wore a pink sports jacket, dark slacks, a white shirt, and a dark tie.

Someone asked Namath if it was true he had received a fancy pink automobile as part of his deal with the Jets.

"That's wrong," answered Namath. "It's green, Jet green."

Werblin smiled. He liked Namath's quip. It was quick and clever. Real show-biz.

"We don't care to divulge the figures," Werblin announced when asked about the amount paid to Namath, "but I believe it is the largest amount ever given to an athlete for professional services."

It certainly was more money than there was in the little town of Beaver Falls, Pennsylvania. Namath was already a legend in his hometown. Everyone in the tiny hamlet kept remembering Namath when he was a spunky, mischievous little kid.

The owners of a local laundry on Fourth Avenue remembered Joe. All they had to do was look up at the steel gates that protect their windows. Joe was responsible for those steel gates.

"When Joe was a little boy he busted every window in the place," recalled his mother. "The laundry people were very mad, and they kept coming around to make us pay for the damages. Finally they put up this steel wiring, which is still there. Joe was throwing a football when he was big enough to walk."

There were a lot of other things that Joe did as a youngster, none of which would have led him to the $400,000 he now had. But at least he had learned what money meant. He hustled a dollar any way he could. Sometimes he would gather soda bottles, take them to the candy store, and collect the deposit on them. Other times he would rummage through the junk yard, swipe a few items, and a few days later sell them back to the unsuspecting dealer.

Once he bet a cop a nickel that he could sneak into a basketball game at Geneva College without getting caught. Namath managed to get inside, walked over to the cop, and collected his wager. The policeman honored the debt all right, but then threw his tormentor out. Undismayed, Joe sneaked back in the same way and watched the rest of the game a nickel richer.

Joe's steadiest job as a youngster was shining shoes at the Top Hat, a shoeshine parlor downtown. He earned fifty cents a week plus tips. A steady diet of hustling convinced him early enough that one day he had to get out of Beaver Falls. The thought of working in a steel mill, as his father did, frightened him.

He channeled all his energy into athletics, playing football, baseball, and basketball in high school. He was determined to excel, especially in football, and did. When he graduated, the offers from colleges came. He wanted to attend Maryland because one of his friends, Al Hassan, was there. He took the entrance examinations but failed them.

"Joe just missed by a point or so," said Tom Nugent, who coached at Maryland at the time. "Just think, if Joe had gotten into Maryland, I'd have still been coaching there instead of being the sports director of a television station in Miami."

Instead, Joe Namath went to Alabama and the tutelage of coach Bear Bryant.

Bryant himself is a legend in Alabama. He played as an end on the undefeated 1934 Crimson Tide team that defeated powerful Stanford, 29–13, in the 1935 Rose Bowl. After serving as head coach at Maryland, Kentucky, and Texas A&M, Bryant returned to Alabama in 1958.

After his first year, Alabama never lost more than two games in any one season and captured national championships in 1961, 1964, and 1965. His eleven-year record is phenomenal: 88 wins, 15 losses, and 7 ties.

Namath has enormous respect for Bryant. He never calls him by any name except "Coach" or "Mr. Bryant." The entire state of Alabama is Bear country. It was often remarked that if anyone could defeat George Wallace for governor, it would be Bryant.

In 1965 the Alabama State Legislature unanimously voted that a new athletic dormitory on the Alabama campus be named in Bryant's honor.

Bryant is a stern disciplinarian. He will tell an athlete only once to do something—and expects it done. He once suspended Namath for two straight games, including the Sugar Bowl game against Mississippi, when his star quarterback broke training.

There is a sign that hangs in Bryant's office: "Winning Isn't Everything, but It Beats Anything That Comes in Second."

Like Bryant, Namath has become a legend in Alabama, and the school's officials protect and preserve the legend. I called the athletic department to find out exactly what Namath had done in 1963 to deserve suspension. The only answer anyone would give was, "You'll have to ask Joe."

Out of this background Namath burst on the pro scene an overnight star before he had thrown a single pass. Yet there was some doubt that he would even be able to play for the Jets. He still had a knee operation to undergo. Dr. James Nicholas, the Jets' orthopedic surgeon, felt that an operation would correct the damage in Namath's troublesome right knee.

The operation was scheduled for Monday, January 25, 1965. Namath entered New York's Lenox Hill Hospital the day before to take X rays and wait. The excitement surrounding Joe was such that television cameras and magazine photographers wanted to cover the operation, but were refused.

At 6:30 Monday morning Namath was aroused from his sleep by a nurse who had a flashlight in one hand and a hypodermic needle in the other. It was time. Drowsily Namath responded long enough to brush his teeth and comb his hair. Within minutes he was on his way to the operating room.

Actually, Namath had not had trouble with the knee until a few months before. Playing against North Carolina State on October 10, Namath had rolled out to his right and then started to cut back to his left. Suddenly his leg gave out, and Namath crumpled to the ground in pain. He was taken out, and immediately ice was applied to the sore area.

He continued to complain of pain after the game. After forty-eight hours the joint was swollen, and the team surgeon, Dr. Ernest Brock, Jr., diagnosed water on the knee. He inserted a needle and relieved the pressure a great deal by withdrawing some of the fluid.

The following week Namath played half the game against Tennessee and played even more the week after. However, against Florida the third week, the knee gave way again and Namath fell to the ground bewildered and in pain. Once more Namath's knee was aspirated, and this time the doctors found blood in the fluid. This meant serious trouble, and Namath was a gimpy-legged quarterback for the remainder of the season.

Inside Lenox Hill Hospital's operating room, Dr. Nicholas worked quickly. He made a three-inch incision just below the knee. Inside the kneecap he discovered that the medial meniscus had been shredded and detached from its outer attachments. It had rolled into a wedge, and the extra thickness prevented Namath from flexing the knee.

Nicholas removed the meniscus completely. He also found that one ligament had been stretched. He pleated it and secured it with a couple of stitches. Nicholas then made another incision, about one and a half inches long, on the outer side of the knee to check on the lateral side. It was undamaged, and Nicholas completed the entire operation in an hour and thirteen minutes.

Namath was returned to his room, and everyone waited for him to regain consciousness. Two nurses in a playful mood observed him asleep. "He's not as good-looking as they say," said one. "Maybe, but look at his beautiful eyes," remarked the other as she flipped open Namath's eyelid.

Nicholas came down from the operating room and waited for Namath to awake. When he did, a short time later, Nicholas told Namath to lift his right knee. When Nicholas assured him it was all right, Namath, feeling the sharp sting of pain, did so.

"There's a sign in the Alabama locker room that says, 'It's all in the mind,' " sighed Namath. "I got something to tell Coach Bryant when I get back. It may be all in the mind, but it hurts just the same."

Through the publicity attending the bidding for, and signing of, Namath, Werblin defended his star system and the money it required. He had authorized a reported $400,000 to Namath; $200,000 to quarterback John Huarte of Notre Dame; $100,-000 to Bob Schweikert of VPI; and another $100,000 to Cosmo Iacavazzi of Princeton, who was signed as a free agent. The total of $800,000 made owners in both leagues wince.

"I want to think that next year no college boy in the country will sign to play pro ball until he finds out whether the Jets are interested in him," said Werblin. "Now it is known that we pay better than anybody else."

"How can I do it?" Werblin answered the question: "I have to. I am dedicated to having the best pro-football team in America. Nobody is going to give me the type of player we need for that, so I have to spend big money on rookies. Maybe I have made mistakes, but I have to trust the judgment of my coaches.

"Maybe they picked the wrong players. This happens. I once bought a horse for three thousand dollars at Keeneland, thinking he would be a winner. I had to sell him back at three hundred dollars and take a loss and try again. I have to expect losses in football until I get the stars who will make us winners.

"The big money we gave out was for bonuses to sign. I try to explain to people that we are not paying big salaries. Our players can see one another's checks, as far as I am concerned, because our salaries are commensurate with the going rate, and no more. If Namath and Huarte don't make the team, we don't have to pay them after next season. If they do, they will help us to be better."

Actually there were conditional clauses involved in signing the bonus stars. They were given a bonus for signing, in some cases an automobile, or deferred payments, but to earn their salary they had to make the team. The bonus was merely an inducement for the athlete to sign with a particular club.

"There won't be any resentment on our squad," continued Werblin. "Matt Snell was our highest-paid player last season, but he was also voted the most popular. You know why? Because he helped make us better. He ran well and he blocked well for the other players. We drew more fans and we made more money.

"I'll tell you why we have six quarterbacks. You need all you can get. They are the stars. I know box office from my thirty-three years with MCA, and I know you have to have stars on the stage. I know the value of names. That is why I don't expect to lose money. I could raise the price of our tickets just fifty cents and pay for all the bonuses we have been giving this year, but I won't. Season-ticket sales have boomed already. They will cover the bonuses.

"I spoke to the players three days before the draft and explained to them that this was the year of the quarterback and that some high bonuses would be paid. I told them that I intended to give raises to them. Larry Grantham, the team captain, also spoke to them. There won't be a morale problem. I'm not worried about Joe. He can handle himself, and he can handle men."

"I'm gonna try like hell," Namath promised. "I can't blame some of the fellows for being skeptical and even sore, but they should understand the circumstances. They should give me a chance to prove myself before they come down on my head like this."

Being a rookie, Namath realized that the publicity connected with his signing would create resentment among some of the veteran players.

Namath's bonus brought a quick reaction from Frank Ryan, a veteran quarterback of the Cleveland Browns.

"If Namath is worth four hundred thousand dollars, then I'm worth a million dollars," snapped Ryan.

Maynard echoed the sentiments of most of the Jet players: "We don't begrudge Joe the bonus," he said. "However, if management has that kind of money to throw around, then why don't they toss some to the veterans?"

"I know they'll be laying for me," said Namath. "It's just natural. But I'm not scared. I don't run scared anymore. I've had all the scare knocked out of me."

Carrying a high price tag, Namath might be a prize target for opposing linemen. Some players through the years had earned their reputation as being quarterback headhunters. They would bust through the protective blocking pocket and crash down on a defenseless quarterback in an effort to knock him out of the game.

"Sure, I know pro football is tough, but ability doesn't change," Namath said. "The difference in pro and college football is that the pros are smarter. They have learned more. They are big and smart and good at every position, but I figure I can learn too.

"I'll learn, and if I have my way, I'll play football for twenty years. I love it."

Namath's signing opened a vast new dimension for the players. It completely upset the mathematics of professional football. Rookies would use Namath's figure as a measuring scale, and veterans would bicker with owners.

If the owners were concerned about the feelings of their veterans, they did not show it. They were busy preparing an intensified campaign for the signing of highly prized rookies. It was a battle for status, and each league was well aware of its importance. New tactics developed. It was simple to wine and dine the prospective athlete, with an added twist—doing anything short of kidnaping to hide the prospect. Some of the kids were innocent prey. They were victims of blackmail and extortion in the ugliest chapter ever written in pro-football history.

The new tactic was called "baby-sitting." It only sounded innocent. The NFL, in its plan to prevent the AFL from signing the prized college chattels, employed a number of agents to watch over a specified college star, sometimes two or three at a time. The agent would take the unsuspecting youngster to some remote hotel and keep him there shrouded in secrecy until the draft by both leagues was completed. It had all the characteristics of kidnaping, yet fell just short of it. If there had been any legal recourse, then some of the unfortunate youngsters who were caught would have certainly resorted to the courts because of the indignities they suffered.

The Jets almost lost Verlon Biggs to one of the many NFL cloak-and-dagger operations. The Jets were going to draft Biggs high on their list in 1964. He was a 6-5, 250-pound tackle at Jackson State, a small Negro school in Mississippi.

However, following Jackson State's final game on November 14, Biggs was taken on a couple of joy rides which amounted to more traveling than he had done in his four years at college. A Detroit Lion scout had invited Biggs and Frank Molden, another Jackson tackle, to Detroit to watch the Lions play the Chicago Bears on Thanksgiving Day. Biggs informed the scout that he had already told the Jets he was going to sign with them.

Since he had not actually signed a contract, the scout told Biggs to come along with Molden anyway for a free trip and a lot of laughs. He said that the Lions would take care of everything and give each of them some walking-around money so they could see the sights. His only request was that the two athletes not tell any of the other players about the trip. After all, he said, everybody wanted to go on this big, beautiful trip, and they could take only a certain number of players.

On Tuesday night before Thanksgiving, Biggs and Molden landed in Detroit. They checked into a downtown hotel, and everything seemed fine, that is, until the next morning. Before they could pack and unpack their bags, the two athletes were taken to three different hotels, finally ending up at the Holiday Inn, which looked like a training camp, with twenty-nine other prospects already checked in.

Then, maximum security went into effect. Biggs could not speak with anyone because a scout was constantly with him and Molden. He stayed in the room with them and began to give them the sales pitch of signing with the NFL. It was the older league, there was a pension plan, more extra money could be made.

Biggs was beginning to get the picture. He knew a selling job when he saw one, and this was the high-pressure treatment. They were so confined to their rooms that they could not go out to eat. Instead, the scout talked them into eating in the room because it was much more comfortable.

At first Biggs thought the scout was trying to keep them segregated. But then he reasoned that they wanted to keep the players completely out of sight so that they would not attract attention. After all, thirty-one football players moving around a hotel lobby are not exactly inconspicuous. When Biggs asked about making a telephone call, the scout told him he would have to give him the numbers, because all the telephone calls were put on his bill, and he would have to give his approval. "After all," reminded the scout, "we couldn't have everybody making phone calls all day."

Biggs realized he was being mouse-trapped, and no lineman likes to be caught in that position. He got up early Thanksgiving morning and made his way to the lobby, trying to be as unnoticeable as any 6-5, 250-pound athlete can be. He went to a phone booth and called his college coach, Rod Paige, to inform him where he was and what was happening. Paige instructed him to take it easy, not to panic, and not to sign anything until he returned to school.

Paige will always remember Thanksgiving morning in 1964. Not long after Biggs called, he received another long-distance call, and getting two such calls in a little town like Jackson could get the whole town talking. This time it was George Sauer, who was calling from New York. After wishing the coach and his family a happy Thanksgiving, the Jets' scout asked about Biggs. The AFL was holding its draft on Saturday, and Sauer wanted to make sure that the Jets still had a fair chance at signing Biggs.

Sauer had scouted the big youngster a number of times during the season and was high on his chances of making it big in the pros. In fact, Sauer was of the opinion that Biggs, with his speed, strength, and mobility, would be as outstanding at defensive end as Namath would be at quarterback.

Rod Paige informed Sauer that Biggs was in Detroit as a guest of the Lions to watch a football game. Although Biggs had given his word to Sauer that he would play for the Jets, he still had not signed a contract. The stakes, risks, and maneuvers of high-powered recruiting being what they were, Sauer quickly got on a plane for Detroit and arrived at the Holiday Inn about an hour after the Lions-Bears game ended.

Sauer would have had an easier time getting information out of the Pentagon. When he picked up the house phone the hotel operator told him that Biggs was not registered. He looked around for Biggs and could not find him, or any other athlete, for that matter. Sauer approached the bell captain and slipped him a ten-dollar bill and told him to see if he could find out where Biggs was. Sauer waited in the lobby, nervously pacing up and down.

About two hours later the bell captain returned. He told Sauer that the players had gone to the hockey game at the Detroit Olympia. Two hours to find out that! Sauer suspected that something was wrong. Nevertheless, he waited for another

AFL Founders (left to right): Bud Adams, Harry Wismer, Lamar Hunt, Robert Howsam, and Sidney Latham (United Press International, Inc.)

Sammy Baugh, the Titans' head coach, with Harry Wismer. Later their parting would not be as jovial (United Press International, Inc.)

Despite this twelve-yard gain by Buffalo's Elbert Dubenion — Larry Grantham is catching the straightarm — the Titans won the 1960 opener at the Polo Grounds, 27-3. Attendance at Titan games always left something to be desired (United Press International, Inc.)

Harry Wismer (right) did everything for the Titans — including arguing with the officials (United Press International, Inc.)

When the Titans fell apart, David "Sonny" Werblin picked up the pieces and called them the Jets (United Press International, Inc.)

Werblin brought in a new coaching staff

Head Coach Weeb Ewbank (The New York Jets)

Walt Michaels (The New York Jets)

Clive Rush
(The New York Jets)

Joe Spencer
(The New York Jets)

Buddy Ryan
(The New York Jets)

Only four Titans made the Jets

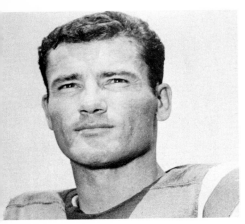

Don Maynard (The New York Jets)

Larry Grantham (The New York Jets)

Bill Mathis (The New York Jets)

Curley Johnson (The New York Jets)

Like the Titans, the Jets dabbled in gimmicks: off-season, linebacker Wahoo McDaniel wrestled — Indian style (The New York Jets)

(Wrestling World Magazine)

The only father-son team in professional football — the George Sauers (The New York Jets)

Sonny Werblin's prize catch: Joe Namath (Photo by Barton Silverman, for N.Y. Jets)

The world's most expensive telephone operators
John Huarte (upper left), who reportedly signed with the Jets for $200,000 and Joe Namath (bottom left), who supposedly received $400,000, worked the phone while Mike Taliaferro played quarterback against the Denver Broncos (United Press International, Inc.)

Tired of bidding huge sums to sign outstanding college players, the rival leagues decided to merge. Making the announcement, June 8, 1966, are Tex Schramm (Dallas Cowboys), NFL Commissioner Pete Rozelle, and Lamar Hunt (Kansas City Chiefs) (United Press International, Inc.)

Weeb Ewbank looks to the future . . . (United Press International, Inc.)

. . . Joe Namath begins to build it (The New York Jets)

two hours in the lobby just in case the players were at the game and were coming back. They never did.

What Sauer did not know was that Biggs was not even in town. After the Detroit game, another NFL agent informed Biggs and Molden that they were welcome to go to Washington to see Sunday's game with the Giants and the Redskins. The proposition was appealing, as Biggs and Molden had never been to Washington. If nothing else, the pair were getting to see the country.

When they arrived in Washington that evening, Biggs and Molden did more moving around than an underworld figure trying to avoid a congressional hearing. No sooner had they checked into the Statler Hilton Hotel than they were transferred to a Holiday Inn. Then they were moved to the Diplomat Hotel, and finally, home at last, at still another Holiday Inn. Apparently there were some AFL spies around, and the NFL boys were not going to make it easy for them.

On Saturday, the day of the AFL draft, Biggs and Molden were extended added hospitality. A tray full of liquor was sent up to their room, and people began to stop by for a friendly drink and a lot of talk about pro football. They did a lot of drinking, which naturally went with a lot of talking. By the time the two well-trained athletes got to sleep, they were pretty well out of condition.

No sooner had they got to sleep than the phone rang. It was just after five A.M., which is a hell of a time to call even a sober man. The call was for Molden. The Pittsburgh Steelers had drafted him, and they thoughfully wanted to tell him so. They wanted Molden to sign a contract right away, which would immortalize him as being the first player in the history of pro football to sign a contract at five in the morning. All Molden wanted was to go back to sleep.

All of a sudden the door opened and in walked an agent with a contract in his hand for Molden to sign. If anything, it must be admitted that any man who is at work by five A.M. after pulling security duty all day is certainly worth what he was being paid. The agent walked in while Molden was still on the phone. The coordination ranks with the best of spy-thriller plots.

Molden told the Steeler agent that he would sign if they gave him an $8,000 bonus. What is $8,000, he figured, compared to all the money that was being thrown around anyway. The Pittsburgh official refused and told Molden that he had better take $4,000, because, after all, nobody in the AFL drafted him.

All Molden wanted to do was to sleep. So, figuring $4,000 was better than nothing, he signed a two-year contract that would give him $12,000 his first year with Pittsburgh and a modest $500 more his second season. The agent left, and Molden went back to sleep.

When he finally woke up later in the day, he could not remember what had happened. The agent came back to remind him cheerfully that he now was the property of the Pittsburgh Steelers and to welcome him to the National Football League. Later Molden got hold of a newspaper and learned that the Houston Oilers had also drafted him.

Biggs kept his word with the Jets and later signed with them when Sauer came to Jackson. On Monday Sauer learned what had happened to Molden, who was still quite upset about his history-making signing. To make matters even worse, Sauer read the contract and made Molden feel sick all over again. He showed him where his $12,000 salary wasn't even guaranteed. He'd have to make the squad to get it. Molden would not get a nickel if he was cut before the season opened.

The same year the Jets also had a chance to land Tom Nowatzke, an All-American fullback from the University of Indiana. The Jets rated him very high. Inasmuch as they had an extra pick on the first round which they had obtained by a trade, they had planned to select Nowatzke after picking Namath. However, the AFL had received word that Detroit had the kid all wrapped up.

A couple of days before the draft, the Jets contacted

Nowatzke. They told Nowatzke that they had learned through reliable sources that he had already signed with the Lions. They did not challenge his decision, but they wanted Nowatzke to assure them that he was signed, the reason being that the Jets would not waste a first-round choice by selecting him.

Nowatzke disclosed that he had not signed and that since he was coming to New York the next day, he would be happy to talk with the Jets and discuss their offer. Fine. The Jets figured they had a chance. The next day Werblin and Ewbank met Nowatzke at the airport upon his arrival. He was accompanied by Dick Pollard, whom Nowatzke identified as a field representative for the Lions but who normally works for the Minnesota Vikings.

Werblin offered Pollard a ride into the city. On the way they stopped at Shea Stadium, which is an appealing place to play football. Werblin and Ewbank asked to have a private talk with the prospect. Pollard did not object and said he would wait. After all, he still had to have a ride into the city.

At the meeting Nowatzke appeared unconcerned. He was in a bargaining position and did not appear interested enough. Werblin and Ewbank both suspected that he had already signed with Detroit. They had to find out quickly. Werblin called his bluff. He offered Nowatzke an extra $25,000 if he would sign with the Jets tomorrow. The youngster finally reacted with a wide-eyed look. However, he remained silent except to say thank you, and he left.

Werblin had made a grandstand play and it worked, but he could not believe it. The Jets figured they had a chance to sign him. They picked him as their draft choice after Namath, and got burned. A half-hour after Detroit selected Nowatzke in their draft, they announced he was signed. They had him under contract all the time.

The manner in which the Jets signed Seth Cartwright, a big tackle from Prairie View College in Texas, could have been the plot for a spy drama. The day before the draft, the Kansas City Chiefs learned that a number of college prospects were being hidden in a motel somewhere in Dallas. They could not find out which one, and there are a lot of motels in and around Dallas.

The Chiefs immediately dispatched one of their scouts, Lloyd Wells, to find out where the players were being kept, because they believed that one of their high-round selections, end Otis Taylor, also from Prairie View, was among the group. Wells was also a photographer, and he took a camera with him, hoping to disguise himself as a newspaperman.

Once in Dallas, Wells traced the two players through some friends. He got to the motel and began to survey the place from the outside. A policeman appeared and asked him what he was doing. Wells told him that he was looking for a friend. It was past midnight, and the officer was suspicious. He then asked Wells if he was registered in the motel. Wells told him he was not. The policeman got tough and told Wells in no uncertain terms that he was prowling and if caught on the property again he would be put in jail.

Wells left and returned a short while later. He got into the motel, located a bellboy he knew, and discovered the players he was looking for were in Suites 101–105. Not knowing exactly what room, he knocked on one of the doors. A man opened the door and asked Wells what he wanted. With the camera hanging around his neck, Wells told him that he was a newspaperman and had come to do a story. He was let in.

Taylor was there and became excited when he saw Wells, whom he had known from high school. The kid had been locked in the hotel for two days. Wells told Taylor that it was best if they left right away. Taylor, however, wanted to wait for his friend, Cartwright, who was out. Wells agreed.

To avoid creating suspicion by remaining in the room too long, Wells decided to go downstairs. He went into the dining room and sat down. He soon realized he was being watched closely by two men at the other end, one of whom was the person who had let him into the room. He felt uneasy and decided to leave.

He got into his car and started to drive off. He gazed into his rear-view mirror and noticed that the two men from the dining room had gotten into a white Ford and were following him. He tried to shake them, but failed. After driving round and round, Wells decided to return to the motel to see if Cartwright was back. The Ford was close behind. When Wells approached the motel, he was refused entrance by the policeman.

At this point the best thing, Wells figured, was to return to his hotel in downtown Dallas. He called Taylor's room to tell him where he could be reached. At 3:30 A.M. Taylor called. The NFL agents had provided them with food, liquor, and girls and had given each of them two sleeping pills, which they had not taken. Wells said to be ready, that he would be right over.

Wells slipped in the back parking lot, evading some plain-clothesmen he had noticed staked out in cars at the front. He tapped on Taylor's window. There was nobody around, and Taylor and Cartwright climbed out of the window with their bags packed, and all three of them ran to Wells's car. They quickly got in, and Wells sped off to the Dallas airport.

They still were not safe. Wells approached the ticket counter and noticed some suspicious-looking men hanging around, even though it was almost five A.M. He decided to drive to Fort Worth and catch a plane from there. Only when all three climbed aboard a 7:40 plane to Kansas City was the great escape completed. Taylor later signed with Kansas City and Cartwright with the Jets.

Taylor proved a valuable addition to the Chiefs. However, Cartwright never played professional football. He injured his knee in training camp that year and had to be operated on. In 1966, he was cut from the squad.

The great bonus war was still in its infancy. The AFL began using the baby-sitting practices employed so effectively by the NFL. They mobilized for the 1965 draft well in advance.

"You have to talk to the college kids before you can sign them," said Kansas City general manager Jack Steadman. "We discovered that the NFL had made elaborate plans for hiding players again this year, like they did in 1964. They planned to set up dates with top players throughout the country.

"Last time the NFL, as far as we could tell, picked up players and took them to four holding areas—Dallas, Detroit, Baltimore-Washington, and California. They hid the players until the draft was over.

"We will counter their moves this time. We will have thirty recruiters out."

Although the baby-sitting phase of the war was not as effective, with both sides playing, as the preceding season, the 1965 college draft was the year of the big dollar. In fact, Namath might well have moaned that he was born a year too soon. Some stadium-shaking bonuses were given out, and not just for quarterbacks.

Bud Adams, with all his oil and real-estate money, was the biggest philanthropist. The biggest offer made by Adams went to Donny Anderson, a halfback from Texas Tech who was big, blond, strong, and good-looking. He was called another Golden Boy after the fabled Paul Hornung. At least the Green Bay Packers thought so, because they outbid Texas money for a Texas boy.

Adams' offer to Anderson had reached $885,000. But it was a long-term deal, and Anderson turned it down. Instead, he accepted the Green Bay offer, which was less, only $700,000.

"It's not beyond the realm of possibility that Anderson will receive eight hundred thousand," said Adams. "It will be an all-cash transaction, too, payable in three years. I learned from a source close to the Anderson family that Vince Lombardi told Donny the Packers planned to trade Hornung and Jim Taylor if they succeeded in signing both Anderson and Jim Grabowski.

"I had called the Miami Dolphins and told them if they had any trouble, if they felt they would lose Grabowski, to let me have a chance at him. They called me one night but couldn't reach me because I was out with Anderson at the time. They then called the Jets, and they made a last-minute offer. I know Grabowski got six hundred and twenty-five thousand or more from the Packers."

The second large bonus offer Adams made was to Tommy Nobis, a powerful linebacker from the University of Texas. Adams dangled a $650,000 package in front of Nobis, but he turned it down. He was the only football player ever to get a recruitment speech from an astronaut. When spaceman Wally Schirra was circling around the moon that December, he sent a message to central control in Houston to tell Nobis to sign with the Oilers.

Even that did not work. Nobis instead signed with the Atlanta Falcons, and Adams lost two home-grown products, which was a blow to Texans everywhere.

"I feel sure Nobis signed for more than seven hundred thousand," claimed Adams. "The offer we had agreed on was six hundred and fifty thousand. It was all cash, payable in three years. I would have raised the ante, but I didn't get a chance."

Another Texan who figured prominently in the bonus war was Carl McAdams, an All-American linebacker from the University of Oklahoma. The Jets had drafted McAdams in 1965, but so, too, had the St. Louis Cardinals. The bidding reached the $300,000 mark, and finally McAdams decided to sign with the Jets.

Werblin provided the clincher. He promised a hunting lodge in White Deer, Texas, as part of the package. Getting the lodge was a novelty in itself, but Werblin really applied finesse in closing the deal. He bought the spread from Carl McAdams, Sr.—the football player's father.

It was obvious that pro football was on a disastrous collision course. The economics of the game could not absorb the incredible bonuses being paid. What started out as an unprecedented $400,000 package for Namath in 1964 suddenly inflated to $885,000 for Donny Anderson a year later. At that rate, by the time the 1966 season came around, pro football would have had its first million-dollar baby.

When 1966 did arrive, pro football stopped short of suicide. The two leagues grudgingly agreed to cooperate.. Gone was the big bonus, the baby-sitting, and the cloak-and-dagger intrigue. The owners awoke one morning and suddenly realized that they were losing the game to the players. The name of the game on the field is the player, but the owners had to pay the bills. The National and American football leagues decided to merge that summer.

7

The Merger

Al Davis, the brand-new AFL commissioner, was caught by surprise. Less than two months after he assumed his office, the AFL merged with the NFL, with two leagues under one commissioner and a common draft. The war was over, and just in time. Some of the weaker franchises—Denver, Boston, and Oakland of the AFL, and St. Louis, Pittsburgh, and Chicago of the NFL—would have been driven out of existence if the war of the dollars continued.

Davis never knew, until it was too late, that members of his league, namely, Lamar Hunt of Kansas City, Ralph Wilson of Buffalo, and Billy Sullivan of Boston, had been secretly negotiating with the NFL. Hunt and Tex Schramm, president of the Dallas Cowboys, were the principal figures. In this day of accelerated communication, they had maintained the best-kept secret in the history of sports.

Secrecy was essential. No one could be sure that a full agreement on terms could be reached. It was much easier for a few persons to negotiate than to hold meetings involving every owner of both leagues. Harmony was necessary, and most certainly Werblin, Davis, and Wayne Valley, owner of Oakland, would have immediately raised objections if they knew what was taking place.

Hunt and Schramm actually had begun peace overtures in the spring of 1965. There was no round table, no meeting behind closed doors. Rather, they met in the parking lot of Dallas Municipal Airport amid the activity of passing motorists and the sound of jets overhead. Six years earlier, Schramm and the Cowboys had run Hunt and his team out of town. Now the two men were together, drawing the guidelines for peace. Over the year they had other meetings in Washington and New York before the merger was signed.

All the while, Pete Rozelle, commissioner of the NFL, was kept informed of every detail. Later, even CBS, which carried the NFL games, was advised of what was happening. NBC finally was informed near the end, which was still a great deal earlier than poor Al Davis was.

Al Davis, however, was not one to suffer publicly such indignity. He just never appeared on June 8, 1966, at the biggest sports press conference ever called, when the announcement of the merger was made.

The weeks preceding the announcement were frantic. The AFL committee of three had notified Schramm that unless they heard from him by June 1, it would be too late to consider a merger for the season and that the war would continue. They had to have a submission of the proposal by the NFL, which would dictate the peace terms. Anyone who surrenders has a right to know the terms of the armistice.

An early peace seemed doubtful until the night of May 31. Hunt called Sullivan in Boston and asked him to be in New York at eight o'clock the next morning for a meeting with him and Wilson. All three met at Wilson's apartment. Hunt brought with him several sheets of handwritten notes for the framework of the peace plan. The three decided to split the long-distance telephone calls to the other owners.

Before they called any of the club owners, however, they

decided to call Davis, whose office was in New York. They panicked when they learned that Davis had just left on a plane heading for Los Angeles. The street fighter was not only signing players but he was aiming another blow at the NFL by meeting Walter O'Malley, the president of the Los Angeles Dodgers, to discuss the possibility of a franchise in Chavez Ravine. And if O'Malley was not receptive to the thunder of professional football, Davis intended to approach Frank Leahy, who had been making overtures from Anaheim.

The Big Three realized it was essential to contact Davis immediately, before he did anything that might upset the impending merger. Luck prevailed, and Davis was reached before he met with O'Malley or anyone else. They beseeched him to return to New York immediately, that an important turn of events was taking place, and they wanted to fill him in on the details. Shortly after midnight Davis returned, was informed of what was about to happen, and, for his part, felt he should have stayed on an airplane.

During the next two days revisions were made of Hunt's handwritten notes, and the revised notes were then given to the NFL. Naturally, the NFL made further revisions, but theirs were phrased more like demands. By the weekend, the owners in both leagues had digested the proposals and counterproposals of the shotgun marriage.

Early Monday morning, Hunt, Sullivan, and Wilson again convened in New York. Sullivan and Wilson filled Hunt in on the reactions of the other AFL owners. By three A.M. Tuesday Hunt had everything in order. He picked up the telephone and called Schramm. It was only one A.M. in Dallas. Everything was okay with the NFL. Schramm was relieved, and he placed a call to Pete Rozelle in New York, where it was 3:30 A.M. Rozelle had not had much sleep the past two weeks anyway. Schramm informed the commissioner that the articles of armistice could now be drawn up. Everybody in the other league was filled with happiness, except Werblin and Valley. It figured. They were the only two AFL owners who had franchises in NFL cities, and they would pay the most for the merger. Nobody cared about Al Davis because he was out of a job anyway.

The curtain was ready to go up on the final act. There were, however, still a couple of scenes to be played. Rozelle told Schramm to meet him in Washington later in the afternoon. Rozelle figured he could get a couple of hours' sleep and catch the noon shuttle, which would get him to Washington by one. Rozelle wanted to inform the Justice Department of what was about to happen. After all, it would be disastrous if some member of the department read about the merger in the newspapers and decided to call it monopoly.

So Rozelle and Schramm quietly made their way into the Sheraton-Carlton Hotel to await Hunt, who was flying down from New York. Hunt was already in the lobby, and Rozelle, who did not want the story to leak out to the press, hurriedly escorted him to a suite upstairs. The final emasculation of the American Football League, born in the spirit of free competition six years earlier, was about to take place. The men met in such secrecy that only a few men knew what was going on.

Jim Kensil, the NFL director of public relations, was one of the few who had to be kept informed of what was happening. He had already summoned a major press conference for six P.M. the next day at the Warwick Hotel in New York. When the announcement of the press conference was made, reporters suspected that the merger would be revealed. They did not know the terms of the merger, and none of their sources of information in the league offices could tell them, because they did not know anything either.

On Wednesday morning Rozelle, Schramm, and Hunt met with Covington and Burling, the attorneys of the NFL. Everything was legal, and Kensil made a hurried trip from New York to prepare Hunt and Schramm for questions that the press would ask later that day. Hunt flew back to New York and again met with Wilson and Sullivan to assure them that everything was settled and that they were all officially members of the same pro-football fraternity.

The scene at the Warwick seemed to many like the setting for a civil wedding ceremony. Metal chairs were lined up neatly in rows on both sides of the room, leaving an aisle in the middle. The bright lights of television and newsreel cameramen illuminated the front of the stage, while NFL writers sat on one side of the aisle and the AFL on the other. Kensil handled the details while everyone waited for the principals.

Finally, but without organ music, Rozelle, Schramm, and Hunt entered the room to meet their guests. They walked over to one side of the room and sat on a small couch that looked like an oversized love seat. Hunt sat on one side, Schramm on the other, and Rozelle sat in the middle. If anybody in the room had not known what they were there for, they certainly knew now. They were witnessing the most expensive wedding of the century, and Rozelle announced over the microphones directly in front of him: "We are gathered here to witness this union," or words to that effect.

The terms of the marriage were hard. Gone was free enterprise. Gone were the players' bargaining powers. Gone was Al Davis, who nevertheless got in a parting shot. A few days before the merger was announced, Davis gave all his key employees, whom he had recruited for the war only two months before, solid legal contracts so that they would not be left unemployed. He was a good street fighter to the end.

Rozelle smiled through it all. Schramm did not say much, and Hunt, looking almost bashful, said even less. The only thing missing was the music. A couple of bartenders at two makeshift bars at the back of the room poured the liquor freely. There were plenty of hors d'oeuvres for everybody. Had Werblin approved of the marriage, he might have had Guy Lombardo there for old times' sake. But he could not conceive of paying a dowry to the Giants.

Then Rozelle, in answer to questions, began to read some of the rules of the union. Some of the guests gagged, at least the ones who were on the invited list of the AFL.

"The American Football League will pay an eighteen-

million-dollar indemnity to the National Football League
over a twenty-year period," began Rozelle.

That was enough. The AFL, which had been winning the
costly signing war, had to pay an eighteen-million-dollar indemnity to be part of a merger they did not even initiate.
They were wooed, and they had to pay roughly $100,000 a
year for each AFL club. There was more. The NFL would
receive the franchise payments resulting from the establish-
ment of two new clubs, which later turned out to be New
Orleans in the NFL and Cincinnati in the AFL.

The two biggest winners in the money exchange were the
NFL clubs in New York and San Francisco. The Giants
would receive about eight million dollars of the total, and
the 49ers six million. They were able to demand a high price
for their approval of the merger, because they were the only
two NFL clubs which had to share their territory with AFL
teams. They were protected by a bylaw in the NFL constitu-
tion which allowed them damages from any encroachment
upon their territories. The Jets in New York and the Raiders
in Oakland violated their domain.

By paying the indemnity, the AFL immediately gained
parity with the older and more powerful NFL. While the NFL
was drawing record crowds in most of their cities, the AFL
attendance had been considerably lower. Through the merger
the AFL could reasonably expect to benefit from the NFL's
stronger promotional campaigns, which would raise gate
receipts for all teams. Perhaps even more important would be
the additional television revenues, which could be gained only
through the NFL's established bargaining power.

The merger guaranteed a common draft for both leagues,
immediately eradicating the costly bonus war. It also prevented players from the National League from jumping to
the American League, which was beginning to happen. In
fact, some players, like quarterback Roman Gabriel of Los
Angeles, quarterback John Brodie of San Francisco, and tight
end Mike Ditka of Chicago, had signed contracts with AFL

teams. This was the result of Davis' effective, if short, term of office.

The peace also set the foundation for interleague play. Interleague games generate extra excitement and attendance, especially if the two teams are from the same city or area. Baseball has established such traditional rivalries over the years. And it shows in ticket revenue. However, regular-season interleague games would not take place until 1970, when the merger would become fully effective. Until then, no interleague trades could be made and no All-Star game played. This was in line with the television contracts of both leagues, which would expire then.

Werblin was upset, and justifiably so. Along with Davis, he had been a hawk who led the fight, and now his wings were clipped.

"I am disgusted, completely disgusted with the way things are going," he told a close associate. "How can I not sell the Jets, considering the way things are going? How can I not sell the club, considering everything, and get out? It is the only thing I can do for myself and my partners. We had the whole thing won, and now we are giving it back."

Jack Kemp, quarterback of the Buffalo Bills and president of the AFL Players' Association, looked favorably upon the merger.

"The players prosper only in relation to how the owners do," said Kemp. "A healthy football situation with twenty-four franchises is a much better atmosphere for veterans to negotiate their contracts than a situation where franchises are in jeopardy." Obviously, no one was speaking for the college players.

At the time, Lamar Hunt appeared to many as the turncoat, the villain of the piece. But even now, several years later, he feels as he did then: "I have no regrets at having worked for the merger." Although the terms of the merger were severe and had been set largely by the NFL, he saw as much more important that they were justified. "The NFL was getting much more TV and gate revenue," he still argues. "And under the merger we were guaranteed preseason games, not just exhibition games, but the kind of games with a special glamour and excitement." And because that does mean more revenue, he feels the indemnity—the one thing at which Werblin really balked—was justified.

8

Welcome to the Club, Joe

Joe Namath detected a certain uneasiness in the Jet training camp in the summer of 1965. He did not expect a rousing reception from his teammates, but at the same time he did not appreciate the coolness the players showed him. So he spoke freely at a squad meeting, and it went a long way toward alleviating misgivings the players had about him.

He did not expect to get away with anything because he was Werblin's pet, he said. And, he added, although he got big money to play football, he was not in the game solely for the money: He loved football. What's more, he wanted to play winning football. All he asked for was a chance to contribute to that end. And then with the brashness that he displayed on the football field, Namath stuck his chin out. "If anybody has any gripes and wants to get them out in the open, this is the time to do it," he said. He looked around the room as if he was challenging every pair of eyes he met. Nobody spoke. Joe Namath, a high-priced rookie, had established his presence.

"I think that meeting cleared the air," Namath says now, as he recalls the situation.

Dainard Paulson, a defensive back, agreed. "If Joe had remained silent at the meeting, or even said the wrong thing, it could have made a big difference. You know how ball players are. Joe earned their respect right then and there."

Werblin had remarked that he had no worries about Namath, that he knew how to handle men. However, he did not completely understand the situation he had projected Namath into.

All anyone heard prior to the opening of training camp was about Namath and his $400,000 bonus. Werblin did everything he could to encourage the hoopla. He took Joe with him to cocktail parties, Broadway shows, fights at Madison Square Garden, dinner at the fashionable restaurants, the big horse races, all with the intention of exposing him to the Broadway columns. That is the quickest way to make a star. It can happen overnight, and to make sure, Werblin and Namath made the whole scene.

Still, Namath had his real work to do when he reported to Peekskill. He knew it. From the very first day there, he would be judged by his teammates. It was as important as appearing in his first game. Instead of driving his Lincoln Continental onto the grounds of the Peekskill Military Academy, Namath had a friend drive him to camp. It was a cautious and intelligent move. He slipped quietly into camp, arriving five or ten minutes before the appointed hour for all rookies to report. The next few months would be crucial ones for him.

They were difficult ones, too. Difficult because wherever Namath went on the grounds of the Academy, he attracted a crowd, usually newspapermen and photographers, and always the kids seeking autographs. If the crowd had been shooed away, there was always Werblin's shadow across the practice field. As any other young athlete would, Namath had enjoyed all the early attention, but now he felt its weight. He had to speak up at the players' meeting. He had to clear the air before the club opened against the Oilers in Houston.

Namath did not perform exactly like a $400,000 quarterback during the exhibition season. He looked good in some games and bad in others. The pressure of his rookie trial was increased by the fact that Ewbank had released the club's two veteran quarterbacks, Dick Wood and Pete Liske. He decided to risk the vital position with Mike Taliaferro, who had only one season of experience; Namath; and the other big-bonus rookie, John Huarte of Notre Dame. Ewbank kept insisting that Taliaferro was his number-one quarterback, but nobody would believe him.

"I'll open the season with the guy who I think will get the ball into the end zone the most times," said Ewbank. "You don't play somebody because you paid him a lot of money. It would be unfair to the customers. Even if you sit on the bench and work the telephone for a year, it makes a big difference. The experience is very important."

When the Jets opened their season against the Oilers, Namath sat on the bench and worked the telephones, just as Ewbank had hinted he would. He sat there in full view of a record Houston crowd of 53,680 in Rice Stadium, relaying messages from the observation booth high in the press box. He sat there sweating from the ninety-degree heat, never once getting close to entering the game as the crowd looked down and wondered about the Joe Namath myth. For one afternoon, Joe Namath was the highest-paid telephone operator in the United States.

Werblin looked on with more disbelief than anyone else. He had concocted the biggest sell job in pro football, and the subject never got to throw a single pass. If it happened at a carnival, the people would have demanded their money back. Werblin wanted to know why Namath had not played. Ewbank explained to him that Joe simply was not quite ready and would not be for at least another four or five games. But Werblin would not wait. He was playing in New York the following week, and he had to have a star. Although Taliaferro started the game, Namath trotted onto the field in the second quarter. The crowd roared its delight, and Werblin felt he had his star.

Werblin had to face reality. Ewbank was right. Namath

was still a rookie and had to learn the rudiments of professional football. There was no shortcut to experience. And although Namath established himself as the club's number-one quarterback by the end of the season, the Jets nevertheless finished with a 5-8-1 record, the first time Namath had played on a losing team since his sophomore year in high school.

The 1965 season was not a complete disaster. Namath's performance earned him Rookie of the Year honors. But, more important, he came on strong near the end of the campaign. Perhaps the key game for Namath was against the Boston Patriots on November 14. He had directed the Jets to a 30–20 victory, completing ten of twenty-five passes in the process. It was not so much his passing that counted, but the manner in which he conducted the game.

Bear Bryant, his coach at Alabama, immediately recognized it. He called Namath after the game and for the first time told Joe that he had made it. "You became a pro quarterback today," said Bryant.

The single most important factor that impressed Bryant was a scoring drive in which Namath controlled the ball for over eight minutes. Namath himself recognized the big difference between the pros and college ball.

"I learned one thing about the game," said Namath, looking back at his first year. "You just don't overpower anybody in the pros like you do in college. Sitting it out for a while helped me a great deal. That's where a quarterback has an advantage. He can see things that are much tougher to spot if he is in there. There's no question that my biggest improvement came in signal-calling. I began to check off more than ever before once I gained that valuable game experience. When I began to read the defense, I knew what to do about it. I want to be known as a football player, not a four-hundred-thousand-dollar quarterback."

Ewbank was pleased with Namath's initial season. "I've always maintained that it takes three years for a quarterback to break in," he emphasized. "There's too much to learn in less time. You just can't do it right away. Joe came along much faster than any of us anticipated. He didn't have any confidence in his leg at the beginning of the season. He threw off balance and didn't have much accuracy. The brace on his leg gave him confidence. He realized finally that he had to learn to live with it, probably the rest of his career. We felt that he could now go right on where he left off when the previous season ended."

The main ingredient the Jets had needed was a quarterback. They had one in Namath, who just needed a little more time to absorb the necessary experience. Everyone knew that Namath could throw a football, perhaps quicker and harder than anyone else in the pros.

Namath's prime receiver was Don Maynard, a lanky Texan who had the distinction of playing with all three New York professional teams—the Giants, Titans, and Jets. Maynard is lean and hard, and to look at him, you doubt that he weighs the 179 pounds listed for him in the program. In fact, he looks more like a Texas ranchhand than he does a football player. He speaks with a soft twang and has a warm smile and laughs easily.

All his professional life Maynard had to fight to survive. When he first broke in with the Giants in 1958, he was labeled a fumbler. He dropped one punt in one game, and immediately the Giant coaching staff concluded that Maynard had bad hands, which to a receiver is like having no hands at all. Allie Sherman took over as the Giants' offensive coach in 1959. Maynard, with his sideburns, boots, dungarees, and plaid shirts, never quite fit into Sherman's image of a pro. So in 1959 Maynard landed in Canada, with his sideburns, boots, dungarees, and plaid shirts, playing for the Winnipeg Blue Bombers. He had heard that a new American league was going to be formed, and he was biding his time.

Maynard played only one year in Canada. Although Canadian football was his style, featuring a fast and wide-open offense, Maynard did not like living in Canada.

"It was a strange feeling being out of the United States,"

said Maynard. "Most of the players were Canadian, and I was considered an import. I was a long way from Texas. I missed my family and friends and couldn't wait to get back when the season was over."

Then Maynard joined the Titans in 1960 and brought his sideburns, boots, dungarees, and plaid shirts back to New York. No one can make Don Maynard change the way he does things. Even his coaches have learned that it is useless to tell Maynard to do something differently if he is convinced he is right.

"Almost everybody I've played for, for instance, has tried to make me change my stride," laughs Maynard. "Why, heck, I can cover more ground with one step than anybody else can with three."

Walt Michaels, the Jets' defensive backfield coach, is a great admirer of Maynard's pass-catching ability. He has studied Maynard's moves closely.

"If I had to prepare to cover a guy like Maynard, my first thought would be to devise several ways to get double coverage on him," says Michaels. "He'd kill you one-on-one. The biggest thing that makes him dangerous is his speed and his change of pace. It's no secret. Everybody knows it. When many guys come downfield fast, they are going all out, but their all-out speed is about three-quarter speed compared to Maynard."

Michaels adds, "He's got good hands." And smiles. "Yes, I've heard the old stories, but how can I believe them? Look what he's done here; he's one of the surest and fastest receivers I've ever seen."

Clive Rush, the offensive coach, waxes enthusiastically about Maynard's knowledge of the game. "Maynard's studied hard to become an expert on patterns," Rush points out. "If he breaks a pattern, it's for a reason. I'm on the phone upstairs during a game, and when he comes off the field, he always communicates well. He reads coverages and constantly informs us of ways to break the defense."

Another thing that impresses Rush is Maynard's tremendous concentration on the ball in flight, regardless of what is happening around him on the field. Rush points out, "Because of this, he catches the long ball better than most people."

Maynard has caught so many passes for so many yards that he stands above the rest in his profession. He is the leading yardage gainer in the history of pro football, accounting for close to 10,000 yards with his receptions. By the time he has finished playing, he may establish a record that no one else can match.

Almost lost in the excitement of Namath's first year was split-end George Sauer, Jr. He had arrived on the scene at the same time, as a redshirt from the University of Texas, with some fine pass-receiving credentials. His father, who recommended that the Jets draft him, had always cast a shadow over him.

The elder Sauer was a standout player at the University of Nebraska. He had also been a successful college coach at Kansas, Navy, and Baylor, producing three Bowl teams. He was elected into the College Football Hall of Fame. And so, George, Jr., has felt he had to try harder than the next man to prove himself.

"It has been a long struggle for him," said the youngster's father. "When he was younger, I couldn't understand why he ignored football. My wife, Lillian, explained it. She told me to stop pushing him, that he wanted to make something of himself without daddy."

In high school in Waco, his track coach, Wayne Gardner, got him interested in track. He blossomed as a runner and was a good quarter-miler and half-miler.

"I told him I wouldn't bother him anymore about football, but that my silence wasn't to be taken as lack of interest," said Sauer. "If he ever wanted to talk football, we would. I remember, sometime later, we were sitting down having dinner when he asked me how an end blocks a tackle in when he's on your outside shoulder. I almost knocked over the table getting to the backyard to work on that one."

The father recognized his son's struggle but never doubted

his ability. "I asked the Jets to draft him as a receiver, even though at Texas they emphasized a running game. I knew how he could catch a pass because I lived with him. We used to spend hours together, and I would throw a ball to him until my arm felt like it was coming off."

It could explain to a large degree why the young, good-looking Sauer is extremely quiet and keeps pretty much to himself. Whatever he does in life, whether it is to catch a pass or write a novel, which he has started, he wants to do it by himself. He shuns the bright lights and much prefers sitting at home reading a book. His favorite author, far removed from the football field, is Albert Camus, who won the 1957 Nobel Prize for literature.

Sauer's reading tastes range through *The Thibaults* by Martin du Gard and Dostoevsky's *The Possessed* to *The Human Revolution* by Ashley Montagu and *Sidney Hook and the Contemporary World* by Paul Kurtz. He has hundreds of paperback books around his Long Island home and is an ardent collector of words. Whenever he comes across a word he does not know, he writes it down and later puts the word and its meaning on an index card and files it away.

George, Jr., has a subtle humor and prefers not to talk about sports. Off the field he wears dark, hornrimmed glasses that give him the appearance of a stockbroker or a young college instructor. He often indulges his dry humor on his wife, Janet, who is quite his opposite. One day George called her his amanuensis. She gave him a quizzical look until he explained it to her. She still does not believe him.

"It wasn't easy coming to the Jets my first year with my father here," admits Sauer. "Then, to make matters worse, I didn't think I was doing well at rookie camp that first year. In the back of my mind, I felt that my father was the reason I was kept on.

"I had reported with a pulled leg muscle, and the team doctor told me to lay off awhile. I sat around for ten days. I just watched the other fellows, and gained weight. I was kept around, and it was always on my mind. But I was told to be patient."

Ewbank was willing to be patient. He detected in Sauer the same potential he had seen in Ray Berry, who was the greatest pass receiver in Baltimore history. Ewbank had had a Unitas and a Berry, and now he expected to have a Namath and a Sauer. A great quarterback and a great receiver need each other. When you have the combination, Ewbank knows, you have the beginning of a winning team.

"Sauer's dedication is amazing," marvels Ewbank. "He reminds me of a faster Ray Berry, with his moves and running patterns. The boy has wonderful hands. He'll be a great one before he's finished."

The Jets began the 1966 season with high hopes. Namath had a year under his belt and knew what to expect from Maynard and Sauer. The Jets also had some highly promising newcomers, namely Emerson Boozer at halfback from Maryland State, Pete Lammons from the University of Texas at tight end, and at center, John Schmitt from Hofstra, who signed as a free agent. The Jets were also counting heavily on the experience gained by Dave Herman at guard, Winston Hill at tackle, Gerry Philbin at defensive end, and Al Atkinson at middle linebacker.

Boozer, a high draft choice, is a shifty runner with excellent speed. He was counted on to balance the Jets' running game by providing outside speed, a breakaway back—something the club had never had in its six-year history.

The team began with a flourish. In their first four games they won three and tied one. Namath had the biggest day of his career, to that point, during the second game, when he broke the club record by tossing five touchdown passes against the Oilers in a 52–13 rout. Namath was not especially accurate that day, completing twelve out of thirty-one attempts, but he did gain 283 yards, mostly with the long ball. He threw scoring passes of 67 yards to Sauer, 25 to Snell, 13 to

Lammons, and 55 and 37 to Maynard. Those five touchdown strikes accounted for 197 yards as Namath left the game with twelve minutes still on the clock.

Although Boozer did not start the game, he scored his first professional touchdown on a memorable play. On his first carry, he was dropped for a yard loss. Again he was given the ball, this time on a halfback draw. He hit the line, found no hole, slid off four players, and turned around left end for a brilliant 39-yard score.

Even the tie, which was a disappointment, was achieved with drama. After three straight victories, the Jets were favored to beat the Patriots in Boston. On a gusty afternoon, Namath could not complete his passes, either under- or overthrowing his receivers. With the Jets behind, 24–7, Namath was well on his way to his poorest performance as a pro when the fourth period began.

Namath's fourth-quarter performance was amazing. He completed fourteen of the twenty-three passes he threw, for 205 yards and a 24–24 tie in the closing minutes of play. During the entire game he had thrown fifty-six passes, breaking the old club mark of forty-eight set by Al Dorow against Oakland in 1960, and he completed twenty-eight for 338 yards, all of which were new personal highs.

"That wind gave me a little trouble out there for most of the game," explained Namath as he was taking off his shoulderpads in the locker room. "It was gusty all through the game. On the long ones, the wind would do tricks with the ball. So, instead of going for the long ball, I went for the button hooks and the square outs."

Two weeks later, disaster struck. In a return engagement with the Oilers in Houston, the Jets were blanked for the first time since the final game of the 1963 season, 24–0. Namath had a terrible afternoon, completing only fifteen of thirty-six passes, with Houston defenders intercepting four of them.

The Oilers played opportunistic football. The defense, which played a major role in the Jets' first five games, was flat and could not reach the passer. This enabled the veteran

George Blanda to set for his passes, and he had a good afternoon. Blanda accounted for 198 yards and two touchdowns.

Meanwhile, the Houston defense did its job. The Oilers' front four poured through, with ends Pat Holmes and Gary Cutsinger applying most of the pressure.

Namath was upset in the dressing room. The situation led to his first blowup with the press. The writers covering the game approached Namath in front of his locker seeking an explanation of what had happened.

"Maybe we've been to too many nightclubs . . . maybe we've been drinking too much . . . maybe we've been doing too much fooling around . . . maybe . . . maybe . . ." snarled Namath in obvious irritation at their questions. "Why can't you say we just got beat, that's all. Give the other team credit for beating us."

The reporters began to walk away. Namath turned to a teammate and said, "What can I say? They just beat us. That's all. They just beat us."

The loss started the Jets on a downward spin. They lost three more games in succession, the fans began to boo, and the heroes were suddenly villains, with Namath the chief one. Actually, the Jets never completely broke down during their losing streak. They were in every game until the very end, but they beat themselves by fumbles and interceptions—one sign of a young team. Their first of three losses was to Oakland, 24–21. They fumbled three times, once when eight yards away from a touchdown and two other times which led directly to Oakland touchdowns.

In losing to Buffalo, 33–23, the Jets gave the ball away six times, five times on interceptions and another occasion on a fumble. Although he completed twenty-four of fifty-three passes against the Bills for 329 yards, Namath was under pressure most of the game. Ron McDole, Tom Day, and Harry Jacobs put the rush on Namath so hard that Joe narrowly missed having two additional passes intercepted.

In their return meeting at Buffalo, a Jet gamble in the closing minutes of the first half enabled the Bills to win a 14–3 game on a muddy field. With less than twenty seconds remaining in a scoreless first half, the Jets had the ball on Buffalo's three-yard line. Instead of going for a field goal on fourth down, the Jets faked a field goal from the ten-yard line. Jim Hudson, who lined up to hold the ball, was supposed to throw a screen pass to Snell. However, Snell was knocked down, and Hudson tried a desperation pass to Lammons which never came close. Instead of a 3–0 lead, the Jets weren't on the board.

In the final period the line failed to hold, and Turner's attempted field goal from the thirty-five-yard line was blocked by Jim Dunaway. The 297-pound tackle picked up the ball and rumbled 60 yards for a touchdown, killing the Jets' hopes.

After a promising start, the club had finished with a 6-6-2 record, which was an improvement over the previous season's performance.

Ewbank's five-year plan reached its final stage at the beginning of the 1967 season. The components were beginning to fit into place. The players' only gripe was that they were back at Peekskill, with its completely inadequate facilities. One night in August it got to Namath.

He told Ewbank that he was going to New York. Ewbank told him not to. Namath said that he had to because his brother was seriously ill and he felt that he had to get away. Ewbank insisted that Namath should not leave, but Namath was adamant.

Namath drove to New York, about an hour away. Any number of things were on his mind. He had thought he was all finished with his knee problem when he had had a second knee operation following the 1966 season, but his leg was still painful. And now bursitis was developing in his good leg, which had buckled on him a couple of times during practice.

And it was Peekskill. The players knew about the training camps utilized by the other clubs and they knew that Peekskill was the worst. The food was bad, the rooms small, and the beds uncomfortable.

Namath failed to make the ten-o'clock bedcheck that night. He did not show up for breakfast the following morning, and he was not even back for lunch. Joe made the most of his night out. He was last seen by a doorman who reported later that Namath had left his apartment with two friends shortly before 4:30 A.M. Later in the morning Namath appeared for an interview with Chip Cipolla of WNEW.

"My knee is fine," said Namath. "I wasn't in camp last night, but it was a personal thing. Possibly, I didn't solve my problem, but I thought I could help this way, and I had to get together with myself. I have no problems with the team or with the coaches, but I will when I get back. I'll play tonight if the coaches let me. If not, well, the hell with it, I guess.

"There's nothing wrong with me physically, maybe mentally, but not physically. My troubles were personal. They had to do with myself and a couple of other individuals, but nothing with the team. I just got angry, and, at first, I just felt like leaving. That's all there was to it. I wanted to be alone, and I wanted to get away."

Namath got back to Peekskill well before the team bus departed for the exhibition game with the Patriots at 3:15 P.M. He looked tired and troubled and appeared at a team meeting called by offensive captain Sam DeLuca, a veteran Jet guard.

"I wasn't concerned with what people think," said Namath. "I was concerned with what my teammates thought. I was afraid that some of them might be under the impression that I might pick up and go anytime, like in the middle of the season. I wouldn't do that to them."

Namath stood before his teammates and apologized. Two years before he had stood up in front of them and asserted himself as being a quarterback who came to play football. This time he was humble. They sat there quietly and listened. And they believed Joe Namath's story of why he had to leave camp and get away for one night.

"The main thing we wanted to determine was whether Joe had a reason to do what he did," explained DeLuca, "or whether he just went on a bender. He convinced us he had a reason. He didn't tell us what his problem was, but we believed him. That doesn't justify what he did, or solve the problem as far as we know, but we were convinced that he did have a problem. It looked like he had been crying."

Perhaps Johnny Sample said the best thing about Joe and that particular situation. He said that as the quarterback and star and with all the money Joe got, the team expected him to be the leader.

It should have ended there, but it didn't. What opened the wound before it had a chance to heal completely was a statement that Werblin made to the press. Sonny said that if it were up to him, he would not fine Namath. That statement pulled the rug out from under Ewbank's authority on the football field. It was the wrong statement for Werblin to have made.

At the end of the month, Namath was charged with assault in State Supreme Court by Charles Parmiter, the sports editor of *Time* magazine. Parmiter maintained that on the night Namath had left camp, Joe and two other unidentified men attacked him at about three A.M. in an East Side bar called the Open End. The affidavit stated that Parmiter walked into the Open End, saw Namath at the end of the bar, and offered to shake his hand. Then, according to the affidavit, Namath grabbed Parmiter, slammed his head over a cigarette machine, and held him there for the next ten or fifteen minutes. Namath and another man then joined in striking Parmiter in the face while the second man stood by the two attackers preventing other persons in the bar from interceding, the complaint charged.

The papers said that Namath was highly intoxicated and made it clear that he was attacking Parmiter because of his dislike for the press. Namath was quoted as saying, "I don't need any of you one-hundred-dollar-a-week creeps to go around writing about me."

An ugly cloud hung over the training camp, and the Jets lost the opener in Buffalo, 29–17, as the Bills overcame a 17–0 deficit in the last period of play. More serious in the process, they also lost their powerful fullback, Snell, for an indefinite period when he injured his knee so badly in the third quarter that it required surgery the next day.

The loss of Snell seemed to galvanize the Jets, and they managed to bounce back, mainly on Namath's passing, and Emerson Boozer's running and defense.

Namath had a masterful day against the Broncos. Down 17–0, he rallied the Jets to a 38–24 victory by hitting twenty-two of thirty-seven passes for 399 yards and two touchdowns.

He continued his accurate passing the following week against the Dolphins. He completed twenty-three of thirty-nine passes for a fantastic 415 yards, three touchdowns, and a 29–7 triumph.

On a windy night against the Raiders, the defense provided the margin in a 27–14 win as Namath had trouble controlling the ball against the gusts. Philbin managed to harass Lamonica most of the game, and Grantham's interception of two of Lamonica's passes led to ten points.

They were held to a 28–28 tie by Houston. They blew a 17–0 lead, and managed to salvage a tie in the last period on a game-saving tackle by Namath, who otherwise had a disastrous day, with six interceptions against him as Jet fans inundated Shea Stadium with boos.

Namath had difficulty with his long passes. He kept trying to hit Maynard, and he kept throwing short, making interceptions easy for the Houston cornerbacks. On certain passing situations, Houston would apply double coverage to Maynard, but because of his stubbornness and headstrong determination, Namath kept throwing deep to Maynard. His own frustration with the challenge and the fans' attitude enraged him.

On successive weeks, the Jets beat Miami and Boston, and approached the second half of the season in Kansas City with a 5-1-1 record, their best first-half showing in the club's history.

John Schmitt, the hard-working center, was relaxing in front of his locker one day before the club began its preparations for the Chiefs in Kansas City. As a center, he is hardly noticed in the mass movement of clashing bodies once the ball is snapped. Every eye in the stadium is focused on the quarterback, oblivious of the fact that the play begins with the snap from the center.

"On the offensive line, we like to say that we're in the Silent Service," says Schmitt. "The only time you hear your name is when you miss a block. You know, a lineman's biggest satisfaction comes from moving one of those defensive horses to open a hole for the back, or picking up a linebacker on a blitz and really knocking his block off. But not many people see it. Our only reward, really, is having Joe say, 'You gave us a lot of time on that pass,' or having one of the backs come by and slap you on the fanny."

It was not easy for Schmitt when he joined the club late in the 1965 season. He was a two-way tackle at Hofstra University and was completely ignored in the 1964 draft. His coach, Howdy Myers, recommended that the Jets give him a look. George Sauer, Sr., went out to Hofstra, liked what he saw in Schmitt, gave him a football, and told him to keep it and learn to snap it the way a center does.

After diligent practice, hour after hour, Schmitt got it down to a science.

"On a regular play, the laces should be up so they come into Joe's hands ready for him to grip it for a pass," Schmitt explains. "On a place-kick, they should be on the bottom, because we've worked it out that at seven yards the ball will take enough revolutions so that when the place-holder catches it, the laces will face the goalposts. Then you worry about the fact that the other team's biggest player is on your nose just waiting to whack you."

Schmitt was flanked by Dave Herman on one side and a rookie, Randy Rasmussen, on the other. Dave Herman was a star lineman at Michigan State and well aware how important it is to protect a quarterback.

Herman, who is called Haystacks by his mates, explains it this way: "The biggest thing you have to do is keep your body squared away in front of Joe. You have to keep yourself as if there's a string hooked on your back in a straight line with Joe. The string should be kept perpendicular to the line of scrimmage at all times."

It's an amazing thing that Herman managed to keep onrushing linemen away from Namath. Herman discovered a year later that he was color blind. "I could see the colors okay on straightaway blocks, or when I had to block inside or outside," Herman said. "But it's on the sweeps that I had trouble."

It's not that Herman went around knocking down his own teammates. He could tell the difference between a dark jersey and a white one. It was just that on a sweep, especially to the left side, when a guard pulls from the line of scrimmage to block for the runner, Herman would look around bewildered for an instant.

As a rookie Rasmussen was doing his job well. He, too, quickly learned the importance of protecting the quarterback.

"I'd start watching the movies the first of the week and try to see what my opponent is doing," Rasmussen explained. "I'd look to see what he'd try to do. Then, of course, I'd try to feel him out the first few plays of the game. You got to find out how hard he comes at you. The thing I have to do is to keep that man out of there. If he hits Joe, I'm in trouble."

Every man was doing his job well. The defense had begun to jell. Atkinson, the middle linebacker, was coming on strong in the middle, and Philbin, the defensive left end, was crashing from his end position. Both were underrated around the league. But it was finally all coming together, offense and defense.

"I'd rather be underrated than overrated," laughed Atkinson. "When you're overrated, you're on the way out."

Michaels, the defensive coach, doesn't overrate Atkinson, he simply rates him highly. He knows a solid linebacker when he sees one, having been a four-time All-NFL linebacker with the Cleveland Browns.

"When I look at the game films, I can hardly ever call him out for a serious mistake," Michaels said in praise. "I believe a linebacker should not gamble on making a spectacular play. I like the solid, dependable type who will not make the mistake that sabotages a defense.

"Gambling linebackers," Michaels adds, "may make nine great plays, but the tenth is a touchdown, and that's no good. Atkinson has great concentration during a game, and that's what counts."

Philbin had begun to shake the effects of a shoulder separation that handicapped him his first year, in 1964. He was becoming a real menace to opposing quarterbacks.

"This has been my best year," claimed Philbin at the time. "It took me three years to get over injuries received in my first season. The most rewarding play I can make is to knock down the quarterback. Nothing else gives me as much satisfaction."

"I wouldn't trade him for any defensive end in football," said Ewbank. "He reminds me of a puppy dog between two kids playing catch. He's always chasing the ball. I have often said that if I had eleven men on defense like Philbin, we'd be champions. I'm talking about things other than physical ability. He's got heart and pride, a will to win, and he's constantly studying the game."

Philbin does not take defeat easily. After a loss, he has an intense look on his face, staring into space and often biting his lip. The fact that he perhaps played a good game offers him little consolation. He just wants to win.

"The glamour of the first year is gone, but not all the excitement. My original goal was just to make the team. Then it was to last for five years to make the pension. But now I want to go on forever, and my goals have moved ahead to divisional championship, the league championship, and the Super Bowl."

The Jets were well on their way to a divisional championship when they met Kansas City on November 6, 1967. The Chiefs, the AFL champions in 1966, were sluggish in their first seven games, winning only four of them. After a close first half, in which they led the Jets by 13–10, they pulled away in the second half to win easily, 42–18.

The Jets probably could have absorbed the loss. What they could not absorb was that Emerson Boozer, who was well on his way to a record-setting number of touchdowns, was hurt and lost for the season. With Snell still on the sidelines, the Jets' ground offensive was dealt the final blow. Without a running threat, the opposition's defense could concentrate on Namath.

The tragedy of Boozer's injury was that it occurred in the last period, when the game was out of reach. He was playing with most of the Jet second stringers when he caught a pass from Taliaferro. Two enemy defenders swooped in on him from different directions—Sherrill Headrick, a linebacker, and Willie Mitchell, a defensive back. Boozer was pincered, and the ligaments in his left knee gave way. He was operated on the next day and was lost for the remainder of the season.

The Jets could not recover from Boozer's loss. They managed to win their next two games against two of the East's weaker teams, Buffalo and Boston, but lost three straight after that. The Jets' opponents began to overplay on pass defense. Realizing that they could not be hurt by the Jets' weak running game, they would send in a corner linebacker to force Namath to hurry his passes. Also, the linebackers would drop back on other passing situations, practically wiping out Namath's targets. More often, Namath had to revert to a pass to a halfback or a fullback in an attempt to neutralize the linebackers.

A final game victory over the San Diego Chargers enabled them to finish with their first winning season, 8-5-1. Ewbank's five-year plan missed by a single game. The Jets, seemingly on their way to their first divisional championship, finished second in 1967.

The players took their defeat hard. At the end of the season they voted for the most valuable player on the squad. Maynard, who had had his greatest season by leading the AFL in yards gained receiving, with 1,434, and in average gain per catch, 20.2, was named by his teammates as the most valuable Jet.

Namath also had his greatest year. He completed 258 passes out of 491 attempts and became the first player in history to gain over 4,000 yards in one season. Namath's passes accounted for a record-breaking 4,007 yards. He also connected for twenty-six touchdowns, his personal high.

But in the players' poll, Namath finished third. Something was still wrong.

9

Something Wrong in the Locker Room

There was definitely something wrong in the locker room. There was also something wrong in the front office. Rumors began to circulate at the end of December that Ewbank wouldn't be back as coach for the 1968 season. He would instead retain his role as general manager, operating on a long-term contract, with the Jets stipulating that there would always be a place in the organization for him.

Werblin did not deny the rumors. Neither did he give Ewbank a vote of confidence, which in itself seemed an indication that he was open to a change on the playing level. Ewbank had been at the helm for five years, and the Jets still were not champions. The blame had to be placed somewhere, and a coach is an easy target.

"I haven't given much thought to a coaching change," answered Werblin when the question was posted. "But," he quickly added, "if I make a change, it will be before the college draft on January 30, and I'll probably make my decision sometime that month. A lot will depend on who's available. This isn't like baseball in that you don't make a change just to make one."

The other owners of the Jets were also becoming disenchanted, but less by what happened on the playing field than by the way Werblin ran things.

Although the club was not making an enormous profit, it nevertheless had started to earn money. The season-ticket list had swelled to over 40,000, and at most of the home games, standing-room tickets were sold. Still, the other partners were not active in the policy-making decisions. Werblin formulated them alone.

In January at the club owners' board meeting, it was obvious the partnership was about to dissolve. Don Lillis told Werblin that he wanted out. The others, Townsend Martin, Leon Hess, and Philip Iselin, also decided that they wanted to sell their shares. They gave Sonny a price, but he rejected it, claiming the overall fourteen-million-dollar price tag was not worth it. When Werblin refused, the other four offered to buy him out. Werblin refused that offer, and the financial structure of the Jets remained in limbo for the next few months.

However, it was obvious that the impasse had to be resolved one way or the other. Werblin, Martin, and Hess each owned 23⅓ percent of the club; Lillis owned 20 percent, and Iselin the remaining 10 percent. Werblin would have to purchase 76⅔ percent, or sell his share for a profit and get out.

Left unanswered was Ewbank's position with the club. Inasmuch as Werblin was not sure where he stood with his partners, he could not make a decision on Ewbank. The college draft came, and as he had done in past years, Ewbank conducted the Jets' business from his office on Madison Avenue.

At the end of May, 1968, the story broke. Werblin had sold his share of the New York Jets to his four former partners. While those on the inside were aware of what was taking place over the previous months, the public and players—with the possible exception of Joe Namath—had no idea what was happening.

Namath probably did know. Werblin had always dealt personally with Namath, and two weeks before Werblin legally broke his connections with the club he signed Namath to a new three-year contract. He did so in Miami, without his usual lavish press announcements. Most certainly he would have made a splash for his star attraction under normal conditions. But it was done quietly and handled routinely by the Jets' publicity department.

Werblin reportedly sold his 23⅓ percent interest for $1,600,000, which would place the dollar value of the Jets at eight million. Now Lillis, Martin, Hess, and Iselin each owned 25 percent. So, from an original investment of $200,000, Werblin walked away from his green-carpeted office with a 1.4 million-dollar profit in a period of five years.

Werblin was taut, subdued, and restrained. Pro football had become a big part of his life. Unlike his other partners, who had various business interests, he devoted his entire time to it. Now there was the prospect of emptiness in his life. People who watched him felt it was eating at him, even though he never publicly displayed any animosity.

"They wanted to run the Jets by committee, and it simply can't be run that way," was all he offered.

As little as Werblin knew about football when he was president of the Jets at the beginning, back in 1963, the new owners knew less. But they admitted as much, and they were all highly successful businessmen who reasoned that, after all, professional football is still a dollar-and-cents operation, sport or not. It was easy for the owners to elect a new president. They all agreed on Lillis, who, because of his retirement from the stock market, had more time to look over things. They also agreed publicly that Werblin had done a "fantastic" job in elevating the club to its present stature.

"You know, when a team rates their star quarterback sixth or seventh in a club's most-valuable-player poll, there must be something wrong. So it wasn't personal jealousy connected with Werblin that brought matters to a head, it was disen-chantment," explained Lillis the week he assumed command. "Disenchantment with being a stockholder instead of a real partner. I came into this originally to have some fun, as well as to make money.

"I was annoyed when Sonny would refer at times to the Jets as 'his' team. Hell, there were four other partners besides him. He didn't treat his partners like partners. We were com-pletely forgotten men. I don't want publicity. I prefer a life of anonymity. I felt that way when I succeeded Larry Mac-Phail as president of Bowie Racetrack, and I still do, but I did expect to have some fun, and it wasn't fun." Elaborating on his complaint, Lillis went on, "All I was getting was a ticket to the game and a free lunch in the director's room. Hell, for the kind of money I invested you could buy a lot of tickets with the interest."

As for his role as president, Lillis said, "I don't intend to invade the locker room or fraternize with the players. Not that I'm a snob, in case that's what it sounds like. I was brought up in a pretty tough part of Buffalo. But the locker room and the players belong to Mr. Ewbank, and I don't intend to encroach. I love football, and I love to watch it, but I'll leave it to the experts. I'll never forget my first meet-ing with Weeb three years ago. I asked him if there was any-thing I could do to help, and he said, 'Yes, stay away from the players.' "

Lillis went on, "I really thought Sonny would buy us out. I don't know why he changed. He seemed to have such a need of the thing. I thought he'd never sell." And then, "I'm sixty-six, and I don't need the job. I don't plan to take a salary. For myself, it's to get some enjoyment and make some money from my investment."

Unfortunately, Lillis didn't do either. He died two months later. His daughter, Mrs. Reynolds Springborn, assumed his shares, while Iselin was named by the others to the role of president.

"I was made president by a process of elimination," smiled

Iselin. "Mr. Hess is a big oil man and is very busy, and he wouldn't take the position. Mr. Martin is retired and a financier, and he wouldn't take the role either. So they looked at me and said, 'You're the guy who's going to have to do it.'

"I took the responsibilities with the understanding that it was a temporary situation. I am president of Monmouth Park, and I am also chairman of the board of my own company, so I have enough to do. I agreed to do it for the time being, inasmuch as nobody else could do it."

Iselin sat back in his chair. He is a short man, dresses neatly, and looks successful. He speaks calmly and is never very emotional. Rather, he prefers to observe a situation intently and then comment. He continued, "I didn't set a cut-off date. There was nothing left for me to do but see what kind of job I could do to get the situation all straightened out."

His idea when he first took over was to place the responsibility where it belonged. As far as the business matters were concerned, he would take care of them. "And," he added, "as far as the coach was concerned, I told Weeb that he was going to run the team, it was his responsibility, and he would stand or fall on what he did. I assured him that he was in complete charge without any interference from anybody."

Iselin made it clear that he didn't want the players to come to him with any small gripes. That was Ewbank's job, and Iselin wanted Ewbank to handle it himself. Iselin did assure Ewbank that he would make the trips and talk with the players, but wouldn't get mixed up in any part of the game. So far as Iselin was concerned, that was Ewbank's domain.

Iselin has been a success because of his lifelong habit of delegating authority to skillful, responsible people whom he then holds responsible for successful operations. In the business world, he has a number of subsidiary companies under his parent Korell Corporation. Only when there is a major decision to be made is Iselin confronted with any problems.

"At Monmouth I've been able to make constant improvements," added Iselin. "I don't know what can be done at

Shea. I haven't consulted yet with anyone in charge, but I wish we could add another fifteen thousand seats. Although New York is the biggest city in the country, that would only make the seating comparable to Cleveland's."

The problems on the field were in Ewbank's hands, the hands of a football man with over thirty years of experience. Ewbank, whose future was so much in doubt when Werblin was on the scene the previous year, finally emerged from the shadows.

The first thing Weeb Ewbank did was to move the team's training headquarters from Peekskill to Hofstra University in Hempstead, New York. The players were jubilant. Werblin had favored Peekskill because one of his sons attended the school.

"It was the greatest move that Weeb made at the beginning," declared Maynard. "I know one thing for sure: Instead of sitting around moaning and griping every night about the food, the showers, the rooms, and everything else, the players began to sit around and talk football. Happy talk, like dating, going out together, and such. They began to enjoy life instead of griping all the time. They had a nice place to eat, air-conditioned dorms, a good practice field. Everything was A-1. You couldn't have wished for anything better. I'm sure this had a lot to do with us winning the championship, because the change sure brought the guys together more, right from the beginning."

Maynard, for all his youth, and he looks even younger than he is, occasionally sounds like the senior citizen of the team, especially when recalling changes.

"I felt that Weeb came a long way too, not necessarily in coaching or winning, but in his relationship with the ball players. Without having someone over his head, Weeb began to treat men like men. The new owners gave him a free rein, and he didn't have to worry about any interference. He was running a football team the way he wanted it to be run."

The players could see that Weeb was much more relaxed, more at ease. "Because he was that way, I was more at ease myself," recalls Maynard. "Before you know it, I am talking more to my roommate, and everyone else is more at ease. The whole atmosphere at Hofstra was better. We had a relaxed team, and all we had to do was play the football we all were capable of playing."

Maynard had personally felt that the Jets could have won the Eastern Division title in 1967. He had enjoyed his greatest season, being voted the team's most valuable player, yet he felt not all of the players on the squad were playing up to their potential.

"For instance, in 1967 we had two guys I felt laid down on us," Maynard explained. "Finally, they benched one and then the other. I jumped on Weeb. Some players, I told him, you can do anything you want to them—bench them, talk to them—but it doesn't do a thing. But I don't care who the man is, you hit him where it counts, in the pocketbook, and it's gonna hurt. I told Weeb he should have fined them five thousand dollars each.

"I was really mad," said Maynard, almost angry about it again as he spoke of it. "We had a chance to win that year. We were ahead by three games, and all of a sudden we lost three games. I work too hard, train too hard, to let some Mickey Mouse guy keep me from winning. That was on my mind all winter. Who kept me from winning? Who kept me from playing in the Super Bowl? Who kept me out of all this money all these years? As soon as I got to Hofstra I walked into Weeb's office and asked him right off: 'Weeb, is this gonna happen again this year?'

" 'Well,' he said. 'Don, we've got a new owner, and everything is going to be just fine.'

" 'I'll tell you what, Coach,' I said to him, 'it's got to be, because these guys cost me money, they cost my family money.' Well, you know what happened? Weeb not only fined them but eventually cut the players off the squad. The other players realized that Weeb meant business. Right then and there, the day the players were let go, we knew that things were different."

Two players that Ewbank released at the time were Plunkett and Harris, two veteran linemen. Plunkett had possibly another year left, but Harris, who was younger, had at least six years ahead. Still, no other team picked them up as free agents.

Ewbank never admitted that Werblin interfered with the club, because he was too loyal, but the players were aware of Werblin's interference, and that Ewbank was never the autocratic coach he should have been. Frequently Ewbank was caught between the players and Werblin. If a player had a gripe, he could carry it right past Ewbank's office to Werblin. It caused Ewbank to walk softly.

Under the Werblin star system, the Jets operated with a double standard, one for the regular cast and the other for the star, Namath. Flattering though it may have been, most times it was embarrassing for Namath. Werblin would offer Namath a ride into town from the airport after arriving from a road game. Joe would politely refuse, but Werblin would insist that he had room. Namath would try to refuse by saying that he was with someone. And Werblin would insist that he could bring him along. All the while, Werblin was oblivious of the rest of the team standing nearby.

Werblin was star-struck with Namath. He treated him as an overindulgent father would, often socializing with him and undercutting the authority of the coach. Some players naturally resented this special treatment. Others felt sorry for Ewbank, and for Namath too. It was a clumsy situation, possibly disastrous.

Most of the players, however, understood Namath's relationship with Werblin. They realized that it was Werblin who pulled Joe away from the team and that it was not Namath who had initiated the relationship.

It was an awkward situation. Namath enjoyed the relationship in the sense that Werblin took him to the best places and introduced him to the right people. But Joe never bragged about his close relationship with Werblin, and, in fact, he did resent front-office politics pulling him away from his teammates.

Sonny's exit from the football scene was an elaborate press party he hosted at Luchow's two weeks after the announcement of the sale was made. It was held in a private room, and Werblin even had a five-piece band on hand. He sent out telegrams inviting his many friends from the press. After the dinner was over, he provided limousines for the writers who had to attend the Bob Foster–Dick Tiger light-heavyweight fight in Madison Square Garden. He was flamboyant to the end.

With some bitterness, perhaps, he recalled that, "When it was a failure, nobody else came around. You didn't see them in Kansas City when it was fourteen below and your feet stuck to the metal floor. But the moment it seemed we were making a profit, suddenly we were running things by committee."

A statement Werblin had made when the club was originally purchased came back to haunt him. At that time he said, "What happened to the many-ownered Los Angeles Rams won't happen here. We'll thrash out our problems within the family."

So Werblin, another showman, left the Jets' scene.

A week before the 1968 season opened, the team named Joe Namath as their captain.

10

At Last

Ewbank began to establish his control by ordering four linemen, Sherman Plunkett, Paul Rochester, Jim Harris, and Verlon Biggs, to report to camp at a prescribed weight. When the four reported with the other veteran players on July 21 for their physicals, only Biggs had come in at his proper weight, 275. Plunkett, an offensive tackle, weighed 337 pounds, 37 pounds overweight; Rochester, a defensive tackle, was six pounds over at 256, and Harris was eleven pounds over at 286, despite the fact that he had come to camp a week earlier at 303 and succeeded in losing seventeen pounds. Ewbank issued his first directive. Plunkett and Rochester would have to win back their first-string jobs, and all three would have to pay their own room and board, fifteen dollars a day, until they shed their excessive poundage.

In his strongest action in five years with the Jets, Ewbank cut both Plunkett and Harris, two veterans, from the squad a few weeks later. The move shocked most of the players, especially the veterans.

Plunkett and Ewbank had been together since Baltimore. When the Colts released Plunkett in 1963, he joined Ewbank and the Jets in Peekskill.

Plunkett was big and heavy. He resembled a giant tortoise, with layers of fat congregating in his midsection. He often weighed over 300 pounds during the season, although the program listed him at 295 pounds.

He lacked speed but was a more than adequate pass-blocker. He was so big that opposing linemen could neither get around him nor knock him off his feet.

Two seasons back, when his weight went substantially over 300 pounds, Ewbank hit him with a small daily fine, something like a dollar a day, until his weight got down. Ewbank said that he would give the money to charity. Plunkett asked the coach if he could name the charity, and Weeb agreed.

"I'd like to donate the money to the Sarah Plunkett fund, since I was always taught that charity begins at home," said Plunkett.

On the night of August 12, more eyebrows were raised. The Jets were in Houston to play their first exhibition game against the Oilers in the Astrodome. In their early years in the AFL, they had played on high-school and college fields and never attracted a large following. On this night, however, over 40,000 fans attended, lured by Namath and the Jets.

The fans, however, never got to see Namath play. Instead, veteran Babe Parilli, who was acquired in a trade from Boston for Mike Taliaferro the previous month, played the entire game at quarterback. Namath claimed that his left knee was acting up. An unconfirmed report before the game said that Namath was holding out for $3,000 an exhibition game. Dick Young, the widely known and respected columnist of the New York *Daily News,* made the statement over television during the exhibition-season telecasts. The disclosure caught everyone by surprise, including some of the principals involved.

"I wanted him to suit up because I thought it would look

better to his teammates," said Ewbank. "He would be one of them."

"If I wasn't going to play, why suit up?" countered Namath. "I know one thing: If it was anybody else but me, it wouldn't make a damn bit of difference."

Namath didn't suit up. Instead, he wore a blue pinstripe sport jacket and white loafers and looked like something out of *Esquire* as he joined his teammates on the sidelines. At times he handled the field phone, walked up and down and screamed at the officials. Joe Namath was making his presence felt even though he wasn't playing.

The story, however, originated months before, when Bite had tried to negotiate a contract with Werblin that would provide Joe with $3,000 for each exhibition game. Werblin turned the demand down, and it was conceivable that Bite renewed talks with the new owners.

Iselin denied it: "It's news to me. All our players get just the American Football League amount for an exhibition game, which is two hundred and fifty dollars. Any agreement he had with the former president doesn't hold now in this case. He won't get any three thousand for a preseason game. I know nothing about any promises Sonny made. We have a contract with Joe, and we intend to have him live up to it."

When contacted in Miami, Werblin denied there was such a contract.

"There's no truth to it," said Namath the next day. "A thing like that can cause a lot of trouble on a team."

This was the first public knowledge of any confrontation between Namath, Ewbank, and the new management since Werblin's departure from the organization. Namath was making news before the season began. The local press kept the public aware of the potentially explosive situation. One *New York Times* writer, William Wallace, even editorialized on the subject three days later. He wrote: "The Jets would do well to trade Joe Namath right now. The reasons are many. The athlete's scant respect for the coach has so diminished that

Namath calls the shots as to when he will play or not play. It is unlikely that the Jets can ever win with Namath and Ewbank out of harmony. These clashing personalities divide the team. One or the other should go. Ewbank is the more secure. What kind of deal could the Jets make for Namath? A good one. Al Davis (Oakland president) would give one of his pale blue eyes for Namath, wobbly knees and privileged contract notwithstanding."

The following day Namath received a double-breasted mink overcoat that supposedly cost $5,000. He made his contractual commitment before the preseason training camp opened and had his picture taken in the coat in the middle of the football field at Hofstra.

The Jets' training camp was not like any other in the past. Namath had not played, neither had Emerson Boozer, and Ewbank had cut linemen Sherman Plunkett and Jim Harris from the squad. The Jets were counting on Boozer, who had burst into stardom the previous season, before being sidetracked with an injury.

Now Boozer, the club's outside threat, just discharged from a tour of active duty with the National Guard, was a question mark. Because of his bad knee, which had required surgery and heavy conditioning exercise eight months earlier, no one expected that he would be activated. He had been, and reported to National Guard basic training in July. However, he was subsequently given a medical release and joined the Jets in mid-August. No one, not even Boozer, could know how his leg would react to contact.

On August 16 Ewbank made a move to bolster his offensive line, which later proved most significant in the success of the club. He signed Bob Talamini, a former All-AFL guard, who had retired because the Houston Oilers, for whom he had played since 1960, refused to renegotiate his contract. Ewbank made the announcement the day before the Jets defeated Boston, 25–6, as Namath and Boozer both looked on from the sidelines. Namath finally made his first exhibition appear-

ance of the season the following week against the Atlanta
Falcons, completing twelve of twenty passes, and led the Jets
to a 27–12 victory. On August 30 against Cincinnati, the
league's new expansion team, Namath played three quarters,
one more than he did against Atlanta. Despite the fact that he
connected on twelve of twenty-five passes for 188 yards, the
Jets failed to score a touchdown and were beaten by the up-
start Bengals, 13–9. It was a satisfying victory for Paul Brown,
who had returned to professional football as coach of the
Bengals after an absence of five years.

"They were ready to play and we weren't," said a terse
Ewbank afterward. "The day before the game Joe's knees were
bothering him so much that I decided he shouldn't play. I
spoke to him about it that night. 'Joe,' I said, 'I don't think you
should work tomorrow.' 'I've got to,' he said. 'I need the
timing.' So I not only started him but let him go longer than I
wanted. But he's a proud man, and when his timing is off he
gets thoroughly disgusted with himself."

The Jets had one more exhibition game remaining, against
the rugged Detroit Lions on September 5, before they would
open the regular-season campaign against the equally tough
Kansas City Chiefs in Kansas City. The Chiefs were one of
the favorites to win the Western Division.

Ewbank had enough to worry about. The Jets had not particularly impressed anyone with their 2-2 record. He also had
several key players who had not signed their 1968 contracts.
He was not sure if Namath had had sufficient work to be
effective and he still did not know about Boozer's knee. The
Detroit game might give him something of an answer.

"This is something I have to find out for myself too," said
Boozer. "No one else can tell what will happen, not even
fellows who have had similar knee operations. How will the
knee react to pounding? I honestly don't know. Sure, I've
been running great in practice, but I am conscious of my
moves then. In a game I'll be making moves without thinking,
quick twists, turns, and breakaways. Besides, those tacklers

will be hitting me. I don't think I've lost my speed. I had difficulty three months ago when I felt as if I was falling forward. I had to regain my strength. I worked with the weights, and I ran up and down the escalators at Shea Stadium. But I haven't been hit as yet. That will be the big test."

Boozer was used sparingly, and Namath threw cautiously, completing five of eleven, for 141 yards, as the Jets slipped by the Lions, 9–6. Namath felt that he was ready, but no one knew about Boozer, who had made only a limited appearance, just to get the feel of contact.

For the Jets to achieve a championship, a healthy Boozer was a must. He represented the club's sole outside-running threat. If the outside run was taken away from the Jet offense, then the opposition could exert a little more pressure on Namath without worrying about getting hurt too badly by a big run. Before he was injured, ironically enough against the Chiefs the previous November, Boozer was well on his way to establishing a new AFL record for touchdowns scored in a single season of play. He had scored ten times on the ground and three more on pass receptions, leaving him six short of a new record. He was injured in the eighth game of the season, and with six contests remaining, it is conceivable that Emerson Boozer would have had his name in the record books.

Boozer is one of football's most exciting runners, with his bouncy, high-kneed style of running. He provided the Jets with a scoring threat from anywhere on the field. On the ground he is the equivalent of a Namath-to-Maynard bomb.

The week before the Kansas City opener, the Jet players elected Namath their captain on offense, a gesture which Namath said was one of the most important honors he had received. The players decided to put all their trust in Namath. It unified the club. Joe Namath was finally accepted by his teammates. This marked an important difference from the previous year, when Namath finished third in a poll among the players in determining the club's most valuable player.

"We all knew Joe could get the job done," said Maynard.

"He was a natural leader, and besides, you can't win anything without a quarterback. We sort of told Joe that it was up to him to take us all the way."

Ewbank invoked some new rules. He would not allow anything stronger than beer on plane trips and ordered the clubhouse to be empty of visitors an hour before game time. This season Weeb had to win or else be fired. The players knew it, and they rallied around him.

Just before the opening game, Johnny Sample, Don Maynard, and George Sauer agreed to terms and signed their 1968 contracts. However, two other key players, Snell and Biggs, remained unsigned. Still, Ewbank had to prepare for the Chiefs, who had opened their regular-season play with a victory over the Houston Oilers, the Jets' chief threat to a divisional crown, the previous week.

A record crowd of 48,871 were in the stands of Kansas City's Municipal Stadium for the three P.M. kickoff. It was a bright, sunny day with the temperature at the eighty-degree mark. A wind from the southeast made it a bit more comfortable. This was the Jets' first test, and a lot of questions would be answered.

It was Namath's first regular game as the Jets' field leader. He might have been trying too hard in the early minutes of play. Whatever the reason, his passing was unsteady.

Of his first seven passes, he completed only one, and that a short swing pass to Boozer. Not until the Jets got the ball for the third time did they score. The touchdown was a beautifully executed fifty-seven-yard pass from Namath to Maynard, who got behind his defender, Goldie Sellers, and caught the ball on the dead run without breaking stride. The Chiefs managed one drive to the New York 26, but the defensive squad battled ferociously, and Kansas City had to settle for Jan Stenerud's field goal from the 33. The period ended with the Jets leading, 7–3.

The Jets continued their savage defensive play in the second quarter. They yielded only two first downs, and held the Chiefs scoreless while providing the offense with opportunities to register additional points. The first was a Turner field goal from the 22 that gave the Jets a 10–3 advantage. New York also scored the next time it received the ball, and Namath and Maynard were again the architects. Maynard for the second time slipped behind Sellers, and Namath responded with a pinpoint-accurate thirty-yard aerial. It provided the Jets with a 17–3 halftime edge in a game that had seen Kansas City's explosive offense controlled.

The Chiefs' first touchdown electrified the large turnout. Noland Smith, a little flea of a runner at 5-6, 154 pounds, took Curley Johnson's punt on his own twenty-yard line and jitterbugged his way eighty yards for a touchdown, which made the score 17–10.

As a result of two successive breaks, the Chiefs added two field goals. The first one occurred when Boozer fumbled on the 45-yard line after he had broken away for a substantial gain. Stenerud had an easy field goal from the 11. Then, after a hard rush by mammoth Buck Buchanan, 6-7, 280 pounds, Namath's hurried pass was intercepted by Willie Lanier on the Jets' 13-yard line, near the end of the third quarter. On the second play of the fourth period, Stenerud was successful with a 21-yard field goal to narrow New York's margin to 17–16.

Namath used four minutes of the clock to get the Jets into field-goal position at the Kansas City 35. Turner was sent in to try for three points from the 42, and he gave the Jets a 20–16 lead. Kansas City, needing a touchdown to move in front, drove to the New York 21 before being stopped. Again they looked to Stenerud, and the Norwegian-born kicker hit from twenty-eight yards out. With 5:56 remaining to play, the Chiefs had moved within one point. Exercising excellent ball control, Namath ran the clock out to preserve the victory, doing so with two key third-down passes to Maynard.

The Jets' defense had asserted itself. They were alert and quickly reacted to Dawson's short passes. Tackle John Elliott was a standout. He made four unassisted tackles and assisted on nine others, and dumped Dawson twice.

Namath also displayed the leadership his teammates had looked for in him. He masterfully ran out the clock in the final six minutes under mounting pressure. Taking the ball over on his own five-yard line he moved the Jets out of field-goal range.

The Jets were in high spirits at Kansas City's Municipal Airport while they waited for their chartered flight back to New York. They were seated in a private lounge, and some of the people at the terminal began to drift into the room seeking autographs. One lady approached Namath and asked him who Joe Namath was.

"He's sitting right over there, madam," answered Namath as he pointed to Babe Parilli, who was reading a newspaper across the way.

"Pardon me, Mr. Namath, can I please have your autograph?" she asked.

"I'm not Joe Namath," replied Parilli. "He's sitting right over there."

The lady turned to look where Parilli was pointing. She looked back at Parilli. "But he told me you were Joe Namath."

"No ma'am, he's Joe Namath," said Parilli.

The middle-aged woman returned to where Namath was sitting. She had a pen and paper in her hand and looked confused.

"Excuse me, but that gentleman told me that you were Joe Namath," she remarked.

"Did he?" asked Namath. "Why, ma'am, he's putting you on. Hey, Joe, why don't you sign your autograph for this nice lady," shouted Namath at Parilli.

Babe looked up and shook his head, but when the lady approached him again Parilli signed "Joe Namath."

Ewbank hardly had time to savor the joy of defeating Kansas City when Snell was quoted as saying the next day that if the Jets did not meet his terms he would not play in the Boston game on Sunday.

"The club was in the driver's seat, but now I'm behind the wheel," Snell was quoted. What Snell was directly referring to was the fact that the club's number-one draft choice, Lee White, a fullback from Utah's Weber College and the prime threat to Snell's first-string job, injured his knee against Kansas City and was out for the season. When Ewbank reached Snell, the veteran fullback told him that he was misquoted and that he intended to play against Boston whether or not he had signed.

As well as a power runner, Snell is an excellent pass-blocker. If he could do little more than pass-block, Snell would still play. Ewbank values his quarterbacks and therefore appreciates the necessity of having the protection of a fullback who can carry out his blocking assignment. Alan Ameche provided it at Baltimore, and Ewbank rated Snell together with Ameche as two of the best pass-blockers he had ever seen.

Obviously Snell was making a power move for more money. He was one of the first big-name stars signed by the Jets in 1964 when the bonus war between the NFL and the AFL was raging. He was considered a prize plum when the Jets succeeded in signing him, and, as a result was paid a bonus somewhere in the neighborhood of $200,000.

Before Namath joined the club, Snell was the big attraction. He rushed for 948 yards in 215 attempts and caught 56 passes for another 393 yards and was voted the Rookie of the Year in the AFL in 1964. He finished second in the league in rushing, behind Buffalo's Cookie Gilchrist, and set club marks for most yards gained in a single season, most yards gained in one game, 180, and most carries in a single game, 31.

Snell does not speak much unless he has good occasion to. Because of his years of service, Snell is the spokesman for the Negro players. They look to him for advice or confront him when they have a legitimate gripe. He advises them, or if the situation requires it, goes directly to Ewbank with the problem. Ewbank respects Snell enormously and almost always has a sympathetic ear for him. In this role, he was bargaining for money—it seemed unlikely he could lose.

The game against Boston was scheduled to be played in Birmingham, Alabama, and designated as the Patriots' home game. Fenway Park in Boston, where the Patriots play their home games, was not available September 15. The baseball season was in its final two weeks, and the main tenants of Fenway, the Red Sox, were playing there.

Why the Patriots ventured so far for a home game is conjectural. Perhaps they figured that Legion Field, where the University of Alabama plays some of its home games, would be a natural site with Namath leading the opposing team. Namath might draw more fans in that one game than the Patriots could with two playing dates in Boston.

However, a hot Alabama sun kept a great many people away. In fact, only 29,192 spectators showed up, but they were Namath fans. It must have been an odd feeling for the Patriots—being designated the home team on the scoreboard and then being booed for every effort.

In any event, Namath knew more about every blade of grass on Legion Field than the entire Boston team together. In a wild scoring game, the Jets easily prevailed, 47–31. When the score mounted to 44–17 in the early moments of the fourth period, Namath left the field and Parilli got some playing time. It was pleasant revenge for the 38-year-old veteran. He had been Boston's regular quarterback for the previous seven years and had led them to two division titles. He was also extremely skilled in the art of holding a football for a field-goal kicker, something which Jim Turner had quickly discovered in Parilli's brief time with the Jets. He placed the ball for all four of Turner's successful field goals against the Patriots.

"Babe is the best holder in football," offered Turner. "It's not coincidence that Gino Cappelletti holds all the place-kicking records in our league. Babe was his holder in Boston.

He has the fastest hands, and he reminds me of things when I go on the field, like to make sure I'm lined up correctly and to check the wind.

"When Babe came in, he moved up the spot where he puts the ball down, a couple of inches less than seven yards. He figured out that those couple of inches would make John Schmitt's snap come out with the laces facing the goalposts every time. This way I don't have to kick at the laces, and he doesn't have to spin the laces around."

After opening with two victories, the Jets were prohibitive favorites to make the Buffalo Bills their third straight victims. The Bills were having all sorts of trouble. They had dropped all three games they played and did not have an established quarterback. Jack Kemp, their regular signal-caller, was out for the season with a broken leg, and their number-two quarterback, Tom Flores, was sidelined with a muscle tear in his right shoulder. Things were going so bad for Buffalo that they fired their head coach, Joe Collier, and asked the club's player personnel director, Harvey Johnson, to take over for the remainder of the season. It was apparent that the club had written off the season and were content to play out the string. Their only consolation was the fact that they would finish the campaign a week earlier than anyone else and more than likely end up with a high choice in the college draft. Although their defensive brigade was still formidable, their offensive fortunes rested on a rookie quarterback, Dan Darragh, who was limping on one leg, and two first-year runners, Ben Gregory and Max Anderson, and a rookie flanker, Haven Moses, who, if he had had anyone to throw the ball to him would have had an outstanding season. It was too much of a load to put on four rookies. All these factors considered, the bookmakers established the Jets as a nineteen-point favorite.

The Jets reported to La Guardia Airport at ten A.M. September 28 for their chartered flight to Buffalo. A light rain and the delay in arrival of the aircraft from Florida postponed the departure until 11:30. The coaches and writers, and any club officials, sat in the first section of the aircraft. The members of the squad scrambled for seats in the second half of the airplane, with the card players pairing off. As usual, the front row of seats behind the partition was left empty for Namath. The first row allowed Namath extra room to stretch his gimpy left leg. Namath propped up his leg and sat on the aisle seat, while Hudson sat next to the window.

The flight to Buffalo took about an hour and a half. It was a half-hour longer flying time than normal because the players had to be served lunch during the flight.

Since the flight left late, the itinerary had to be altered slightly. Instead of going straight downtown to their hotel, the two buses which transported the players from the airport headed directly to War Memorial Stadium for their scheduled 1:30 P.M. workout. The day was warm, and the sun shone brightly, which made it easier for the players to loosen up. They were in a relaxed mood in the old wooden dressing room at the top of the stairs. Some of them started to kid Bob Talamini, who was still a relative newcomer on the squad.

"Hey, Parilli's been talking about you again," said one of them as he came out of the shower and passed Talamini. "He says you're still too heavy and out of shape. You should hear him talking about you in the shower. He's saying you're lucky the Jets picked you up and got you out of retirement."

Talamini did not say a word. Finally, when Parilli emerged from the shower, Talamini spoke.

"Now listen, Babe, I heard what you've been saying about me. If you don't behave yourself, I'll mash your finger and ruin your career."

The players laughed. It was an obvious reference to the fact that Parilli would not be doing much more than holding the ball for Turner's field goal and point after touchdown attempts.

Quickly the players dressed and hurried to the buses, which were parked outside of the old stadium. They were anxious to check in at their hotel and watch the Notre Dame–Purdue game, a battle of two unbeaten college teams.

I sat with Namath and Hudson at the hotel and watched the game on television. Namath felt that Notre Dame's secondary did not play aggressively enough.

The telephone rang every ten minutes or so. All of the calls were for Namath. After a while, Hudson kiddingly complained, "I'm going to quit answering the phone. I'm not your secretary. Besides, I want to watch the football game. Next time the phone rings, I'm not going to answer."

Hudson and Namath are close friends and always room together on the road. They are a study in contrasts. Hudson is a tall, quiet Texan. He speaks seldom, and when he does, he talks in low tones. He has great admiration for Namath, and Joe likes the toughness Hudson displays on the field. Hudson is a born competitor. He loves nothing better than a one-on-one challenge, and in most cases he emerges as the winner. He has a quick temper, which is triggered by his fiery desire to win.

Hudson's chances of becoming a professional football player had been remote. He was signed as a free agent, because no team in professional football felt he had enough ability to risk selecting him in the draft. Then he had to overcome illness and injuries as a rookie to make the club. His desire and hard tackling impressed the coaches. Hudson has gained prominence as the Jets' strong side safety, and Namath and many other players feel that Hudson is the most underrated safety in the league.

Joe took a nap and when he awoke, Hudson called down for messages. He handed the notes to Namath, and Joe looked them over. He always returns the calls of his friends. One call was from Ernie Warlick, a former Buffalo player who was now a sportscaster. He wanted to do an interview, and Joe accommodated him.

"Warlick will be over at six o'clock to do a tape," said Joe. "It won't take long. After I finish, we'll go out and get something to eat."

We ate in a restaurant on the outskirts of the city to ensure more privacy. We finished dinner by 9:30 and then returned to the hotel in time for the 10 P.M. snack which all the players and coaches are required to attend. By eleven o'clock all the players were in their rooms in time for bedcheck.

Buffalo being Buffalo, Sunday morning was cool. By game time it had become cloudy, and there was a slight wind. A crowd of 38,004, lured chiefly by Namath and the Jets, were in the stands when Bruce Alford, who had been signed only that Thursday by the injury-depleted Bills, kicked off to New York. Earl Christy brought the crowd to its feet by taking the opening kickoff on his own six-yard line and racing down the sidelines to the Buffalo seven-yard line. The Jets were in excellent position for a quick score, and on third down Namath drilled a four-yard pass to Sauer for a touchdown.

A Buffalo punt had given New York possession for the second time on the Bills' 39-yard line. But on second down, Tom Sestak, Buffalo's massive tackle, blitzed Namath and brought him to earth on the 44 for a nine-yard loss. The sight of 6-4, 270-pound Sestak landing on Namath brought a roar from the crowd. Then Namath was intercepted by Tom Janik, who brought the ball back to New York's 36. Four downs later, Alford kicked a 35-yard field goal to cut New York's advantage to 7-3.

On the ensuing kickoff, Buffalo's defense held the Jets. Curley Johnson punted from deep in his own territory, and Buffalo took over on its own 40. Eleven plays later, with only four seconds remaining in the first period, little Max Anderson scored from two yards out. Alford made good on the extra point and the Bills led, 10-7.

Inspired by their lead, Buffalo's defense in the second quarter put a strong rush on Namath, who was forced to release his passes a second quicker. Finally, on their third series of downs in the quarter, Namath maneuvered the Jets into field-goal range, but Turner's attempt from the 37 fell short.

For an instant the Jets got lucky. On second down, Darragh fumbled on his own ten-yard line, and Ralph Baker recovered the ball. Seeking a quick touchdown, Namath, releasing the ball too quickly, missed on his first two passes. On third down, he dropped back again. Janik intercepted on the goal line and ran 100 yards untouched for Buffalo's second touchdown and a 17–7 edge, with four and a half minutes remaining in the period.

New York launched its offense from their own 34. Namath decided to pass on first down. He threw to Sauer, but Butch Byrd swooped in front of the intended receiver on the Jets' 48 and flew downfield for an apparent touchdown. However, Buffalo's defensive end, Tom Day, was off-side on the play, and the touchdown was nullified. The Jets maintained possession, and six plays later Boozer slipped across the goal line from one yard out to narrow Buffalo's lead to 17–14.

Anderson ran the kickoff back to the Jets' 34, with less than two minutes left in the first half. On fourth down, Alford connected on his second field goal of the afternoon, to increase Buffalo's margin to 20–14. The Jets went on the attack from their own 33, with only 48 seconds left in the half. Buffalo used a prevent defense, in which they take out a lineman and use an extra linebacker to defend against the pass. With 32 seconds left Namath dropped back from his own 45, and Maynard broke down the right sideline. He got behind Janik, and Namath deposited the ball in Maynard's arms for a touchdown that enabled the Jets to walk off the field with a 21–20 edge at halftime.

The Jets weren't playing like nineteen-point favorites. They had scored on the Bills, all right, but the left side of the Bills' line had put an effective rush on Namath. Ron McDole, the Bills' veteran defensive end, had continually burst into the Jets' backfield.

McDole had been getting the best of Sam Walton, the Jets' rookie offensive tackle. Walton, who had played well in the Jets' opening two games, looked confused and had trouble holding off McDole. If Namath, who saw McDole coming at him from the corner of his eye, had not released the ball a little quicker than usual, he would have been on the ground looking up at McDole most of the half.

After an explosive first half, the game settled down in the third quarter. The only scoring in the quarter was Alford's third field goal, which returned the lead to Buffalo, 23–21. In the opening minutes of the fourth quarter, a Namath-to-Sauer pass was intercepted by Byrd, who once more took off untouched down the sidelines for another Buffalo touchdown. It was the third time they had intercepted Namath for a touchdown. Buffalo's lead rose to 30–21, and the Jets were in deep trouble.

With twelve minutes remaining, the Jets had a third and one on their own 38. Ignoring the run, Namath chose to pass. Booker Edgerson, the right cornerback, figured the play. He lifted his arms on the Jets' 45, speared the ball, and ran unmolested for a touchdown that provided the underdog Bills with a 37–21 bulge. Namath walked off the field, obviously furious with himself. He roughly unloosened his chin strap and paced up and down in a small area away from the bench. He wanted to be alone. Then he stood there with his hands on his hips staring on the playing field with utter disbelief. After two solid games, he was being plagued with the interceptions that had marked his first three years as a pro.

Within minutes Namath was back on the field directing the offense. He began on his own 35 and in seven plays brought the Jets their fourth touchdown, the payoff being a three-yard pass to Snell. After holding Buffalo, New York shifted to the attack from its own 20. In seven plays they had reached the Bills' 34-yard line. On second down Namath went to the air. He wanted to hit Sauer, but Byrd again intercepted. The Bills took over on their five, with 2:37 left to play. The defense held, and Paul Crane broke through the Buffalo defense to block their kick, and the Jets recovered on the 11. On second down Sauer caught Namath's ten-yard pass for a touchdown and took the Jets to within 37–35. There was 1:04 showing on the clock, still time for the Jets to recover an onside kick and boot a game-winning field goal. However, Paul Costa covered Turner's attempt, and with just 59 seconds remaining, ran out the clock for an unbelievable victory.

There was no question that Namath was rushed hard during most of the game. The chief reason was the pressure applied by McDole, Buffalo's tenacious left end. The 6-4, 265-pounder completely outplayed his counterpart, rookie Sam Walton. He kept coming at Namath all day, and a great many times Namath threw without clear vision. Walton was so outclassed that Ewbank sent in Talamini and Jeff Richardson, redesigning his offensive line in an effort to stop McDole. At one point Walton became so frustrated that he tackled McDole in order to stop him.

"Sam's a rookie, and he made some mistakes out there," explained Ewbank in the quiet Jet dressing room. "He's got to learn some things. He had a fine exhibition season and did well in our first two games, but today he ran into some trouble. Why, we never teach our players to tackle a lineman the way he did. He just lost control."

Namath was the last to dress. As he slowly buttoned his shirt, he took the blame for the loss. "I was bad out there today," said Namath, reaching for his tie. "How many times did they intercept me?"

No one had to answer him. He was making his point.

In reality, he was protecting Walton, whose confidence could easily have been shattered after the terrible day he experienced. The bus ride to the airport was long and quiet. Namath stood most of the way sipping a large cup of soda and ice. He pierced the silence by yelling to Ewbank: "Hey, Weeb, are we going to practice tomorrow? I for one could use it."

"We'll talk about it later, Joe," replied Ewbank from the front of the bus. It was quiet the rest of the way.

San Diego was coming up, and the coaching staff had one

day less to prepare for the meeting. The contest was listed for Saturday night, October 5, at Shea Stadium, the Jets' first home game of the season. Like Kansas City, the Chargers were also considered strong contenders for the Western Division championship, the other club being the defending kings, the Oakland Raiders.

Ewbank approached the Charger game with caution. He instructed Namath to control the ball, since the Jets had won the coin flip and had elected to receive. Namath followed the game plan. In their first two series of downs, they ran the ball eleven times, managing only three first downs, one an eighteen-yard run by Boozer on the opening play of the game, and another a twelve-yard maneuver by Snell. It was after Snell's effort that Namath threw his first pass of the night, overshooting Maynard down the right sideline. Another pass by Namath went incomplete and was nearly intercepted, as the crowd groaned. The Jets did manage a field goal as a direct result of Randy Beverly's interception of John Hadl's pass on the San Diego 35.

Turner seemed to be kicking with more confidence than any season before. Parilli had made a big difference. Turner's kicking had provided the Jets with another offensive threat; if they drove down in close, they could always look to him for three points if the touchdown drive stalled.

After two minutes of the second quarter, San Diego scored on a seven-yard pass from Hadl to Lance Alworth. Turner kicked an important field goal, with just over five minutes remaining in the opening half. He then kicked another from the 26-yard line, which was nullified when the Jets were detected holding on the play. Turner tried again from the 45 and split the uprights, to carry the Jets to within one point of the visitors, 7–6. The kick seemed to provide the Jets with a lift.

Philbin and Biggs began crashing from the end positions and applying a great deal of pressure on Hadl. The Charger quarterback was getting less time to throw and as a result had to hurry his passes.

Finally stopped by Dave Grayson (45), Snell picks up good yardage against Oakland (United Press International, Inc.)

Emerson Boozer and Matt Snell started the Jets running game in 1966

Boozer got tangled in Boston traffic ... but he broke through for the score (United Press International, Inc.)

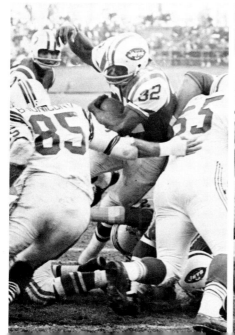

Oakland's Ben Davidson instructs Namath in the perils of a passing game (United Press International, Inc.)

In 1967 Snell continued to go outside — this time, against Kansas City, after a handoff from Namath (12) and lead by Randy Rasmussen (66) (United Press International, Inc.)

And Boozer went inside, against Houston, all alone (United Press International, Inc.)

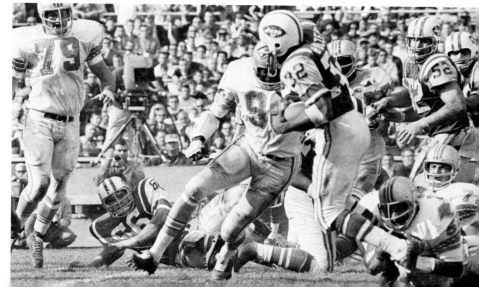

Fu Manchu in 1968 (United Press International, Inc.)

Despite all the Jet defenders, Buffalo's Ben Gregory squeezed through and the Jets lost, 37-35 (United Press International, Inc.)

Namath got determined protection — note Snell's (41) hands — against Denver (United Press International, Inc.)

Following Dave Herman (67), Snell ran through the Bronco line (United Press International, Inc.)

But Denver's Fran Lynch flew over the line and the Jets lost to another underdog (United Press International, Inc.)

Against tough teams the Jets got tougher

Randy Beverly intercepted a Houston pass and ran it back twenty-eight
yards (United Press International, Inc.)

With forty-eight seconds left, Snell drove into the end zone to win the game, 20-14 (United Press International, Inc.)

The touchdowns nobody saw

With the Jets beating Oakland in the fourth quarter, NBC switched its cameras to *Heidi* (National Broadcasting Company), and Jet fans were spared watching Raider's Charlie Smith score and . . . (United Press International, Inc.)

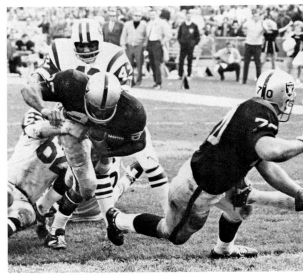

Preston Ridlehuber (37) recovers a Jet fumble and is escorted by five teammates into the end zone. If you missed *Heidi*, Oakland won, 43-32 (United Press International, Inc.)

The Jets got revenge, beating Oakland for the AFL Championship. Jim Turner — season's high scorer for the Jets — attempts a field goal (United Press International, Inc.)

Oakland's Davidson continues, too late, his lessons to Namath (United Press International, Inc.)

An escort for Coach Ewbank (United Press International, Inc.)

Don Maynard and Joe Namath celebrate (United Press International, Inc.)

To the quarterback go the spoils — at the Shea Stadium victory party
(Wide World Photos)

OFFENSE

SNELL
FB

BOOZER
RB

NAMATH
QB

MAYNARD
FL

LAMMONS
TE

HERMAN
RT

RASMUSSEN
RG

SCHMITT
C

TALAMINI
LG

HILL
LT

SAUER
SE

THE JETS LINEUP FOR
THE SUPER BOWL GAME

PHILBIN
LE

ROCHESTER
LT

ELLIOTT
RT

BIGGS
RE

BAKER
LLB

ATKINSON
MLB

GRANTHAM
RLB

SAMPLE
LC

HUDSON
LS

BAIRD
RS

BEVERLY
RC

DEFENSE

(The New York Jets)

Earl Morrall: Namath said there were five better quarterbacks in the AFL (United Press International, Inc.)

Bubba Smith: He said nothing, but was supposed to make Namath long for Davidson (United Press International, Inc.)

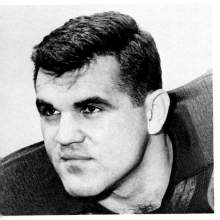

The enemy

Lou Michaels: Supposedly he wanted to take care of Namath, on or off the field (Langhead Photographers)

But . . . Philbin (81) took care of Morrall (United Press International, Inc.)

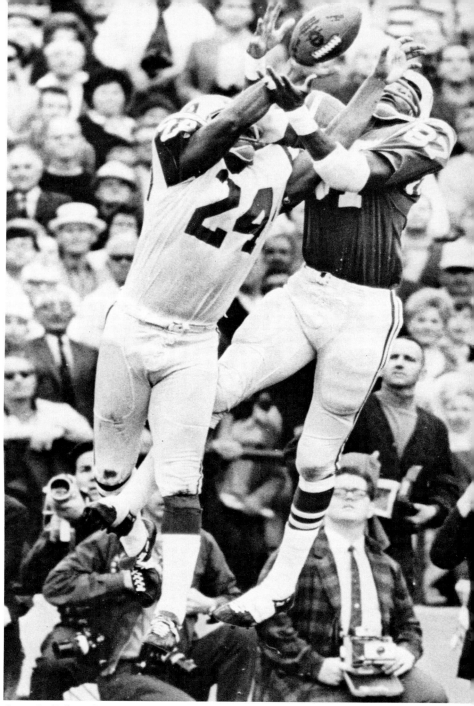

Sample (24) took care of everyone who came his way — in this case, batting down a Morrall-to-Richardson pass (United Press International, Inc.)

Namath handed off to Mathis who went around end, or . . . (United Press International, Inc.)

to Snell who tore through the Colts for the first score (United Press International, Inc.)

Jim Turner kicking one of the three field goals that provided the margin of victory (United Press International, Inc.)

It wasn't easy. When Bubba Smith broke through, he was terrifying (United Press International, Inc.)

Injured Johnny Unitas replaced Morrall, managed one scoring drive, but to no avail (United Press International, Inc.)

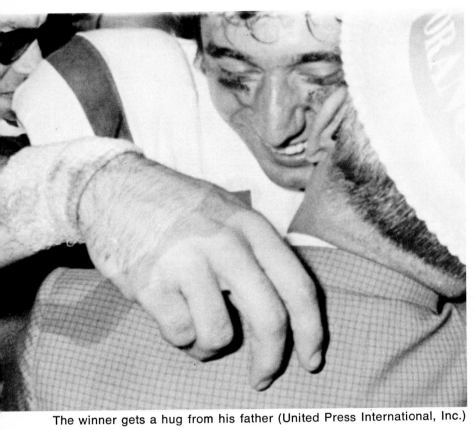

The winner gets a hug from his father (United Press International, Inc.)

Seconds from the end of the quarter, Turner delivered again, this time from eleven yards away, to send the Jets into the lead, 9–7.

Instead of a wide-open offense, the Jets had played it close in the first half. Namath threw only thirteen passes, completing seven but for short yardage. His longest completion was a 23-yarder to Maynard. Instead, the Jets leaned heavily on their ground game.

New York did not produce its first touchdown until Snell hurdled the San Diego line from one yard out at the end of the third quarter. But Hadl retaliated with an 84-yard touchdown pass to Walt Garrison. The Chargers missed the extra-point attempt but Hadl again teamed with Garrison, this time from five yards out, for a touchdown that put the Chargers ahead, 20–16. New York took the ensuing kickoff on its own 25, and Namath directed them on a twelve-play, 75-yard scoring march, culminated by Boozer's drive from a yard away, that won the game.

Ewbank analyzed the 23–20 victory in the dressing room: "We played it close out there," he said. "After a game like the one in Buffalo, you don't want something to go wrong right away. We ran the ball the first eleven plays. Joe needed a little time to get his confidence back. I didn't want him to be forcing things when he shouldn't."

The players enjoyed two days off before reporting back to Shea on Tuesday to prepare for the Denver Broncos. Like Buffalo, the Broncos were having their troubles in a rebuilding season. They had only one victory in four games, and the Jets were twenty-point favorites.

Most of the 62,052 spectators at Shea that day looked on with amazement. The young Broncos, who had upset the heavily favored Jets the year before on the same field, were doing it again. In almost a replay of the Buffalo game two weeks ago, the alert Bronco secondary picked off Namath passes with unceasing regularity. When the game had ended, they had intercepted five of Namath's passes, to upset the Jets

21–13, and boos reverberated throughout the huge stadium for the high-living quarterback.

Namath was visibly upset in the dressing room. As the reporters congregated around his locker, Namath refused to answer any questions. He was about to walk away from his locker when he spoke. "I ain't saying nothing except that I stink," Namath said woodenly. "I know it's your job, but I stink, and that's it, period. I've been talking for four years, and I've never refused to talk, but today I ask you to respect my wishes. I only want to say one thing—that I stink!"

Namath then went directly to the trainer's room, which is off-limits for anyone other than players. The silence throughout the room disclosed the players' feelings. For the second time in three weeks they had blown a game they were supposed to win easily. They were almost in shock. Philbin dressed slowly, biting his lip at times, his eyes showing his anger. Hudson sat on his stool with his head down, his elbows resting on his knees as he dragged on a cigarette. Even Johnny Sample, at the adjacent locker, kept shaking his head as he dressed. The Jet loss was even reflected in Houston, where Oiler coach Wally Lemm remarked, "We're back in the race."

Ewbank was philosophical. He said he always maintained that on any given Sunday any team can rise up and beat the other. He was trying to brush off the losses lightly.

Throughout the losses, the Jet defense had performed effectively. They had exhibited steady, solid play. The offense was erratic. The running attack still hadn't established itself, and the passing phase of the offense was ineffective when it resorted to the long ball.

The Oilers were next. The Jets arrived in Houston on Saturday afternoon and went from the airport to their hotel and then to the Astrodome for a workout. The players were somber. They knew the importance of the game against Houston.

Namath and Hudson went to their room, joined by Bite and myself. Bite had brought some brochures on a chain of drive-ins that were going to be franchised under the name of Broadway Joe's. The first one was scheduled to be opened in Miami in December. Namath was casually dressed in a mod print sport shirt and slacks. Hudson was wondering how he could get twenty-five tickets for his relatives and friends for tomorrow's game.

The telephone rang. It was for Namath. He joked with the caller and then said, "Hey, Lou, somebody wants to talk to you."

It was Cookie Gilchrist, a former Buffalo star, who was in Houston on a business deal. "So you dropped me and took up with Joe," kidded Cookie.

"Of course not, Cookie. I'm running with Hudson, and Joe happens to be along."

Cookie laughed. After a minute or so he talked with Joe again. He was primarily interested in securing a franchise in Denver.

That evening we had dinner at Frank Chicarella's apartment, a genuine Italian dinner. Cookie had come by, and we had all gone down to the cocktail lounge on the mezzanine for a drink before we left for dinner. Gilchrist spoke briefly with Joe and Bite over a drink and then left on a business appointment.

Chicarella is originally from Youngstown, Ohio, but was working in Houston. That night's dinner was extra special because Frank's mother came down to Houston to visit and to prepare a big home-cooked meal for Joe, like the old days. When we arrived, Joe warmly embraced Frank's mother, who was busy cooking in the kitchen.

As usual with any home-cooked Italian dinner, there was more than enough food. Joe was moved by Frank's mother, who had traveled all the way from Youngstown on her vacation to visit her son, and then stood in the kitchen cooking for hours. When we finished eating, just after nine o'clock, she still had not sat down to eat. Joe made a final toast to Mrs. Chicarella, and as we departed, Joe again embraced the wonderful woman, and we returned to the hotel for the ten-P.M. snack. Just before eleven o'clock we all went up to Namath's room. Frank also wanted a brochure on Broadway Joe's. We spent only five minutes in the room, and then Frank, Bite, and I departed. As we were leaving, Namath handed Frank a basket of flowers that he had received that evening.

"Give these to your mother, and I'll see you all tomorrow at the game," said Joe.

Namath's affection for Mrs. Chicarella is a direct reflection of his close relationship with his own mother. He worries about her and often calls her in Beaver Falls. Joe's mother and father have been divorced for years, and while his father manages to attend the Jet games whenever he can, she always watches Joe play on television.

There is nothing Joe would not do for his mother, or anyone else in his family for that matter, but his mother comes first. Two seasons ago his mother made Joe promise her he would stop smoking. Joe did, and he has never broken the promise.

Like most mothers, she is both proud of her son and worried about him. Whenever he comes home, she delights in cooking stuffed cabbage, one of his favorite dishes, for him.

A testimonial luncheon honoring Namath as the hero of the Super Bowl had to be postponed a day because Joe had to see his mother in Beaver Falls. The magazine tried to get him to postpone his visit. He simply told them that he had promised to go to Beaver Falls that day and nothing would change it. The magazine finally pushed the luncheon back to the following day.

Joe's mother is just as fiercely loyal to him. She is his number-one fan. Last March she wrote a letter to the Jets' office saying she was Joe Namath's mother, that she was starting a fan club for Joe in Beaver Falls and wanted permission for it to be recognized as the official club in the area. She signed it, "Sincerely, Mrs. Rose Szolnoki."

The game against Houston was one of the most vital of the entire season. A New York victory would just about finish the Oilers as serious challengers. A loss, however, would move

Houston within a half-game of the Jets and reestablish them as a contender.

It was a tightly played first period. The Jets failed to produce a first down, while the Oilers collected only three. Both teams seemed tense as they probed the defense with caution. It was like waiting for a time bomb to go off.

Bite was nervous on the sideline. "C'mon, baby, get on the board," he prayed. "Get a touchdown and make 'em chew awhile."

The Jets finally broke the scoreless struggle, with only twenty-five seconds left in the quarter. Crane, as he had done in the Buffalo game, barged through Houston's protective wall to block Jerry Norton's punt in the end zone for a safety, to give the Jets a 2–0 lead.

"Who got that?" yelled Namath as the Jets came running off the field. When informed that it was Crane, he slapped the former Alabama center on the rump and exclaimed, "Way to go."

It wasn't until there were just over six minutes left to play in the first half that the Jets finally succeeded in making their initial first down against the rugged Oiler defense. After he had missed the target on his first nine passes, Namath finally zeroed in on fullback Billy Joe on a third-and-ten situation from his own 40. Joe reached the Houston 49 for an eleven-yard advance. Four more first downs carried the Jets to the Oilers' one-yard line. Snell tried to go in but was thwarted. Then Namath took the ball in himself around left end with only 1:17 left. Braced to try and prevent the extra-point conversion, the Oilers were caught by surprise. Kneeling to await the snap from Schmitt, Parilli got up and spun around to his right. He hit Mathis in the end zone for a two-point conversion that provided the Jets with a 10–0 edge as the first half terminated.

The titanic defensive struggle continued in the third period. Twice the Jets had the ball, and both times they failed to generate a drive. Three times Houston tried to mount an attack, and three times they were repelled.

"C'mon, Sam, we gotta get something going," yelled Herman on the sidelines at Sam Walton.

"We gotta get some more," shouted Namath. "The defense is going to shut 'em out."

On the last series of downs of the third period, the Jets began to fashion an attack. Starting on their own 48, they reached the Houston five-yard line when time elapsed. On fourth down, Turner, opening the final period with a twelve-yard field goal, expanded the Jets' lead to 13–0.

The Oilers' fortunes turned on an injury to second-string quarterback Bob Davis, who had been filling in for the sidelined Pete Beathard. Little Don Trull, a scrambler, went in and ignited the Oilers. In three plays he produced a touchdown, and Houston was back in the game, 13–7.

New York's offense failed, and Trull continued to spark the Houston attack. He guided them sixty-three yards to a touchdown in ten plays. Walker kicked the extra point and the Jets trailed for the first time all afternoon, 14–13, with less than five minutes to play.

Ewbank was upset. He hurriedly walked up and down the sideline. "Where's Joe, where's Joe?" he screamed.

Namath stood at the far end with his chin strap unsnapped and his hands on his hips looking at the clock. He motioned for Ewbank to calm down.

"Take it easy, Weeb," he assured him. "I know what I have to do, and there's plenty of time left."

Namath demonstrated extreme confidence. He was not the least bit excited. He fastened his chin strap and trotted onto the field. In a daring series of plays, he threw three passes to Sauer and completed all of them.

On the first two passes, Sauer ran a square out pattern. He ran straight upfield and then made a sharp cut to his left. On the third pass play, he started upfield the same way, but instead of cutting to his left, he went to his right.

The Jets now had a first down on the Houston 44, as the clock disclosed only 2:58 remaining.

Then Namath threw to Boozer over the middle for seventeen yards and another first down on the Oilers' 27. Boozer then carried for two yards to the 25, and the Jets signaled for a time out, with 1:59 left. Namath trotted over to the sidelines to meet with Ewbank.

"I'm going to let Snell and Boozer run the ball right up the middle and get all they can," Namath told Ewbank.

Namath figured it perfectly. He called Boozer's number, and the shifty halfback manipulated for fifteen yards. Then he called on Snell, and the hard-running fullback churned for eight yards to the Oiler two-yard line. He asked for Snell again, and the fullback went in standing up, dragging a tackler with him. There was only 48 seconds of action remaining when the Jets virtually sealed a 20–14 verdict.

The key to the Jets' defensive efforts was the linebackers. They had an edge and made the most of it. Realizing that the Oilers had to depend on a second-string quarterback, they weren't concerned with Houston's passing attack. They figured the secondary, aided with a good rush from the front four, would handle any air threat.

So they cheated a little. They played up tight and sealed off Houston's running game. With Houston's best runner, Hoyle Granger, sidelined with an injury that wasn't disclosed until game time, all they had to stop was Bob Hopkins. They did.

It was unquestionably the Jets' biggest win of the year. Namath was greatly relieved after the game. Chicarella waited for him to finish dressing in order to drive him to the airport. I went along too, as did Bite. It was becoming obvious that Namath was determined to lead the Jets all the way.

"I don't need the money," he exclaimed on the way to the airport. "But, hell, if we win the AFL championship, that one game alone is half a season's pay to a lot of the guys on the team. Boy, my mother must have gotten a heart attack after a game like this. I'll call her tomorrow the first thing. By the time we get back to New York tonight, it'll be late and she'll be asleep."

Before the Houston encounter, a number of the players made a vow not to shave until they had clinched the Eastern Division title. The defensive linemen also had something going, a quarterback pool. They started it just before the Boston game in Birmingham. Each of the front four would put up ten dollars, and whoever got to the opposing quarterback the most times that particular day would collect the sum. The investors were Verlon Biggs, Gerry Philbin, John Elliott, Paul Rochester, and Carl McAdams, who alternated at tackle with Rochester. Biggs had suggested the idea, and it became a popular head-hunting game.

"I thought it would give us something extra to work for," explained Biggs. "I made forty dollars on it that day."

Others began contributing to the pool. Ewbank, defensive line coach Buddy Ryan, and Mike Martin, a front-office official who loves to watch the games from the sidelines, all added ten dollars, which made an eighty-dollar bounty every game. Elliott hit for $160 against San Diego; he was the only one to throw Hadl. The pool does not pay off in a losing game, and the San Diego prize carried the previous week's amount from the Buffalo loss. The $160 was also the amount for the Oiler game, and Philbin, Rochester, and Elliott, who each got the quarterback once, left the money in the pool instead of sharing it, which brought the pot to $240 for this Sunday's game against Boston.

Elliott had been the biggest surprise of the front four. In his rookie year the previous season he had filled in at three different positions—end, linebacker, and tackle. He was also a member of the kickoff and punt-return teams and had impressed the coaches with his speed and hard tackling. By the end of his rookie season he had made his way into the starting defensive unit as a tackle. Another in a long line of Texan Jets, Elliott was one reason why the Jets' front four had jelled as a solid unit.

"We don't let the linebackers in on the pool," disclosed Rochester. "If we did, Larry Grantham would blitz every play.

We're probably the smallest front four in the league, but we've got quickness and speed. With the emphasis on the pass rush, it's going to come to that. You just can't stand around anymore. You've got to move."

The Boston game was a rout, the easiest win of the season. Leading by 20–0 after the third quarter, Ewbank inserted Parilli to give him some work, and the ex-Boston quarterback directed the Jets to four more touchdowns in a 48–14 romp. And while Parilli and reserve fullback Billy Joe had their day in the sun, Philbin was the biggest winner of them all. He got to Boston's two quarterbacks four times to win $240.

"We wanted to hold them to a shutout," pointed out Philbin, who departed with the rest of the first team in the final seven minutes. "I was very disappointed after they scored. Sure the offense scored a lot, but we have pride in our own unit.

"We want to be the best. Why give them the extra one hundred and eighty yards? After the game Walt Michaels and Buddy Ryan, the defensive coaches, blasted a couple of guys. The coaches have a lot at stake too. If we wind up number one defensively at the end of the season, it helps their future. You know, they like to make more money too."

The Jets' outlook had brightened considerably. They had won two straight games and had reached the halfway station of their season with a 5–2 record. If they could duplicate the performance in their final seven games, they would easily win their first divisional crown.

New York's next opponent was Buffalo. The Bills had won only one game all season, and nobody needed reminding that it was enjoyed at the expense of the Jets. Buffalo was experiencing an agonizing campaign. Six players had already undergone surgery, and a number of others were forced to play with injuries because there was no one else. It prompted Jack Horrigan, Buffalo's vice-president, to quip: "We're the only club in the league with three sets of uniforms—home, road, and hospital gowns."

Yet, somehow, the Bills always play some of their better

games against the Jets. Although Namath did not have the same horrendous day he experienced the first time the two clubs met, the Jets had to come from behind in the final quarter to win, 25–21. Instead of Namath's arm, it was Turner's leg that provided the margin. In fact, the defense scored the only New York touchdown. Sample intercepted a pass on the 31 and raced for the score.

Turner set an AFL record by attempting eight field goals, tied one by making six, and set a new club record by scoring nineteen points in one game. He missed his first two tries, one wide and the other blocked, before he booted six straight.

Part of Turner's success comes from his intensity as a performer. He sulks. He thinks a great deal. He gets so wound up at times that it is best to leave him alone. He has always been that way, and the players understand his moods.

It took him a little time to relax in the dressing room. A locker-room attendant reached past Turner, who was sitting on a stool in front of his locker, and picked up his shoes.

"Where you going with them?" he snapped. "Leave those alone."

"I was only going to clean the dirt out of them," the youngster replied meekly.

"Dirt doesn't bother them," answered Turner.

Then Turner turned around to the group of reporters and continued, "I don't like anybody to touch my shoes. Not that I am superstitious. It's just that one time someone was messing around and took my shoes.

"I get a mental picture. If you don't have a mental picture, you just can't go in and kick. I think of what yard line we're on, what the angle is, how the wind is blowing, and how much I have to put in the kick.

"Usually Parilli tells me something when we go out. He might tell me he can kick better than I can, so I better make it. He does it to relax me. But when we went out there to try for the thirty-five-yarder, he didn't say a thing. No one did. That's the first time no one has said anything. They were being kind to me. They knew what the kick meant.

"To tell the truth, though, I really didn't get excited about making it until I was off the field and talking to some of the guys."

Turner's magic was essential to the Jets' offense. Buffalo's defense had always been troublesome for Namath. Their front four, led by Tom Sestak and Ron McDole, manage to put a hard rush on Namath. They are big and always come in with their hands up, making it difficult for him to see over them.

It causes Namath to lose the range. He has a tendency to overthrow his receivers when he lacks good vision. Or, if they cause Namath to scramble, he is forced to throw off balance, and his accuracy drops.

The difference in 1968 was that the Jets were no longer a one-man passing attack. The defense had matured. The enemy not only had to concern itself with stopping Namath, but they also had to find a way to launch a successful offensive. The Jets' defense was respected by the other clubs. It had come of age, and no championship is possible without a solid defense. Philbin, Biggs, Elliott, and Rochester had blended into the best front four in the league.

The offense wasn't a "hurry-up-and-pass, there's-nothing-else" type of attack. They had a running and a kicking game, and Namath had matured as a quarterback. He threw fewer passes and emerged in his new role, directing the club on the field. He no longer played for the touchdown all the time. He could get on the board with a field goal, and in Turner he had the most effective kicker in the business.

The remaining stumbling block on the schedule was Houston. The Jets' record was 6–2, and the second-place Oilers were 4–5. A New York triumph would balloon their lead to three and one-half games, which for all practical purposes would ensure a title.

Despite the fact that it rained and the field was muddy, the Jets had an easier time against the Oilers than in their previous clash in Houston. Leading all the way, New York had sealed Houston's doom with a 26–7 conquest. Mathis scored both touchdowns, and Turner booted four more field goals, and the Jets were flying high.

The Jets flew to the West Coast on Thursday evening to meet the Oakland Raiders, who were battling for Western supremacy with San Diego and Kansas City. Only one game separated the three title aspirants. Past New York and Oakland battles have always been rough affairs. There is no love lost between the two clubs. In last year's game at Oakland, rugged 6-8, 280-pound Ben Davidson, a Paul Bunyan–type man with a long handlebar mustache, cracked Namath's cheekbone. He and his big playmates, like 6-5, 270-pound Ike Lassiter and 6-3, 240-pound Carleton Oats, and 6-4, 240-pound Dan Birdwell, like nothing better than sticking it to Broadway Joe.

Namath does not hide his feelings about the Raiders.

"Every team has a couple of individuals who are that type of player. Around the league they talk about our guys. But on Oakland, they all want to hurt the quarterback. It's one thing to give a guy a good lick and he gets hurt, that's the game. But it's another thing to twist my leg in a pile-up, like Davidson did when I was a rookie, or like he did last year when the play was over.

"I was looking downfield watching the flight of the ball; I didn't even know it was him until I got up and saw him. I like Oakland less than any other team. It's mostly because we've been frustrated against them.

"Until last season, the best we had done against them was a tie out there two years ago. We beat them here early last season, but then we lost to them out there, and if we had won that one we would have tied Houston for first place in our division."

The Jets had plenty of reminders for the remaining five games. Namath and Sample had called a meeting the week before of their respective units. They told their teammates that they must sacrifice the rest of the way. They asked the players to sacrifice their Friday and Saturday nights so that Sunday afternoons would not be sacrificed instead. A number of other players rose and made the same speech.

There were other reminders pinned up on the bulletin board. Signs that read: "Will Jets Blow It Again?", a copy of a telegram from the Houston Oilers last season which read: "Good luck in your game with the Chargers, we saved second place for you," a huge copy of a bank check made out "To the order of each New York Jet" in the amount of $25,000, their potential share for winning the AFL championship and the Super Bowl.

"That's a lot of money," said Billy Joe. "It's a big incentive. Football instinct is the main thing, I guess. But this is professional football. They don't call it that for nothing."

"In past years," offered Grantham, "we haven't come through at this point of the season. This year the primary difference is dedication. We're in good shape, but we've got five more Sundays to go. If we don't win it this year, then forget it."

The Oakland game began normally enough. As was expected, it was a hard-hitting clash of two teams battling for a championship. There was a penalty on the opening kickoff, and so it went. The Jets got on the board first, with two field goals by Turner, from 44 and 18 yards out. Near the end of the quarter, quarterback Daryle Lamonica hit Warren Wells with a nine-yard scoring pass, to provide the Raiders with a 7–6 lead after one period of play.

On the first series of downs in the next quarter, Oakland scored again. Lamonica called a screen pass to Billy Cannon, and the veteran tight end rambled forty yards untouched behind some magnificent blocking, to increase Oakland's advantage to 14–6. Just eight seconds from the end of the half, Namath scored from one yard out on a keeper play. Parilli then, faking a kick, tried for a two-point conversion that would have tied the score. However, his pass dropped to the ground untouched in the end zone, and the Raiders led, 14–12.

The rough first half was marked by a number of penalties. Oakland was reprimanded four times for 63 yards, while New York was slapped with seven infractions for 86 yards. The second quarter alone consumed 49 minutes. It looked like a long afternoon.

New York gained the lead early in the third period. A Hudson interception gave the Jets an excellent field position. Six plays later, Mathis made his way into the end zone from four yards out, to provide the Jets with a 19–14 edge. Then the game went wild. Hudson was singled out for unsportsmanlike conduct on an Oakland scoring drive. The Jets were penalized to the shadows of their goalposts, and Hudson raved at the officials. He was ordered to leave the field, and more Jet tempers raged on the sidelines. The Raiders went in for the touchdown, and a two-point conversion from Lamonica to Hewritt Dixon put them on top at the end of the third period, 22–19.

On the first play of the fourth period, Philbin recovered Charlie Smith's fumble on his own three-yard line to undermine a Raider scoring threat. Then, in two similar pass plays to Maynard, Namath covered 97 yards by air for the lead touchdown, 26–22. The next time the Jets got the ball, Namath moved them in position for a Turner field goal from the twelve-yard line, as the Jets moved in front by 29–22.

Just 3:55 from the end, the Raiders tied the score on a Lamonica-to-Fred Biletnikoff 22-yard touchdown pass. The Jets received the kickoff and quickly moved downfield. With 1:08 left on the clock, Turner was called upon to attempt a 26-yard pressure field goal. He delivered, to give the Jets an apparent 32–29 victory.

At least millions of television viewers thought so. They were deprived of the final 1:05 of play because NBC had a special children's movie, *Heidi*, scheduled for seven P.M., and it was now 7:10. The network switched from the football game and presented their regularly scheduled program.

It was not until later that football fans discovered that the Jets had lost, 43–32. Oakland had unbelievably scored two touchdowns in 50 seconds to deprive the Jets of a victory. Could it possibly happen?

The NBC switchboard was flooded with thousands of phone calls, so many that the switchboard broke down. Unable to get through to NBC, thousands of irate callers called the Police

Department and tied up the emergency police number for hours. Still other bewildered callers telephoned *The New York Times* and the *Daily News* to find out what had happened.

The Jets' switchboard was also flooded with calls the next day. The irate callers wanted to know why the Jets had cut off the game before it was over. Lynn Donohue, the switchboard operator, had a hard time convincing some of the fans that it wasn't the Jets' fault.

The game had far-reaching effects two weeks later. Pro-football commissioner Pete Rozelle fined the New York Jets $2,000, one of the largest in history, for the club's criticism of the officials. Individual fines were also meted out. Hudson and Michaels were fined $150 each. Hudson and Elliott, who was ejected after the final Oakland touchdown, were assessed $50 each for their removal.

Rozelle's office cited complaints to reporters about the game officials by Ewbank and Michaels; the intrusion of the Jets' physician, Dr. James Nicholas, into the officials' locker room; and the showing of controversial game-action films to reporters, thereby prolonging the dispute. If anything, the already strained feelings between the Jets and Raiders worsened.

The loss did not seriously hamper the Jets' title chances. It just delayed the inevitable another week or so. The Jets had only four games remaining, with only the following week's opponent, San Diego, considered a tough game. In fact, New York had little difficulty in beating the Chargers, 35–17. Now, either a Houston loss or another Jet victory would clinch the divisional toga. They had two games remaining with the Miami Dolphins and one with Cincinnati.

The divisional title became official just before four P.M., when the Kansas City Chiefs eliminated Houston, 24–10, in a Thanksgiving Day game. The players, their wives, and club officials had gathered at Shea for a family dinner. Champagne corks popped, and the players and their wives were all excited, jumping and moving about the room, hugging and congratulating everyone.

Maynard seemed relieved. He had that quiet smile of his and shook his head in a soothing way.

"I'm sure glad it finally came about," he sighed. "I've waited for this day for nine years, first when we were Titans, and now the Jets. I was just watching the game and kind of hoping. In pro football you don't expect anything, you just hope."

The remaining three regular-season games would merely be used as tune-ups and a chance to get some of the injured players ready for the AFL championship game. Ewbank planned to let Namath play only half a game, with Parilli finishing out the clock. In this way Namath would remain sharp and Parilli would get some badly needed playing time just in case he should be wanted for other duty besides holding the ball for Turner's kicks.

The Jets won all three of their games, to finish with their best mark in history, 11–3. They defeated Miami, 35–17, Cincinnati, 27–14, and then the Dolphins again, 31–7. They were sharp and had momentum for the title game. Their opponent in the Western Division would be either Kansas City or Oakland, who had finished in a tie. The play-off game on December 22 was won by Oakland. The stage was set for a natural return game with the Raiders on December 29 in Shea Stadium. There was no looking back now.

11

First Oakland

The Jets had mustered at Shea to study films of both the clubs until they knew that only Oakland had to be studied.

As in their normal weekend practices, the Jets worked out lightly. There was no contact. There was no need for it. The players worked speed drills and sharpened their timing. Some of the injured players tested their ailments, Maynard's knee and Boozer's leg being the primary concerns.

Maynard had pulled up slightly lame against the San Diego Chargers four weeks earlier. He suffered a pulled hamstring muscle in his leg and did not play in the final game of the year against Miami. Boozer played the entire game against the Dolphins. It was the longest he had played all season, and his legs were a bit sore. The men both reported that they would be ready to play against the Raiders.

Following Sunday's playoff game, in which Oakland emerged the winner, the Jets' coaching staff assembled on Monday at eight A.M. to begin their week's preparations for the Raiders. Whatever they had previously gathered in the way of information about Kansas City was immediately scrapped.

The sting of the loss to the Raiders just over a month ago still stuck in the minds of the Jets. Michaels for one was reluctant to talk about the Raiders.

"We need full-time people officiating who are as dedicated to their jobs as we are to ours," Michaels said at the time. "I can't believe we had that many face-mask penalties."

The Jets were penalized a total of 143 yards in the game. It angered Michaels—so much so that he tried to get into the officials' dressing room to express his displeasure.

Michaels is spartanlike. He is a tough taskmaster who not only played hard during his career with the Cleveland Browns, but who demands a great deal of effort from his players. He is a serious coach who does not fraternize with the players. He has his job to do and wants a player to do his.

At times Michaels reveals his temper. He will scream at a player if he feels the player is not putting out. In Oakland he had wanted to scream at the officials.

It was Michaels' responsibility to devise pass coverage for the Raiders' three top receivers, Biletnikoff, Wells, and Smith. Biletnikoff caught seven passes that day, Smith four, and Wells two.

"You have to remember a few people had been thrown out of the game," recalled Michaels. "But I'm not going to say anything else about it."

The players assembled at noon Tuesday to begin rehearsals for the Raiders. They needed no reminders about their first fracas with them. Some of the players, like Philbin, had their own personal objective driving them. He sat with his back resting against his locker, enjoying a brief break in the day's routine.

"Get Lamonica. That's the best defense against their passing attack. If we can get to Lamonica early, then we won't have to play catch-up football. We've got to keep him on his back. We have to get him and throw him for a loss; you can get to him, because when he's hot, he's hot. Even if you can't tackle him and throw him for a loss, get your hands in his face.

"He throws so quick, you have to get in on him or he'll hurt you. He's also one of the toughest quarterbacks around. We've given him some good shots, and he just bounces right back. You can't rattle him mentally either."

The quarterback head-hunting pool wasn't in effect this time. The Jets' front four didn't need it. "We don't have anything going on this game," said Philbin. "It's all or nothing. We don't need any extra incentive."

The weather was cold. The wind lashed around Shea Stadium and stung the faces of the players. They took part in a forty-minute drill with winter gear—gloves, hooded sweatshirts, ski masks, and heavy sweat pants over their long underwear. When the players were not in motion, they huddled around with their hands in the pockets of their sweatshirts. The wind, gusting at forty miles per hour, made it feel even colder.

The next day was Christmas. It was also another day given over to preparing for Oakland. Following their workouts, the players and their families were invited to a Christmas dinner given by the club.

Turner worried about the wind. As the AFL's leading scorer, he was often asked about his secrets for kicking field goals with regard to certain weather conditions. Now he was mum.

"I'm not going to tell you anything about it, not this week. All you do is kick, and the wind does the rest. The wind here is the worst in the league. It doesn't matter what kind of day it is. The wind is always there. There's nothing about the wind I don't know, but that doesn't help get the kick through."

"Weather plays a part in all games," Namath added, "but the wind factor is the biggest thing. Cold weather and rain are bothersome, but they don't bother you nearly as much as the wind. I have this game more on my mind than I've ever had any other. You know, all season long people talked about how we weren't getting any touchdown passes. But all along we kept winning. Statistics don't mean a thing. Everything has to be compared to winning. Man, if you're winning, that's all that counts."

The cold continued on Thursday. Again the Jets managed a brief workout under icy conditions. In the dressing rooms Bob

Talamini, a nine-year veteran, figured he could earn more money in the next two games than he did in his first three years in pro football.

"Three years in the pros is like an eternity," he said. "You go through three years of exhibition games and three years of playing fourteen games a year and three years of bumps and bruises, and then you can make more money in just two games. It's not just the twenty-five thousand dollars. Being on a Super Bowl team helps in the off-season earnings too."

Schmitt said it simply enough as he peeled off his practice togs. "The biggest thing to keep guys going is the reminder that there's one more game to go to get that twenty-five thousand dollars. If the guys start slacking off, all you have to do is remind everyone about the Super Bowl, and they get going again."

The snow came down heavily on Friday. It forced the Jets inside, and Ewbank took the team to a nearby armory for a workout. The tarpaulin was placed on the field as soon as it began to snow that morning. It would remain there until a few hours before game time on Sunday.

Regardless of the weather on Sunday, Sample expected a busy afternoon. Lamonica and Biletnikoff would never give him a chance to relax. "Biletnikoff had such a great game last week against Kansas City, you know they have to throw to him. I've got something in mind, but I'm not going to talk about it. I've looked at films every day this week. I'm ready now. If the game was today, I'd be ready. We're only one game away."

On Saturday the Jets worked indoors once again. The Raiders, who had planned a light workout at Shea, were forced to cancel their plans. Instead, they ran through their paces in Oakland before boarding their chartered jet to New York. And so, neither of the teams would test the Shea Stadium turf until their meeting on Sunday. Only then would they truly know the conditions of the field.

By Sunday the weather had warmed to thirty-seven degrees. However, the wind whipped around the park in gusts of thirty to thirty-five miles per hour. Turner said there was always a wind at Shea, and today was no exception. Now all he had to do was figure it, just as he had all season long.

The game was blacked out in New York. As a result, tickets were hard to obtain. Somehow the scalpers managed to do business, even on a cold day. A couple were outside of the Diamond Club entrance to the big stadium, asking if anybody needed tickets.

They were asking $25 for a $12 ducat. They caught some live ones. Two fans in their late thirties had a short talk with the scalper. Very discreetly $50 was counted, and cautiously tickets changed hands.

The Raiders won the toss of the coin and elected to receive. A crowd of 62,627 spectators, who had paid a top price of $12 a ticket, were witnessing the first professional championship game in New York in six years.

Oakland failed in their first offensive thrust. A short punt gave the Jets operating room on the Oakland 44. Namath and Maynard quickly went to work on cornerback George Atkinson, who was no match for the speedy Jet flanker the last time they met. Namath's first pass gained fourteen yards. Maynard ran straight down, gave a head fake to his left, and cut to his right. On second down Namath again threw to Maynard, and Atkinson was caught for pass interference, to give the Jets another first down on the 20. A well-timed draw play by Snell gained six yards, and New York broke from their second-down huddle on the 14. Maynard, at full speed, had again run straight down and cut sharply to his right toward the corner of the end zone. Namath dropped straight back and rifled a bullet into Maynard's hands. In less than four minutes the Jets had a 7–0 advantage.

The Jets' defensive unit limited the Raiders' offense to only one first down the first four times Oakland had the ball. They put a strong rush on Lamonica, making him hurry his passes. Philbin and Rochester applied the pressure from the left side. Rochester dropped Lamonica for a two-yard loss. Philbin nailed fullback Hewritt Dixon for a three-yard loss when he attempted to go outside. They both stopped halfback Charlie

Smith at the line of scrimmage. As a result, they presented their offensive team with field position. Beginning on their own 44, the Jets marched to Oakland's 25-yard line before bogging down. Turner, with the wind blowing, attempted his first field goal from the 32. He split the uprights, to give the Jets a 10–0 lead, and the happy patrons championship aspirations.

The Raiders finally got their offense going in the opening minutes of the second quarter. Lamonica completed a 23-yard swing pass to Hewritt Dixon and a first down on the Jets' 29. After an incomplete pass, Lamonica connected with Biletnikoff for a touchdown. Biletnikoff ran a post pattern and got past Sample on the inside. The Raiders trailed by only 10–7.

A Jet scoring drive ended in failure. They had moved from their own 11 to the Oakland 37 before they stalled. Turner was sent in to try a 44-yard field goal, but his kick fell short by a few yards. Near the end of the first half the Jets mounted another offensive. They reached the Raiders' 28 before being stopped. Again Turner was summoned, and this time he made good on a 36-yard field-goal attempt, for a 13–7 edge.

The Raiders managed to retaliate with a field goal just after the two-minute warning. George Blanda, a 41-year-old veteran, kicked one from 26 yards away, to narrow New York's halftime advantage to 13–10.

Midway through the third quarter the Raiders managed to even the score. Two Biletnikoff receptions and another by Wells carried the Raiders to the Jets' six-yard line. New York's defense stiffened. In three downs Oakland managed to reach the one-yard line, but no farther. Hudson, the left safety, had diagnosed Oakland's plays perfectly. He combined with Baker to stop Smith on the first carry and then came up fast to drop him when Smith tried to turn the end. On the third running attempt, Hudson, aided by Atkinson, stopped Dixon on the one. Going for the tie on the fourth down, Blanda booted a field goal from the nine-yard line, to deadlock the struggle at 13–13.

Then, in a long, time-consuming drive, the Jets came back.

They began on their own 20. Namath hit on four of the seven passes he threw, the score coming on a twenty-yard touchdown strike to tight end Pete Lammons. As the third period ended, the Jets were in front, 20–13.

Gaining possession on their own 30-yard line, the Raiders realized they had to score quickly. Although there was still 11:39 remaining to play, they needed a touchdown and at least a field goal to win.

Lamonica went for the big play. After Dixon got a couple of yards to the 32, Lamonica set up to pass on second down. He dropped back, and behind good protection, waited until Biletnikoff shook loose from Sample. He did, and Lamonica sent the football spiraling to him for a 57-yard completion on the New York 11. However, once more the Jets' defense was unbeatable. Smith tried to go outside but was repelled by Philbin for a yard loss. Lamonica's pass for Wells was overthrown, and then Hudson batted away a pass that was intended for Cannon. Failing to collect the tying touchdown, the Raiders had to settle for Blanda's twenty-yard field goal, to trail by 20–16.

The Jets put the kickoff in play on their own 22. In one play, the game suddenly was turned around completely. Dropping back to pass, Namath attempted to isolate Maynard on Atkinson. However, this time the young rookie didn't falter. He intercepted the ball on the 37 and brought it all the way back to the five-yard line before being tackled. On the first play, Pete Banaszak went into the end zone standing up with 6:42 remaining, to give the Raiders a lead for the first time all afternoon, 23–20.

Namath and the Jets were coming down to the wire. The whole season hung in the balance. Christy gave them some working room by running the kickoff back to the 32. Namath went to the air. His protective pocket held firm, Talamini and Hill on the left side and Rasmussen and Herman on the right. Schmitt helped out on the blocking assignments, always keeping an eye out for any blitzing linebacker up the middle.

Namath hit Sauer for a first down on the 42. Then he sent

Maynard deep down the right side and fired a 52-yard pass over Atkinson for the biggest play of the game. The play was blown dead on the six-yard line, and the Jets were in striking distance for the biggest touchdown of the year. Namath took the snap from Schmitt, faked a hand-off to Snell, and then fired the ball accurately to Maynard in the end zone, to move the Jets in front, 26–23. The Jet players were jubilant on the sideline. Turner lined up to kick an important extra point. It was one that would lift the Jets out of a game-tying field goal should Oakland be confronted with such a situation. He booted the point, and now the Raiders needed a touchdown to win.

They tried. On the ensuing kickoff, they put the ball in play on their own 34. Lamonica passed on first down and completed a twelve-yarder to Billy Cannon, for a first down on the 46. With the Jets braced for the anticipated pass on the next down, Lamonica caught them vulnerable to a run up the middle. He called for a draw play, and Dixon burst through for twenty-eight yards before Baker dropped him on the Jets' 26.

He went right back to Dixon, who failed to gain anything. Two passes fell incomplete. On fourth down Lamonica tried to pass but was smothered by Biggs for a six-yard loss. The New York defense had held again.

The Jets' front four, led by Biggs and Philbin, had succeeded in putting an effective rush on Lamonica. Lamonica had to rush his passes, even though it appeared that he had open receivers downfield.

Oakland got another opportunity, with 3:27 on the clock. They had a long way to go, starting from their own 15-yard line.

Oakland's offensive line slowed down the Jet charge and gave Lamonica a little extra time. He used it. Lamonica hit Biletnikoff for a 24-yard gain that carried the ball to the 39. On the next down Lamonica looked for Wells and reached him with a 37-yard pass. The Jets were penalized twelve yards on the play, moving the ball to the New York 24. Now the

Raiders were in striking range, with exactly 2:00 left on the clock. They had momentum and plenty of time.

Lamonica stepped back quickly. He wanted to throw a swing pass to halfback Charlie Smith, the same receiver he had found to give the Raiders their winning touchdown in the first game with the Jets. But Lamonica threw behind Smith, and the football dropped harmlessly to the ground. However, the ball was still in play. Inasmuch as it was thrown behind Smith, it was a lateral and a free ball. Smith, in a momentary lapse, failed to go after it. Ralph Baker did, and the Jets had possession of it. Oakland lost it all on the bounce of a football.

When the field judge's gun signaled the end of the game, a number of Jet players lifted Ewbank on their shoulders and carried him off the field. It was the first public display of emotion they had shown him.

They carried Ewbank all the way to the tunnel underneath the stands that led to the dressing room. They were ringed by fans, some of whom yanked at Ewbank's leg. When they reached the safety area underneath, Ewbank limped into the locker room.

It was the defensive team's turn to award the game ball to the person of their choosing. Johnny Sample asked for quiet in the middle of the room and then said that the team was awarding the game ball to Weeb.

"We wouldn't be here if it wasn't for *our* Coach of the Year," exclaimed Sample. The remark was a reference to the fact that Hank Stram of Kansas City was named Coach of the Year two weeks earlier.

Philbin then led the group of players who carried Ewbank to the showers, where they doused him, to the cheers of the players.

Namath asked for the champagne, and Ewbank, toweling his wet head, told him there were a couple of cases in the back room.

"Let's bust it open," yelled Joe.

Namath then turned to Maynard. "Are you ready for Baltimore?" he asked.

"I'm always ready," Maynard assured.

"It took a long time to make it," added Namath.

"He thinks that's a long time," laughed Maynard. "What should I say?"

The crowd in the Jet dressing room was delirious. The champagne flowed like water. Philbin threw announcer Bill Mazer under a shower. Johnny Carson entered the tumultuous room to offer his congratulations. He walked over to Namath's locker, and Broadway Joe poured champagne over his head.

The celebration continued far into the night, later at a closed party at the Bachelors Three, an Upper East Side bistro owned by Namath and former Jet player Ray Abruzzese. When the night ended, the Jets' owners picked up the tab. Everything was fine.

The excitement of the victory celebration was to be maintained for the next two weeks by one event or another. At Shea Stadium the official victory party would give every guest an opportunity to reflect on the fortunes of a team which had been transformed from terrible Titans to champion Jets. The man who was largely responsible for the chaos of the Titans would not be at that party, nor would the man who had started the Jets toward the championship. During those coming two weeks, while preparing for the invincible Baltimore Colts, Joe Namath would fire his club and the national press with the flat prediction: "I guarantee that we are going to win the Super Bowl game."

12

Then
THE Game

Ominous low clouds moved swiftly in a northerly direction. There was still a small chance of rain. It had rained heavily the night before, but now the sun was trying to struggle through. Rain would definitely favor the Colts. They had the heavy runners, and a quarterback with two sound legs. A lot of the smart money waited until the final day before putting down a bet on the Super Bowl game. If you send in a lot of action, you have to figure the elements. The odds which favored the Colts by eighteen points thirteen days earlier had not fluctuated much, a half-point either way, depending on the local bookmaker.

There was no wake-up call for any of the players, but most of them got up early. Their first order of the day was to assemble at 10:30 A.M. in the dining hall for the pregame meal. It was the same ritual they had observed all season long: Super Sunday was no different. Even the food was the same: fruit juice, fruit, steak, eggs, toast, tea, coffee, and milk. That's the way it was all season long in the previous seven road games.

The players slowly made their way into the dining hall.

They ambled in quietly, often in pairs—Snell and Boozer, Namath and Hudson, Elliott and Johnson, Grantham and McAdams, Atkinson and Baker. They conversed in subdued tones. Occasionally Ewbank would make an announcement.

"Remember," he said, "if anybody needs taping, Jeff is all set up in the back.

"We'll return here right after the game, so any personal belongings you have can be kept in your rooms.

"Does anyone have any questions?"

Nobody spoke.

It was like a scene from a well-rehearsed play. Players kept right on eating while the announcements were being made, almost as if they knew what was going to be said. Trainer Jeff Snedeker was off to one side of the room, already at work. This was the busiest part of his day, taping ankles. He arranged a couple of tables in front of him. On one were rolls of adhesive tape and gauze and a number of pill bottles. On the other sat the athletes, one by one, with their ankles propped.

Snedeker, in a T-shirt and white pants, worked quickly and effectively. He had done this thousands of times. Between tape jobs he would straighten up, wipe the sweat from his face, and take a puff from his cigarette. Another athlete would jump on the table, and Snedeker would put down his cigarette and quickly resume work.

When all the players had finished eating, they congregated in their respective groups for a final briefing with the coaches. Clive Rush handled the offensive backs, Joe Spencer the offensive line, Walt Michaels the defensive backs, and Buddy Ryan the defensive line. The coaches spoke in low tones, and the players listened quietly and intently. This was the final time they would meet together as a separate unit.

Ewbank had one more announcement.

"Just one more reminder, boys. The buses will depart for Miami at twelve noon. There will be two buses waiting outside in front of the door."

The squad broke and left for their rooms to collect their gear. Namath returned to his suite on the fourth floor. He answered a knock on the door. A bellhop entered the room holding a basket of flowers. He placed it on a table and smiled as he left the room. Namath had received flowers before from friends and admirers. This was something different. There was no card. Just one dozen red roses. They were ordered from Buning Florist in Ft. Lauderdale by Don Cuddy of the Diplomat Hotel in Miami, on orders from Lou Michaels.

There were three buses chartered to make the hour-long journey to the Orange Bowl. Two buses were for the squad, while the other was for the writers covering the club and various members and associates of the Jets' organization. They were parked one behind the other like troop carriers. The equipment men herded the gear to the side of the bus, where the driver placed the bags in the luggage compartment underneath. The players boarded the buses, and when they were all accounted for, the buses began to roll southward toward Miami.

It was a few minutes after twelve. The departure went smoothly, according to the timetable. The players sat quietly. Some stretched their legs, and others sat erect. There were few conversations. Most of the players stared out the window, while a number of others leaned back and closed their eyes. You could feel the tensions starting to build. Maynard tried to nap but was unable to. He would close his eyes and then open them again, moving around in his seat trying to get comfortable. He had never had trouble sleeping before on trips.

Beverly rested his head on the back of the seat, staring idly at the roof of the bus. From time to time he would look out the window.

"I'd rather see players quiet and a bit on edge," Michaels remarked. "Then I know they're ready. I don't like it when they're too loose. Most people think that's the best. I like to see them a bit on edge, not too much, mind you, but just a little. This way they have their mind on what they're about to do. Once the game begins, they'll loosen up enough. The important thing is being ready to go once the whistle blows."

In Michaels' eyes the Jets were ready.

The buses arrived at the north end of the Orange Bowl a few minutes after one P.M. It was much too early for any of the expected 75,000 fans to arrive. There were a number of kids in sneakers running around trying to get a look at the players. "Hey, there's Joe Namath," one yelled, his eyes flashing with excitement because he had spotted him first. "Go get 'em, Joe," shouted another. And then the other youngsters ran over to catch a glimpse of the star quarterback.

As the Jets moved into the dressing room, you could feel the tension just by looking at them. They walked at a normal pace. No one spoke. For the most part they looked straight ahead.

Almost leisurely they went about preparing for battle. The first lockers to the left as you walked into the room were assigned to Jim Turner, Namath, and Babe Parilli. The quarterbacks always remain together. That is the way the squad is quartered. The offensive backs dress in adjacent lockers, as do the defensive backs, linebackers, defensive linemen, and offensive linemen. The remainder of the room is for the players who operate on the special teams, the kickoff and punt-return units.

The Jets were assigned the dressing room normally used by the Miami Dolphins. It is a long, rectangular-shaped room with individual locker stalls. Above each stall was a wide strip of adhesive tape with the name of the player who would use the stall. There were four separate rooms adjoining the one used by the players. One was for the coaching staff, another for the trainer, the lavatory facilities, and the showers. Ewbank and his assistants were in the first room. As he had done throughout the season, Ewbank assigned Michaels, Rush, and Spencer to the telephone in a booth high above the stadium. Sitting like hawks on their high vantage point, they would observe the individual play of the twenty-two combatants below to detect strengths or weaknesses. The final outcome of a contest could very easily be determined by what they detected. They are in continuous contact with the bench with the second-string quarterback, whose primary function during the course of a game is to man the field telephone, charting plays on instructions from the three-man observer team above. Ryan, the other assistant, would operate with Ewbank on the sidelines, making any necessary substitutions and carrying out any special instructions from the head coach.

George Sauer, Sr., stood in the middle of the dressing room. He too would be on the sidelines, for any special details that might arise. He had his own special interest going for him in this game. George, Jr., was one of the key links in the Jets' accelerated offense. There was pride in his eyes as he glanced over at his son. It was as if he was remembering a lifetime in a quick second.

"This is really something," said Sauer. "I think the boys can do it." Then he walked over to his son, offered some words of encouragement, and walked away.

Maynard had trouble adjusting his shoulderpads. He fastened them once, then unfastened them. He pulled them down, then fastened them again. Then he swung his right arm in a circular motion and adjusted the band underneath his arm. Now they felt comfortable.

Grantham came over and said something to Maynard. Don nodded. Grantham patted him on the shoulderpads and walked back to his locker, which was at the other end of the room. He was still in his stocking feet, wearing only his uniform pants and gray T-shirt. He proceeded to finish dressing.

Atkinson stood at his locker frowning, as if he had forgotten the next move of the routine. He caught my eye, winked at me, and nodded, then reached into his locker for a T-shirt.

The entire atmosphere had a certain stillness about it. You wanted to talk but were afraid to.

The one person who did not appear tense was Namath. He came up behind me and gave me a playful bear hug.

"Hey, Lou, look at you, you sharp cat. You look like a native with those white pants and white shoes."

We spent a few minutes discussing his press interview for the league after the game which I would be handling for him.

"We're going to be all right," Namath said, as if I had

asked a question. "We're going to get the ball and try to get us a touchdown right fast. Got to get those points up on the board real quick. Yes, sir, everything is going to be okay." He then entered the training room, where Snedeker was waiting to tape his weak right knee. Joe stood up on a table and braced his hand against the ceiling while Snedeker carefully applied the protection. Joe Namath had learned to live with it.

When all the Jets had donned their battle gear, they waited for the signal to enter the arena. By now the early birds were arriving in the stands. The sun would break through the clouds every now and then, and the threat of rain diminished. The Orange Bowl terrain was colorfully manicured. The white chalk marks contrasted brilliantly against the green sod. In the middle of the field, against a blue background, was a silver replica of the Super Bowl trophy. The east end zone was sprayed a rich blue, with the words "Baltimore Colts" and their helmet design emblazoned in white, along with the shield of the NFL. The west end zone was painted green, with the inscription "New York Jets" and their logo printed in white, together with the emblem of the AFL.

In less than an hour the field would be a battleground for crashing bodies, without any regard for the needlework that is designed for the spectators' delight and the mechanics of color television. The players were completely unconcerned with the decor as they briskly went through their pregame warm-ups, the Jets at the east end of the field and the Colts at the west side. This was the first time the two champions had felt the ground of the Orange Bowl since they began preparations for their Super Bowl confrontation.

By some strange reasoning, the Jets were designated as the visiting team. They were playing in an AFL stadium, in a league city where only weeks before they had finished their regular-season play against the hometown Miami Dolphins. They were also assigned the north side of the stadium, which is also the sidelines used by the local team.

The Jets wore their road uniform of white trimmed with green, while the Colts were dressed in their traditional home jerseys of blue with white piping and white pants. After their allotted loosening-up drills, both squads returned to their dressing rooms for final instructions.

"The boys were a little tight, and I tried to relax them in there," Ewbank told me later. "I told them I knew that we were going to win, but this time, please, not to lift me up and carry me off the field, as I didn't want to have my other hip hurt by someone trying to shake my leg in congratulations."

Some ten minutes before the kickoff, the squads returned to the pit of battle. The Jets entered first, cheered in their underdog role by wild-screaming supporters who flashed hand-painted signs and waved New York Jets banners. One obvious banner read: "Broadway Joe We Love You." Namath had brought to the underdog role more color and glamour than ever in the history of sports. This was the hour in which all his taunts and candid remarks of the previous week might be stuffed down his throat. That is what the odds-makers figured, and a lot of people went along with them. When was the last time any bookmaker gave anything away?

The Colts trotted onto the field. The rabid Baltimore fans made their feelings known.

This was a team that was considered one of the finest defensive machines of all time.

Baltimore had won fifteen of the sixteen games it took to get them to the Super Bowl. In four of those games, Baltimore blanked the opposition. In two others, they prevented the opposition from scoring a touchdown, yielding only field goals. In five other games they surrendered only one touchdown. It was an awesome defensive combine that challenged its foe head to head. They wanted their rivals to come at them. They would think nothing of putting a safety man at the line of scrimmage, seemingly leaving themselves vulnerable to the pass. The Colts were known for their great ball pursuit. They would snuff out the ball carrier and bring him down to earth with a thud. They hit quick and hard, from all sides. Sometimes the ends would crash; tackles would charge, after a split second delay; linebackers were noted for the blitz, and even the safety man would penetrate to spill the quarterback behind the line of scrimmage.

The Colts were considered almost impregnable on defense. They possessed a blend of age and youth and a savage ferocity for attacking a ball carrier. Their indefatigable pressure again and again had forced their opponents into numerous errors throughout the season. Regularly they had provided their quarterback with excellent field position. Their game was to force the opposition into a mistake and go for a quick score. If a touchdown was unattainable, then they had an excellent scoring weapon in field-goal-kicker Lou Michaels, a powerful left-footed performer. Ordell Braase, a 6-4, 245-pound end, a twelve-year veteran, was the oldest member of the defensive unit at 36. Next to him was tackle Fred Miller, a 6-3, 250-pounder who at 28 was in his sixth season. Alongside of Miller was the other tackle, Billy Ray Smith, a 6-4, 250-pound All-Pro. Another veteran performer, the 33-year-old Smith was in his tenth campaign. The remaining end was big Bubba Smith, a 6-7, 295-pound behemoth. Only in his second season, Smith had come into his own and made a big difference on Baltimore's defensive line. Any one of them could look down on Namath and come away laughing.

Baltimore's linebacking was greatly respected. Right linebacker Don Shinnick, 6-0, 228, was the leader. At the age of 33, he was in his twelfth campaign. Dennis Gaubatz, 28, a 6-2, 232-pound, sixth-year veteran operated in the middle, while All-Pro Mike Curtis, 24, a 6-2, 232-pounder in his fourth campaign, covered the left side.

The defensive secondary, which intercepted twenty-two enemy passes, was supposed to provide additional trouble for Namath. If the front four or the linebackers didn't get to the Jet quarterback, then the secondary would effect the final death blow. The youngest member of the quartet was Rich Volk, a safety man who was an All-Pro despite the fact that he was playing only his second season of professional football. The other safety was Jerry Logan, who was a six-year campaigner. The cornerbacks, who have the unenviable mission of guarding the swift pass-receivers, the flanker, or the split-end, were both hard-nosed veterans. One was Lenny Lyles, in his eleventh season, and the other was Bobby Boyd, an All-Pro in past seasons who was playing his ninth year in the NFL. They knew their assignments. In the manner in which the Jets attacked, Lyles would cover Sauer, an All-Pro split-end, while Boyd would cover Don Maynard, the deep receiver, who was also an All-Pro. These were two of the great individual battles that could determine the final outcome.

This very same defensive brigade had dealt the Cleveland Browns an ignominious 34–0 beating in the NFL championship game just two weeks before. So convincing was the Baltimore defense that they limited Leroy Kelly, pro football's leading runner, to a mere twenty-eight yards. So cohesive was the Colts' defensive unit that they permitted the Browns to cross midfield only twice, with the deepest penetration being only the 35-yard line. It prompted Cleveland head coach Blanton Collier to remark after the game that the Colt defensive team might be one of the best of all time. So complete was the Baltimore triumph that head coach Don Shula handed out a game ball to every member of his forty-man squad. It was an added piece of psychological warfare that Shula had employed, with the Super Bowl and Joe Namath waiting just two weeks away.

Going against Namath, the Colts were going against pro football's most explosive quarterback. He had it all—the arm, the release, the knowledge, and the guts. Yet, the eighteen-point spread delegated by the bet parlors was the largest spread of any of the three Super Bowl encounters. That's how much respect the bookies had for the Baltimore defense. Everyone knows the name of the game is quarterback first and defense next, and despite the fact that the Colts were going against the best, they were odds-on choices to make it a runaway.

The Colts' quarterback, Earl Morrall, was something of a Cinderella. He had been discarded by four other professional teams and for years was considered nothing more than a back-up man. Mechanically he was sound. But in leading a team to a championship, he never was considered able. The only time in his uneventful career that he held a job was with the New York Giants three years before. That was the only time in his long career that he actually felt he belonged. He had sparked the beleaguered Giants for two years and brought them some measure of respectability. It was all short-lived. Morrall fractured his wrist, and the Giants quickly acquired Fran Tarkenton from the Minnesota Vikings. It was obvious that Morrall would never be a starter again, a role he had fought for throughout his frustrating career.

Finally, with his rag-arm reputation, he was traded to Baltimore in August, 1968, and suddenly in one season, it was all rags to riches. It was ironic. Where an injury deprived him of his regular job with the Giants, an injury to the great Johnny Unitas had opened up a job for him in Baltimore. He made the most of it, and despite the fact that Unitas was healthy again, it was Morrall who earned the respect of his teammates and the right to start in the Super Bowl.

Johnny Unitas, a living legend in Baltimore, would be on the sidelines, while a trencherman quarterback would lead the Colts.

Baltimore's running attack wasn't overpowering. Not having a breakaway runner who could quickly change the course of a game, they chiefly depended on Tom Matte, a heavylegged halfback whose greatest distinction in eight professional seasons was the time four years earlier when he courageously played quarterback after injuries had struck down Unitas and his back-up, Gary Cuozzo. Matte earned plaudits for almost leading the Colts to a playoff victory over the vaunted Green Bay Packers in a sudden-death skirmish in Green Bay. Alex Karras, the outspoken Detroit Lion tackle, termed Matte "a garbage-can runner." Nonetheless, Matte was an effective runner. He got the hard yards inside and could also run well, although without any great speed, to the outside.

At fullback, Shula alternated Jerry Hill, a seven-year veteran, and Terry Cole, a fine rookie. Hill is regarded as the better blocker of the two, and in the Baltimore way of doing things, a blocking fullback is an important asset. Both could get the tough yards inside, while Cole could move better outside. All three were methodical workhorses, neither of whom could electrify a crowd. They hit away, for three or four yards at a clip, and from this attack approach the Colts could employ the pass to better advantage.

Baltimore's biggest threat was a Morrall pass to either of three excellent receivers, flanker Willie Richardson, split-end Jimmy Orr, or tight end John Mackey. Richardson had the speed to burn a defender. He was expected to work on left cornerback Johnny Sample and beat him to the inside. This was the pattern employed by Oakland's Fred Biletnikoff in the AFL championship game against the Jets.

Orr, a cagey eleven-year veteran, was expected to teach the Jets' young Randy Beverly, only a second-year pro, a few lessons in the art of catching a football. Mackey, the Colts' leading pass-receiver, is one of the game's most dangerous receivers. Once in the open field, Mackey moves with speed and power. He would operate against safety Jim Hudson, a give-nothing performer who is one of the hardest tacklers in either league.

The Jets' game plan was not expected to deviate from the successful plans they had employed the final ten weeks of the campaign. They were primed to set up the running game and then revert to the passing game. Namath had two fine runners to work with, fullback Matt Snell and halfback Emerson Boozer. Snell, an excellent blocker, was most effective on a draw play. He was also a threat as a secondary receiver coming out of the backfield. Boozer, although bothered by a troublesome knee most of the campaign, was the club's outside-running threat. He, too, could be employed as a secondary receiver on a flare-pass pattern.

Namath's primary receivers were three of the finest in the AFL. Sauer, who led the league's receivers in total number of receptions in 1967, finished second to San Diego's Lance Alworth by just two catches. Maynard, the deep receiver, finished fifth in receptions but second in total yardage, despite being handicapped by a painful hamstring pull. Maynard and Namath had perfected their timing on long passes down the sidelines. Lammons, the tight end, had good hands. Namath looked to him in the middle when Sauer and Maynard were covered. At times Namath would keep the defense off-balance by throwing a quick one, down and in, to Lammons.

The New York defense, although not as distinguished as Baltimore's, nevertheless established itself during the year's campaign. There weren't many teams that generated a successful running attack against them. They took pride in allowing fewest yards rushing when the season was over. They did it on the final day of the season, when they contained Miami's ground game. They weren't expected to encounter any great difficulty with Baltimore's minimal ground attack. Only the Jets' secondary remained a bit suspect, and if Morrall got time to throw, he could pierce the defense.

Namath had to have generous protection. His offensive wall had provided him ample time, except for a couple of contests, all season long. This game would be their biggest challenge, against the most-talked-about defense in pro football. They also were aware that if anything happened to Namath, they would quickly lose any chances of earning the lion's share of $15,000 each for their day's work. It was as simple as that, and no game plan could spell out how to protect the passer. It had to be done by individual effort in the predetermined match-ups. Could Dave Herman hold back Bubba Smith? Could Randy Rasmussen handle Billy Ray Smith? How successful could Bob Talamini be against Fred Miller? And could Winston Hill hold his own against Ordell Braase, while center Johnny Schmitt formed the point on the protective pocket? Here is where a game is won, in the trenches, with the one-on-one hand-to-hand combat. The offensive linemen are the unsung heroes in the violent world of professional football.

There was nothing left anyone could do. It was five minutes until kickoff, and the officials signaled both benches for the respective captains to meet at midfield. Unitas, Lyles, and

Preston Pearson trotted on the field first, to represent the Colts. Unitas carried his helmet in his left hand, still displaying the boyish crew-cut he has maintained all these thirteen years. Namath and Sample completed the meeting a few seconds later. It was somewhat of a memorable occasion for the two Jets. Namath, as a youngster in high school in Beaver Falls, had always admired Unitas. And Unitas, like Namath, was from a small town outside of Pittsburgh. For Sample, it was the sweet taste of revenge. This was the closest he got to a Colt uniform since Baltimore released him as a player eight years ago. He was branded as a troublemaker, and Sample could never quite forgive them for the rap. Like Namath, he too was an open target for Baltimore. He was the one defensive player the Colts figured to beat, and nobody knew it better than old John.

Although the toss of the coin was held an hour before, referee Tom Bell had to go through with the ritual for the benefit of the 75,377 partisans and the countless millions watching on television. He indicated that the Jets had won the toss and had elected to receive, while Baltimore chose to defend the west goal, which was at the closed end of the stadium. The temperature was recorded at 73, with the wind blowing north at 18 miles per hour.

Because of the number of highly distinguished guests, the game was delayed for almost ten minutes. Sitting in the north stand were President-elect Richard Nixon; Vice-President-elect Spiro Agnew; Senator Edward Kennedy and his father, Joseph Kennedy; Senator William Eastland of Mississippi; Governor Claude Kirk of Florida; Governor James Rhodes of Ohio; astronauts Frank Borman, Bill Anders, and Jim Lovell; and comedian Bob Hope. Another familiar comedian, Jackie Gleason, sat on the Jets' side in the south stand as a guest of the Dolphins' managing director, Joe Robbie. The moment was at hand. Michaels signaled to the referee that he was ready, and he approached the ball in his customary manner. Boom! He got off a good kick that Earl Christy caught on the fly two yards deep in the end zone. He began his ascent upfield looking for a convoy of blockers. He managed to extract a little running room before he was tackled by Alex Hawkins on the 23. That was the first sound of contact, the one that's supposed to ease all the tensions of the players. The fearsome Baltimore defensive legion trotted onto the field, as did the New York offensive unit. It was time for the first test.

The Jets broke the huddle fast. Namath barked the signals. Baltimore's defense focused on Namath. The Jet quarterback took the snap, turned, and cleanly handed the ball to Snell, who picked up three yards on the right side of Baltimore's defense. Everyone made contact, which is why they often open a game with a running play. New York again came out of the huddle quickly. Namath again gave the ball to Snell, who this time tested Baltimore's left side. The crowd's roar indicated that Snell had found some running room. He maneuvered nine yards for a first down before being stopped by Volk on the 35. Now it was Boozer's turn. The lithe halfback tried to go outside but was repelled by Shinnick for a four-yard loss. This was Baltimore's defense in a familiar performance. On the fourth play of the game, Namath elected to pass. He hit Snell coming out of the backfield, for a nine-yard gain. Satisfied with the result, Namath slapped the part of the shoulder pad which protected him around his chest. On third down and five, Namath designated a draw, with Snell carrying. It was the same thing Miller figured, and he dropped the New York fullback, for a two-yard loss.

A Curley Johnson punt gave the Colts their first opportunity on offense from their own 27-yard line. Morrall also broke the huddle quickly. He received the snap from center Bill Curry, quickly dropped back to pass, and hit Mackey, for a first down on the 46. On the next play Morrall sent Matte around the right side, for a ten-yard advance to the New York 44. Two plays, two first downs.

The people who laid the eighteen points were happy.

Now it was Hill's turn. He made his way around the left side, for seven yards, before Hudson came up to drop him. Matte then went inside, for only a yard. Hill again carried, this time inside right tackle, for five yards and a first down on the Jets' 31. In five plays the Colts had produced three first downs. They appeared to be going in for a score.

Hill tried to go outside but was upended by Philbin three yards behind the line of scrimmage. In a passing situation, Morrall tried to hit Orr but threw the ball short. However, on third down Morrall went back again to throw and connected with Tom Mitchell, for another first down on the New York 19.

Morrall in eight plays had accounted for four first downs and brought the Colts to within a shadow of the goalposts. He decided to go for the quick kill while he had the Jets on the run. On first down he looked for Richardson, hit him in the hands, only to see him drop the ball. The Jets on the sideline were all standing yelling encouragement to the defense. "Hold 'em, defense," shouted Namath. Still sensing the quick score, Morrall once more stepped back to pass. He had tight end Tom Mitchell running a pattern toward Sample, but overthrew him.

Burning with the desire to produce a fast touchdown, Morrall faded back to throw for the fifth consecutive time. Finding no one open, he was forced to run and made it back to the line of scrimmage, where middle linebacker Al Atkinson met him head on. The situation now dictated a field goal from the 27-yard line, almost automatic for the pros. Michaels' kick sailed wide to the left, and the Colts, who seemingly were headed for seven points but were willing to settle for three, suddenly had nothing.

The missed placement seemed to pick up the defensive unit as they made their way to the sidelines. Ewbank talked to a few of the players, as did Ryan. Namath went to work on his own 20 and went for a pass play before the Colt defense could assert themselves. He hit Snell in the open, only to have his fullback drop the ball when he heard the footsteps of the fast-closing Gaubatz. On a quick move, Namath deposited the ball in Lammons' hands, for a short two-yard gain. He then requested a halfback pass to Bill Mathis, who made his way for 13 yards before being stopped by Gaubatz. Then, in rapid succession, Namath called for three pass plays. On the first, he sent Maynard deep downfield, and although the swift flanker had Logan beat by several steps, Namath overshot him, as the crowd moaned. Next, he hit Sauer, for a six-yard gain, but when he went to his split-end again on the same pattern, he overthrew him.

Again the Jets were forced to punt. Timmy Brown gave the Colts excellent field position by returning Johnson's punt 21 yards to the Baltimore 42. Morrall seized the opportunity to move quickly and threw a pass into the arms of Mackey, who dropped the ball in the open. After Hill made three yards, Morrall positioned Richardson on Sample. It was their first confrontation of the game, and Sample emerged the victor by breaking up the play.

David Lee's first punt of the afternoon for Baltimore was a beauty. The ball rolled dead on the Jets' four-yard line, where Baltimore's vaunted defense moved in to take advantage of the situation. Snell almost got the Jets out of the hole by carrying for nine yards on two trips. With a third and one, Namath called a smart play. Detecting the linebackers in close to stop the impending one-yard run for a first down, he sent Sauer breaking into the middle. He connected, for an apparent first down, only to have Sauer fumble when he was brought to earth by Lyles. Ron Porter, a linebacker, recovered the loose ball on the Jets' twelve-yard line, and the Colts got the first break of the game.

Once again the Jets' sideline yelled encouragement to the defensive troops. "Dig in . . . hold 'em . . . get tough," echoed the players. On the last play of the quarter, Hill tried to go wide but was dumped, for a yard loss, by Philbin.

Matte took a pitchout and stepped his way around the left side, for a seven-yard gain, as the second period opened. With a third down and four on the New York six, Morrall slipped back to pass. He located Mitchell in the end zone and threw on target. However, the ball bounced high off Mitchell's left shoulder. It ricocheted so high that Beverly caught it in the manner of a baseball player settling under a high fly ball.

Once again Baltimore blew a scoring opportunity, and the Jets' defensive team came off the gridiron elated and fired-up. Twice Baltimore had penetrated dangerously deep into New York territory, and both times they had come away empty-handed.

The Jets put the ball in play on their own 20. Namath gave Snell the ball three consecutive times, and he moved for one, seven, and finally six yards and a first down. Checking off at the line, Namath signaled for a draw play, which meant that Snell again was designated as the ball carrier. He responded with a twelve-yard advance and another first down on the New York 46. The Jets, who managed only two first downs the entire first period, quickly had two the last two times they put the ball in motion.

Then Namath went to his aerial game for four consecutive passes. Shinnick broke up the first one, intended for Sauer. Namath hit Mathis, for six yards, and then reverted to Sauer, for fourteen more and a first down on the Baltimore 34. Again he dispatched Sauer on the left side, and he rifled one that accounted for eleven yards and still another first down on the 23. The north stands were on their feet. They sensed a Jet touchdown or at least a Jim Turner field goal. Boozer got only two yards as Namath switched to the run. Returning to the pass, Namath zeroed in on Snell, who found an opening in the middle, for twelve yards and another first down on the nine.

Nobody was any happier than Billy Joe, the Jets' reserve fullback, who was on crutches on the sidelines. "They're working, they're really working out there," he remarked. "They're going to go in, they're going to go in," he added. Once again Namath asked Snell to carry, and the hard-working fullback bulled his way over the right side, for five yards. One more time Namath called Snell's number in the huddle, and this time the gritty fullback went all the way in from the left side.

The Jets were on the board.

Jet fans, thousands of them who flew down from New York, were ecstatic. They jumped up and down in their seats and in the aisles. They waved their banners furiously. If this was going to be their only thrill of the afternoon, they were going to let everyone know about it.

Snell and Namath were glad-handed by their teammates as they made their way to the sidelines, and they received congratulations from Ewbank and Ryan. Parilli then handed the field telephone to Namath, and he spoke with the coaches on the opposite side of the stadium for about a minute.

Walt Michaels told him he had detected where they were using a zone pass coverage. "In this situation, you won't be able to connect with Maynard. Don't worry, you can get to Sauer, and Sauer can beat Lyles."

The elation of the Jets' first touchdown broke all over the face of Mike Bite, Namath's lawyer from Birmingham. Throughout the entire 80-yard drive, Bite had remained stationary on the 30-yard line, nervously puffing away on a couple of cigarettes. "I'm not going to move the rest of the game," he announced. "I found me a holy spot. No, sir, there is no way anyone can get me to move from here. You wanna know something, the Jets are going to win the game. We're going to win it sure as Birmingham is in Alabama."

Following the kickoff, Morrall tried to mount an attack from Baltimore's 28. On a first-down pass, he threw over the head of Richardson. However, on the next down, he found connections with Matte, with a 30-yard pass that provided the Colts with a first down on the Jet 42. Hill managed to bang his way for four yards up the middle. Morrall tried to send Matte wide around the right side, but Biggs turned him in, for no gain. Then Morrall tried to complete a pass to Mackey, but it was foiled by Sample. On fourth down Michaels, who missed a 27-yarder in the first quarter, tried to boot a field goal from the 46. Like the previous one, it was wide, and a third Baltimore scoring chance was wasted.

On the next series of downs Namath directed the Jets from their 20 to a field-goal situation from the Baltimore 41. However, Turner's try was wide, and the Colts took over on their own 20, with 4:13 remaining to play in the first half. Sample yielded a short one of six yards to Richardson. Matte electrified the huge throng by breaking away behind some beautiful blocking around right end, for 58 yards before being cut down by Billy Baird on the New York 16. After Hill made only a yard, Morrall again isolated Richardson on Sample. Richardson broke down the sidelines and then cut inside on a spot pattern that was supposed to embarrass Sample. However, the wily veteran defender reached in front of Richardson and intercepted the ball with a picture-book catch.

Sample had it figured all the way. "I moved a step to the outside, but I played him to the inside," he explained as he took a breather on the bench. That one play made up for his poor performance two weeks before against Oakland, which had almost cost the Jets the championship.

Johnson had to punt from his end zone to get New York out of danger. There were only 43 seconds remaining when Baltimore took over on the Jet 42. Morrall collected only one yard on a safety-valve pass to Hill. Then, in a key play that brought the crowd to its feet, Morrall handed the ball to Matte, who appeared as if he was going to run around his own right end. However, Matte suddenly stopped and threw the ball back to Morrall on the left side with nobody near him. Morrall had four receivers downfield. Orr was wide open, frantically waving his arms in the end zone. Morrall never saw him.

The confused Jet secondary was trying to collect itself when Morrall threw the ball in the direction of Hill. From out of nowhere, Hudson picked the ball off on the 12 and fell down on the 21, clutching the ball as the half ended.

"I don't know what happened," confessed Hudson. "I fell down, and when I got up I picked out the first blue shirt I saw. Man, I'm winded."

The first half ended in bitter frustration for the Colts. On four occasions they saw scoring opportunities evaporate. No one would mention the Jets' defense in the same breath with Baltimore, and yet the Colts were held scoreless. New York had gotten on the scoreboard first. Their defense rose to the occasion when they had to. Holding the Colts without a point was a bonus. The offense revealed that they could move the ball, and the defense showed that they were equal to the challenge.

The teams lined up for the second-half kickoff. Baltimore received, and they knew they had to move quickly. On the first play of the half, Matte fumbled, and Ralph Baker covered the ball for New York on the Colt 33. Namath worked his way down to the 11 with two first downs. However, the Colt defense met the challenge. They spilled Boozer, for a five-yard loss. And then, for the first time, Baltimore got to Namath. Bubba Smith charged like a bull and dropped Namath like a broken doll, for a nine-yard loss. Namath's third-down pass fell incomplete, but Turner made good on a field goal, for a 10–0 New York lead.

After the kickoff, the Colts bogged down. They failed to produce a first down, and a Baltimore punt presented the Jets with the ball on the New York 32. Once again Namath moved the club. He engineered three first downs, which brought the ball to the Colt 24. Mathis could extract only a yard from the middle, and Namath stepped back to pass on second down. He tried to hit Maynard deep in the end zone, but Don caught the ball over the base line.

Suddenly, before anyone realized it, Namath came running toward the sideline shaking the thumb on his right hand. Just as quickly, Parilli was dispatched into the lineup.

"It's my thumb," cried Namath as he walked up and down shaking his hand. There was nothing anyone could do. It had happened before during the season, and Namath himself is the only one who can work it out.

Namath cannot explain what happens. He just loses the feeling in his thumb. He suffered a dislocated thumb the year before, and Dr. James Nicholas, the club's physician, diagnosed the condition as a "subluxation of the thumb."

Turner kicked his third field goal of the day from thirty yards out, and the Jets' lead rose to 13–0.

Almost forgotten in the excitement of Turner's field goal was Namath. "Someone catch me," he yelled. "C'mon, Lou, catch me, I've got to work this thumb out." We moved behind the bench in full view of the stands. Namath was twenty yards away and he began to throw. He did not throw lobs, but fired with the same force he uses under game conditions. I clutched each toss as if it meant life or death, realizing the importance of his being able to warm up properly and knowing that a dropped throw would result in valuable lost time. Namath threw four passes. Four times I returned the ball to him. Harvey Nairn, a receiver on the Jets' taxi squad, was then sent over to relieve me. On the very first toss Namath threw, Nairn dropped the ball. My fame was established. The crowd booed. Namath fired one more, which Nairn caught, and then Joe was ready to go again, his thumb back to normal.

Namath stood on the sidelines and looked on as Unitas took over for the Colts. There was his boyhood idol, and they were going to meet on the field in the final half of the third Super Bowl. Unitas failed to generate an offense on his first series of downs following the kickoff. The Colts had to punt once more, and the Jets gained possession on their own 37, with 2:24 remaining to play in the third period. Time was now a factor working in favor of the Jets.

The elder Sauer liked the way things looked as the offensive team lined up for play. "We're going to do it," he said quietly.

Another who liked the way things were going was Father Ed, a Catholic priest from Graymoor, New York, who had befriended Namath when the Jets used to train at Peekskill. "Isn't Joe doing wonderful?" He smiled. "I think we're going to win. Say a prayer, Lou."

"We'll leave that for you," I said. "You got a lot more going than I do."

Namath, sensing the kill, wanted to get some more points on the scoreboard. After Snell gained three yards, Namath tried to reach Sauer with a pass but threw it a little too high. Apparently he and Sauer detected something. Lyles was playing Sauer too deep, playing him loosely for fear the clever end might slip behind him. Namath came right back to his split-end the next two times, once for 11 yards and the next for 39, and suddenly the Jets were on Baltimore's ten-yard line. Snell picked his way for four yards to the six as the quarter came to a conclusion. It was obvious the Jets were ready for more points. Three running plays failed to get the touchdown, and the Jets had to settle for a Turner field goal nine yards away from the goalposts. Their lead was now 16–0, and Unitas had only 13:10 left to rally the Colts.

Johnny U. tried hard. He was out there with an arm shot full of medicine trying to produce a garrison finish, as he had done many times in the past. Putting the ball in play on his own 27, Unitas brought the Colts to the Jet 25. He threw over Richardson's reach on first down, and then turning to Orr, one of his favorite targets over the years, he threw a bit short, and the ball was intercepted by Beverly in the end zone. From the 20, Namath wisely stayed on the ground as he moved his club upfield, while at the same time running out the clock. Two first downs and a penalty brought the Jets to within field-goal range from the 42. This time, however, Turner couldn't deliver. Nevertheless, Namath used up almost five minutes on the drive, and when the Colts put the ball in action on their 20, there was only 6:34 showing on the clock as the shadows grew long and the Orange Bowl lights were turned on.

Baltimore had one last gasp. Unitas inspired them on an 80-yard march, despite the fact that he completed only three of the ten passes he attempted. On fourth down from the New York one, Hill finally reached the end zone, to give Baltimore its first touchdown, with just 3:29 left to play.

The Colts were successful with an on-side kick that Mitchell recovered on the New York 44. Unitas jumped into the breach, trying to effect a miracle. He connected on his first three passes, which carried the ball to the Jet 19, where it was second down and five for an all-important first down. Unitas tried Richardson, and Sample once again broke up the play. Third and five. He looked for Orr and threw short. Now it was fourth and five, and a lot of experts figured the Colts would go for the field goal from twenty-six yards away and then try another on-side kick, the reasoning being that you take three points whenever you can get them. The Colts would still need a field goal, along with the necessary touch-down, if they expected to win. But coach Don Shula decided to go for the touchdown, and the last hope rested on Unitas' erratic arm. He went to Orr again, but threw behind him, as the ball and Baltimore's hopes fell to the ground.

Some of the Jet players on the sidelines had begun yelling disparaging remarks to the big, bad Colts. Namath stopped them. "If we're going to be champions, then let's act like champions," he said. They listened. Broadway Joe had made them believers.

Namath succeeded in running out the clock, Baltimore finally gaining possession of the football on their own 34, with just eight seconds left. For the records, Unitas tried two more passes and completed just one. But no one will ever remember that. The moment they will remember is when the gun sounded to end the game. The crowds spilled onto the field, pouring out their joy and congratulations to any Jet players that ran by. In the wildest days of Ebbets Field and the tales of the Brooklyn Dodgers, there was never an ending to equal this one. An eighteen-point underdog completely outplayed the favorite.

The attendant at the Jets' dressing-room door was almost crushed under the force of hundreds of bodies. Finally some semblance of calm settled, and the attendant managed to pull open the door and let the jubilant players inside. One by one the players made their way inside, through the pulling and the tugging of the multitude. As soon as all the players, coaches, and club officials assembled, the team meditated in prayer for a moment. Then shouts of joy broke the silence. Sample jumped on top of a large table and announced that it was decided to award the game ball to the American Football League. It was a great honor.

The room was getting crowded as members of the press began to arrive. In a tender moment, Namath and his father, John, who was wearing a styrofoam hat with the words "Orange Bowl" on the band, embraced. "I told them you could do it," exclaimed the father. "You can talk," laughed Joe. "You didn't have to play. Where did you get that hat?"

Before the father could answer, Ewbank warmly offered his congratulations to Joe's father as he made his way through the crowd. "Mr. Namath, you've got a remarkable son," he began. "You've got a son who makes some big statements and then goes out there and makes every one of them come true. I take my hat off to a man like that and to a man like you, sir."

John Namath's eyes were filled with tears of joy. "Thank you," he said, touching his own hat. "Joe is a good boy."

Winston Hill moved toward a TV mike held out to him. He reflected a moment. Then he spoke directly to the boys in a Lincoln, Nebraska, correctional school where he had been the athletic director the year before.

"You guys," he said with intense emotion, "this shows that you can accomplish anything if you try hard enough." Hill went on, oblivious of how even those few words had moved everyone—some even to tears—"We were the underdogs today and we proved that you can accomplish your goal if you work hard towards it."

The entire mood of the clubhouse was strangely restrained. There was something missing. Maybe it was the champagne—the same champagne that's used to toast a World Series victory. It was conspicuously absent, and that piqued Namath. When the Jets defeated Oakland for the AFL championship two weeks before, there was champagne, lots of it. Namath made it a point to request champagne of Ewbank and told him he personally would pay any fine if the league reprimanded the club for allowing it in the dressing room. Now, in the greatest moment of glory, there was no champagne for Broadway Joe and his teammates. Direct orders from Commissioner Pete Rozelle had forbidden it.

Namath seethed. He walked up and down and then sat in front of his locker. By now the room was mobbed with reporters. Television crews had turned on tremendous floodlights, which quickly added to the heat of the room. It was oppressive as the reporters ringed around Namath. They wanted answers, and Joe indicated that he didn't want to talk, at least not until everybody moved back and gave him some room. Then Phil

Iselin made his way through the group. He leaned over and whispered something in Joe's ear.

"I don't want to," replied Namath, "but if you want me to I will." Iselin nodded that he did, and Namath got up and picked his way through the reporters until he reached the makeshift television platform for a brief interview. That concluded, Namath returned to his locker and the cordon of writers that waited for him there. "Now, I'm not going to answer anybody until you all move back and give me some room," ordered Namath. Bite, who was standing on a bench next to Namath, motioned the group to step back. "Hey, Mike," Namath called, "get me a tape cutter." Then he remembered something else. "Hey, Lou, do me a favor and make sure the boys get in, they're waiting outside," he asked.

In a few seconds Joe's boys were in the room. Al Hassan, a speech instructor from the University of Maryland; Bobby Skaff of Cleveland, vice-president of Liberty/UA Records; Tad Dowd, a record distributor from New York; and Jimmy Walsh, Namath's attorney in New York. Namath shouted at each one of them as they walked by.

Now Namath was ready to talk. He was calm, and whenever a particular question rankled him, he would snap back, "What are you, an NFL writer?" Some of the writers tried to goad him, but Joe wouldn't be trapped.

"A whole lot of people were wrong," Namath replied when asked about the game. "Eighteen-point underdog, gee whiz," he moaned, shaking his head. Then he continued talking while cutting the tape from his sore right knee. "Baltimore is a damn good football team. They didn't give me any mouth out there, and they didn't take any cheap shots. They're a good hard-nosed club. Our team did everything well. We didn't have one offensive penalty. I felt I wasn't throwing good to my left, and I told Sauer so. I can't say enough about our defense. Ordinarily, sixteen points isn't enough to win, so that should tell you something. Now, if you'll excuse me, fellows, I want to take a shower."

Namath disappeared into the mob, his dark black hair a

bit ruffled and the protective black shoe polish under his eyes
starting to smear. His ruddy face was sweaty from the stifling
heat.

The shower offered Namath the relief of hot water soothing
his muscles and the escape from the hundreds of questions.
The only other player in the shower was Ralph Baker, and
the two made with some small talk as they lathered their
bodies. Every once in a while they would laugh, like two kids
who pulled a prank on some bullies down the street and got
away with it.

The Jets all headed back to Ft. Lauderdale for a victory
party. Broadway Joe and the Jets would finally get their
champagne. They had earned it, and no one could take it
away from them.

APPENDIX 1

American Football League Standings 1960–1968

1968

EASTERN DIVISION

	W	L	T	Pct.	Pts.	OP
New York	11	3	0	.786	419	280
Houston	7	7	0	.500	303	248
Miami	5	8	1	.385	276	355
Boston	4	10	0	.286	229	406
Buffalo	1	12	1	.077	199	367

WESTERN DIVISION

	W	L	T	Pct.	Pts.	OP
* Oakland	12	2	0	.857	453	233
Kansas City	12	2	0	.857	371	170
San Diego	9	5	0	.643	382	310
Denver	5	9	0	.357	255	404
Cincinnati	3	11	0	.214	215	329

* Oakland beat Kansas City 41–6 in playoff

AFL Championship Game
New York 27, Oakland 23
AFL–NFL Championship Game
New York 16, Baltimore 7

1967

EASTERN DIVISION

	W	L	T	Pct.	Pts.	OP
Houston	9	4	1	.692	258	199
New York	8	5	1	.615	371	329
Buffalo	4	10	0	.286	237	285
Miami	4	10	0	.286	219	407
Boston	3	10	1	.231	280	389

WESTERN DIVISION

	W	L	T	Pct.	Pts.	OP
Oakland	13	1	0	.929	468	233
Kansas City	9	5	0	.643	408	254
San Diego	8	5	1	.615	360	352
Denver	3	11	0	.214	256	409

AFL Championship Game
Oakland 40, Houston 7
AFL–NFL Championship Game
Green Bay 33, Oakland 14

1966

EASTERN DIVISION

	W	L	T	Pct.	Pts.	OP
Buffalo	9	4	1	.692	358	255
Boston	8	4	2	.667	315	283
New York	6	6	2	.500	322	312
Houston	3	11	0	.214	335	396
Miami	3	11	0	.214	213	362

WESTERN DIVISION

	W	L	T	Pct.	Pts.	OP
Kansas City	11	2	1	.846	448	276
Oakland	8	5	1	.615	315	288
San Diego	7	6	1	.538	335	284
Denver	4	10	0	.286	196	381

AFL Championship Game
Kansas City 31, Buffalo 7
AFL–NFL Championship Game
Green Bay 35, Kansas City 10

1965

EASTERN DIVISION

	W	L	T	Pct.	Pts.	OP
Buffalo	10	3	1	.769	313	226
New York	5	8	1	.385	285	303
Boston	4	8	2	.333	244	302
Houston	4	10	0	.286	298	429

WESTERN DIVISION

	W	L	T	Pct.	Pts.	OP
San Diego	9	2	3	.818	340	227
Oakland	8	5	1	.615	298	239
Kansas City	7	5	2	.583	322	285
Denver	4	10	0	.286	303	392

Championship Game
Buffalo 23, San Diego 0

1964

EASTERN DIVISION

	W	L	T	Pct.	Pts.	OP
Buffalo	12	2	0	.875	400	242
Boston	10	3	1	.769	365	297
New York	5	8	1	.385	278	315
Houston	4	10	0	.286	310	355

WESTERN DIVISION

	W	L	T	Pct.	Pts.	OP
San Diego	8	5	1	.615	341	300
Kansas City	7	7	0	.500	366	306
Oakland	5	7	2	.417	303	350
Denver	2	11	1	.154	240	438

Championship Game
Buffalo 20, San Diego 7

1963
EASTERN DIVISION

	W	L	T	Pct.	Pts.	OP
* Boston	7	6	1	.538	317	257
Buffalo	7	6	1	.538	304	291
Houston	6	8	0	.428	302	372
New York	5	8	1	.384	249	399

WESTERN DIVISION

	W	L	T	Pct.	Pts.	OP
San Diego	11	3	0	.785	399	256
Oakland	10	4	0	.714	363	288
Kansas City	5	7	2	.416	347	263
Denver	2	11	1	.153	301	473

* Boston beat Buffalo 26–8 in playoff

Championship Game
San Diego 51, Boston 10

1962
EASTERN DIVISION

	W	L	T	Pct.	Pts.	OP
Houston	11	3	0	.786	387	270
Boston	9	4	1	.692	346	295
Buffalo	7	6	1	.538	309	272
New York	5	9	0	.357	278	423

WESTERN DIVISION

	W	L	T	Pct.	Pts.	OP
Dallas	11	3	0	.786	389	233
Denver	7	7	0	.500	353	334
San Diego	4	10	0	.286	314	392
Oakland	1	13	0	.071	213	370

Championship Game
Dallas 20, Houston 17
(Sudden death—12:06 of Sixth Quarter)

1961
EASTERN DIVISION

	W	L	T	Pct.	Pts.	OP
Houston	10	3	1	.769	513	242
Boston	9	4	1	.692	413	313
New York	7	7	0	.500	301	390
Buffalo	6	8	0	.429	294	342

WESTERN DIVISION

	W	L	T	Pct.	Pts.	OP
San Diego	12	2	0	.857	396	219
Dallas	6	8	0	.429	334	343
Denver	3	11	0	.214	251	432
Oakland	2	12	0	.143	237	458

Championship Game
Houston 10, San Diego 3

1960
EASTERN DIVISION

	W	L	T	Pct.	Pts.	OP
Houston	10	4	0	.714	379	285
New York	7	7	0	.500	382	399
Buffalo	5	8	1	.385	296	303
Boston	5	9	0	.357	286	349

WESTERN DIVISION

	W	L	T	Pct.	Pts.	OP
Los Angeles	10	4	0	.714	373	336
Dallas	8	6	0	.571	362	253
Oakland	6	8	0	.429	319	388
Denver	4	9	1	.308	309	393

Championship Game
Houston 24, Los Angeles 16

APPENDIX 2

American Football League Records Held by New York Jets Players

MOST YARDS GAINED PASSING, SEASON—Joe Namath 4,007 1967 (pro record)

MOST GAMES 300-PLUS YARDS PASSING IN ONE SEASON—Joe Namath 6 1967

MOST YARDS PASS RECEIVING, CAREER—Don Maynard 9,349 1960–68 (pro record)

MOST TOUCHDOWN RECEPTIONS, CAREER—Art Powell 81 (New York, 27, 1960–62; Oakland, 50, 1963–66; Buffalo, 4, 1967)

MOST FIELD GOALS, SEASON—Jim Turner 34 1968

MOST FIELD GOALS TRIED, GAME—Jim Turner 8 1968

MOST FIELD GOALS TRIED, SEASON—tied, Jim Turner 46 1968 (with Pete Gogolak of Buffalo, 1965)

MOST SEASONS LEADING LEAGUE IN PASS INTERCEPTIONS—tied, Lee Riley 1962; and Dainard Paulson 1964 (tied for one season each with 10 others)

MOST INTERCEPTIONS, SEASON—tied, Dainard Paulson 12 1964 (tied with Freddie Glick of Houston, 1963)

MOST CONSECUTIVE GAMES, PASSES INTERCEPTED BY—tied, John Bookman 5 1961 (tied with two others)

MOST SEASONS ACTIVE PLAYER—one team: Larry Grantham, Bill Mathis, Don Maynard, 1960–68; more than one team—Curley Johnson, Dallas 1960, New York 1961–68; Paul Rochester, Dallas-

Kansas City 1960–63, New York 1963–68; Bob Talamini, Houston 1960–67, New York 1968; Babe Parilli, Oakland 1960, Boston 1961–1967, New York 1968. Tied with many others.

MOST SEASONS LEADING LEAGUE, PUNT RETURNS—Dick Christy 2 1961–62, tied with two others

HIGHEST AVERAGE GAIN ON PUNT RETURNS, SEASON—Dick Christy 21.3 1961

HIGHEST AVERAGE GAIN ON PUNT RETURNS, GAME—Dick Christy 45.7 1961 (3 returns)

MOST TOUCHDOWNS ON PUNT RETURNS, CAREER—Dick Christy 4 (tied with Les Duncan of San Diego)

MOST TOUCHDOWNS ON PUNT RETURNS, SEASON—Dick Christy 2 1961 and 1962 (tied with three others)

MOST TOUCHDOWNS ON PUNT RETURNS, GAME—Dick Christy 1961 2

MOST TOUCHDOWNS ON KICKOFF RETURNS, SEASON—Leon Burton 2 1960 (tied with two others)

LONGEST GAIN, FIELD GOAL ATTEMPT RETURN, TOUCHDOWN—Marshall Starks 97 1963

TEAM RECORDS

MOST TOUCHDOWNS RUSHING, GAME—6 Oct. 27, 1968 vs. Boston

MOST SEASONS LEADING LEAGUE IN FIRST DOWNS—2 1960–67, tied with Houston

FEWEST FIRST DOWNS RUSHING, SEASON—52 1963

FEWEST RUSHING ATTEMPTS, SEASON—306 1963

FEWEST YARDS GAINED RUSHING, SEASON—978 1963

FEWEST FIRST DOWNS ALLOWED, SEASON—178 1968

FEWEST TIMES TACKLED ATTEMPTING PASSES, SEASON—9 1966

FEWEST YARDS LOST ATTEMPTING PASSES, SEASON—92 1966

HIGHEST AVERAGE GAIN, PUNT RETURNS, SEASON—17.8 1961

MOST KICKOFF RETURNS, GAME—10 1960 (tied with 5 others)

FEWEST FUMBLES, SEASON—15 1964 and 1967

FEWEST OPPONENTS' FUMBLES RECOVERED, SEASON—6 1967

1968 Season

New York Jets Individual Statistics

RUSHING

	Att.	Yards	Avg.	Long	TDs
Snell	179	747	4.2	60	6
Boozer	143	441	3.1	33	5
Mathis	74	208	2.8	16	5
Joe	42	186	4.4	32	3
Sauer	2	21	10.5	15	0
Smolinski	12	15	1.3	5	0
Namath	5	11	2.2	4	2
Parilli	7	—2	—0.3	10	1
Johnson	2	—6	—3.0	0	0
Rademacher	1	—13	—13.0	—13	0
	467	1608	3.4	60	22

PASSING

	Att.	Comp.	Pct.	Yds. Gained	Tkld./ Yds.	TDs	Long	Int.	Pct. Int.	Avg. Yds. Gained
Namath	380	187	49.2	3147	15/112	15	87	17	4.5	8.28
Parilli	55	29	52.7	401	3/23	5	40	2	3.6	7.29
Snell	1	1	100.0	26	—	0	26	0	0.0	26.00
	436	217	49.8	3574	18/135	20	87	19	4.4	8.20

PASS RECEIVING

	No.	Yards	Avg.	Long	TDs
Sauer	66	1141	17.3	43	3
Maynard	57	1297	22.8	87	10
Lammons	32	400	12.5	37	3
Snell	16	105	6.6	39	1
Boozer	12	101	8.4	23	0
B. Turner	10	241	24.1	71	2
Mathis	9	149	16.6	31	1
Smolinski	6	40	6.7	19	0
Johnson	5	78	15.6	18	0
Joe	2	11	5.5	11	0
Rademacher	2	11	5.5	6	0
	217	3574	16.5	87	20

PUNT RETURNS

	No.	FC	Yards	Avg.	Long	TDs
Richards	4	7	57	14.3	37	0
Christy	13	1	116	8.9	39	0
Baird	18	6	111	6.2	20	0
Philbin	1	0	2	2.0	2	0
D'Amato	0	1	0	0.0	0	0
Hudson	0	1	0	0.0	0	0
	36	16	286	7.9	39	0

KICKOFF RETURNS

	No.	Yards	Avg.	Long	TDs
D'Amato	1	32	32.0	32	0
Christy	25	599	24.0	87	0
B. Turner	14	319	22.8	36	0
Smolinski	1	17	17.0	17	0
Snell	3	28	9.3	15	0
Neidert	1	0	0.0	0	0
Rademacher	1	0	0.0	0	0
	46	995	21.6	87	0

PUNTING

	No.	Yards	Avg.	Long
Johnson	68	2977	43.8	65

INTERCEPTIONS

	No.	Yards	Long	TDs
Sample	7	88	39	1
Hudson	5	96	45	0
Beverly	4	127	68	1
Baird	4	74	36	0
Baker	3	31	20	0
Atkinson	2	24	22	0
Gordon	2	0	0	0
Christy	1	16	16	0
	28	456	68	2

SCORING

	TDs	Rush-ing	Pass-ing	XP	XPM	FG	FGA	Safety	Total Points
J. Turner	0	0	0	43	0	34	46	0	145
Maynard	10	0	10	0	0	0	0	0	60
Snell	7	6	1	0	0	0	0	0	42
Mathis	6	5	1	2*	0	0	0	0	38
Boozer	5	5	0	0	0	0	0	0	30
Joe	3	3	0	0	0	0	0	0	18
Lammons	3	0	3	0	0	0	0	0	18
Sauer	3	0	3	0	0	0	0	0	18
Namath	2	2	0	0	0	0	0	0	12
B. Turner	2	0	2	0	0	0	0	0	12
Beverly	1	0	0	0	0	0	0	0	6A
Parilli	1	1	0	0	1**	0	0	0	6
Sample	1	0	0	0	0	0	0	0	6A
Smolinski	1	0	0	0	0	0	0	0	6B
Crane	0	0	0	0	0	0	0	1	2
	45	22	20	45	1	34	46	1	419

* Ran for 2-pt. conversion.   ** 2-pt. conversion pass attempt failed.
A = Interception return.   B = Rec. blocked punt.

New York Jets Statistics
Club Comparison
(11-3)

	N.Y.	OPP.
FIRST DOWNS	249	178
Rushing	80	59
Passing	144	104
Penalty	25	15
RUSHING		
Net Yards Gained	1608	1195
Average per game	114.9	85.4
Rushes	467	368
Average per rush	3.4	3.2
PASSING		
Total Yards	3574	2567
Passer Tackled and Yards Lost	18/135	43/399
Net Yards Gained	3439	2168
Average per game	245.6	154.9
Passes Attempted	436	403
Completed	217	187
Percentage	49.8	46.4
Had Intercepted	19	28
COMBINED NET YARDS RUSHING AND		
PASSING	5407	3363
Average per game	360.5	240.2
BALL CONTROL PLAYS	921	814
Average per play	5.5	4.1
INTERCEPTIONS BY	28	19
Yards Returned	456	455
PUNTS	68	98
Yardage	2977	3766
Average distance	43.8	38.4
PUNT RETURNS	36	38
Fair Catches	16	8
Yards Returned	286	531
Average per return	7.9	14.0

KICKOFF RETURNS	46	82
Yards Returned	995	1664
Average per return	21.6	20.3

FUMBLES	19	29
Own Recovered	10	14
Opponents Recovered	15	9

PENALTIES	76	65
Yards penalized	742	695

SCORING		
Touchdowns	45	36
Rushing	22	9
Passing	20	17
Returns	3	10
Extra Points	45	37
Field Goals	34	9
Field Goals Attempted	46	17
TOTAL POINTS	419	280

ACCUMULATIVE SCORE BY PERIODS, GAME SCORES, AND ATTENDANCE

JETS	103	113	64	139 —	419
OPPONENTS	44	69	41	126 —	280

Jets	20	Chiefs	19	Away	48,871
Jets	47	Patriots	31	Away	29,192
Jets	35	Bills	37	Away	38,044
Jets	23	Chargers	20	HOME	63,786
Jets	13	Broncos	21	HOME	62,052
Jets	20	Oilers	14	Away	51,710
Jets	48	Patriots	14	HOME	62,351
Jets	25	Bills	21	HOME	61,452
Jets	26	Oilers	7	HOME	61,242
Jets	32	Raiders	43	Away	53,318
Jets	37	Chargers	15	Away	51,175
Jets	35	Dolphins	17	HOME	61,766
Jets	27	Bengals	14	HOME	61,111
Jets	31	Dolphins	7	Away	32,843

Home Total — 433,760		Away Total — 305,153		Total — 738,913	
Home Avg. 61,965		Away Avg. 43,593		Avg. 52,778	